A Forgotten Legacy

A FORGOTTEN LEGACY

Canadian Leadership in the Commonwealth

JOHN KENNAIR

Order this book online at www.trafford.com
or email orders@trafford.com

Most Trafford titles are also available at major online book retailers.

Printed in the United States of America.

ISBN: 978-1-4669-0713-3 (sc)
ISBN: 978-1-4669-0712-6 (hc)
ISBN: 978-1-4669-0711-9 (e)

Library of Congress Control Number: 2011962032

Trafford rev. 12/30/2011

www.trafford.com

North America & international
toll-free: 1 888 232 4444 (USA & Canada)
phone: 250 383 6864 ♦ fax: 812 355 4082

Table of Contents

TO THOSE WHO BELIEVED IN ME

Preface

When the Commonwealth Games came to Edmonton, Alberta, in 1978, I remember the fervor that it generated. People, old and young alike, were excited by this international event that was going to bring Edmonton into the world's spotlight. As a child, its meaning had a limited significance. I was, like most people, unaware of the problems of racism and the affect this had had upon the 1976 Olympics in Montreal, nor how these problems threatened the Commonwealth Games in Edmonton. I was wrapped up in the excitement that my parents had for this event. I remember being dragged to the parade to see the Queen; attending sporting-events; and looking for my father on television. He was the team doctor for Canadian Boxing, and we were so proud of him.

Having been raised around sport, and knowing my father's involvement in Boxing, I was aware of his responsibilities—his job was to protect the 'fighters'. But when my father came home after one fight during the Games, explaining how he had to intervene to save a Zambian boxer, my first glimpse into the disparities in this world took place. Not every country could afford doctors for these Games. His reward for this act of diligence and kindness was to be given the most beautifully crafted Zambian badge by their High Commissioner. I remember the weight of the badge, as it was crafted with threads of precious metals. I also remember asking about Zambia and where it was, not knowing of the problems that had been occurring in that part of the world. Why would I, as I was but a child.

This encounter with politics would affect my life, as it would become a passion to learn about it, along with the Commonwealth in general.

As a Canadian, I was aware of our multicultural society, and I knew that there were other countries, but this was the first time these two concepts came together in my mind. I wanted to know more, but few could give me satisfactory answers as to what the Commonwealth was, and what did this mean to Canada. This has led to a 30 quest for knowledge that has culminated in this book.

No journey of this nature is taken alone, and many have offered assistance and guidance along its way. There are far too many people who have helped, encouraged and guided me in my life, probably far too many to mention. From the encouragement to attend university from the Royal Canadian Mounted Police; from my professors and mentors in university; to colleagues and friends, all of you have helped me along the way, believing in and seeing something in me when I did not believe in myself. For this, I am grateful. As this project started out as my doctoral thesis, I thank the guidance of my doctoral committee at the University of Kent, so many years ago—John Groom, Andy Williams, Stephen Chan, and Jarrod Wiener. Finally, I would like to thank my friends and family who supported me, through good times and bad, on this odyssey. The mistakes and misunderstandings within this book are but mine alone, and for those I apologize. I have learned a lot about the Commonwealth and what it has meant to Canada, and I would like to share this history with you.

JK
St. Albert, Alberta

Commonwealth Heads of Government Meetings—1965 to 1987

London
1965 *Agreed Memorandum* established the Commonwealth Secretariat
Arnold Smith becomes the first Secretary-General

Lagos, Nigeria
January 1966 Unilateral Declaration of Independence by Rhodesia on 11 November, 1965 was the subject of discussion
London
September 1966 Further discussion on the Rhodesian crisis

London
1969 Further discussion on the Rhodesian crisis

Singapore, Singapore
1971 Proposed British Arms Sales to South Africa
Introduction of the Commonwealth Fund for Technical Cooperation and the Commonwealth Youth Programme

Ottawa, Canada
1973 Introduction of the Commonwealth Retreat
Limited discussion on the South African and Rhodesian crises

Kingston, Jamaica
1975 Shridath "Sonny" Ramphal becomes the second Secretary-General
Problems facing the Third World are the central theme of discussion.

London
1977 Problem with Uganda and the Idi Amin Government
Gleneagles Statement on Racism and Sport

Lusaka, Zambia
1979 Problems over the Smith/Muzorewa Constitution for Rhodesia
This led to the Lancaster House talks, 1979/1980.

Melbourne, Australia
1981 Central theme at this meeting was the UNCTAD conference at Cancun
Creation of the Women's Division in the Secretariat

New Delhi, India
1983

Nassau, Bahamas
1985 Discussed the possibility of sanctions on South Africa
Creation of Eminent Persons Group headed by Malcolm Fraser

Vancouver, Canada
1987 Commonwealth decides to place sanctions on South Africa
Creation of the Commonwealth of Learning Institute
Commonwealth Okanagan Statement on South Africa

Introduction

A Forgotten Legacy: Canadian Leadership in the Commonwealth

FOR DECADES, CANADA has played a leading role within the Commonwealth. Not as a power-wielding hegemon, but as an intellectual, moral leader, preserving and shaping this organization. Since its inception in 1931, with the Statute of Westminster, the Commonwealth's and Canada's histories have been entwined. Just as Canada has shaped the Commonwealth, it too has defined where Canada finds its origins, linking it back to Britain and serving Canadian trade and foreign policy ambitions. It has been a medium through which Canada could reach out to other regions of the globe. Indeed, the Commonwealth has been Canada's primary vehicle for bilateral aid, and in later years, it became a means through which Canada pursued its human rights ambitions. As a non-hegemonic state, Canada has had limited resources to project itself and its interests, but the Commonwealth has enabled it to have relations with states around the world. Yet this legacy has been forgotten.

Little research on the importance of this association to Canada, as evidenced by the lack of literature exploring Canada's relations with the Commonwealth, has been done. A few pages, here and there, have been awarded that describe its relevance in an ancillary fashion, but only in a general framework of international concerns that have won Canadian favour. At best, it has received a chapter in texts on Canadian foreign policy, but these have been few. The most prolific writer has been Margaret Doxey, who has focused on Commonwealth affairs, producing three articles that have explored Canada's relations with the Commonwealth.[1] These articles, however, have been descriptive in nature, providing a general overview of these relations with little depth of political analysis. More recently, Evan Potter, David McIntyre and David Black have written on Canada and the Commonwealth,[2] but these too have been superficial in character, intimating that there is a lack of literature out there on this subject. There are some works that have been published that deal with specific issues of interest, as they pertain to Canada and the Commonwealth,[3] most notably the crises in southern Africa over *apartheid*,[4] but rarely do they give an analysis, beyond a recounting of Canada's actions. Most of the literature on Canada's international affairs has, instead, concentrated on its relations with Britain or the United States, juxtaposing Canada to the hegemons of recent history. Alternatively, Canadian historians have concentrated on interesting elements of international relations, such as the development of Canadian foreign relations in the post-war years. However, much attention has been focused on international organizations such as the United Nations and the North Atlantic Treaty Organization (NATO),[5] touching on the Commonwealth only in a superficial fashion.

It is the intent of this book to fill this gap in the literature on Canada's diplomatic history with the Commonwealth, examining Canada's relations with this association between the years of 1963 to 1987. These are the years when Canada was most active in the Commonwealth. In fact, it will be demonstrated that Canada has played a leadership role during these years that helped to preserve this association, and further show how Canada helped to re-shape it into a more functional body that could serve Canada's interests. During this time frame, the Commonwealth would change from its initial form as an association of states, echoing old ideas of empire, to an international organization, with Canada playing a part in this transition. Lester Pearson, in 1963, as Canada's new Prime Minister, led these new developments in the Commonwealth. Subsequent Canadian Prime Ministers, namely Pierre Trudeau and Joe Clark, also played a leading part in the shaping of the Commonwealth. After the Vancouver Commonwealth Heads of Government Meeting (CHOGM), 1987, this book ends its survey when Brian Mulroney led the Commonwealth in making a stand against *apartheid* in South Africa. At the heart of this work, therefore, is the question of Canadian leadership within the Commonwealth.

Canada, the Commonwealth, and Middle Power Leadership

In the mid-1980's, some writers postulated that Canada was no longer a middle power, as proclaimed by John Holmes in the 1960's, but a principle power.[6] When Canada joined the G-7, it became a part of the core of states whose economic policies were setting the tempo for the international system. If Canada was not quite part of the core yet, it was definitely on the edge of this core. This was supported by Bernard Wood's arbitrary upper line that found Canada to be the world's seventh richest state.[7] Juxtaposed to this position were those theorists that placed Canada as a satellite of the United States, soon to be subsumed by its southern neighbour through the Free Trade Agreement of 1988.[8] More common, however, has been the assumption that Canada is a middle power, and does not envisage itself to be anything other than a middle power.[9] In 1989, as Canada's Secretary of State for External Affairs, Joe Clark emphasized this point, stating that Canada did not seek, nor could it ever achieve, great power status. Clark states:

> There are foreign policy choices open to some countries which have never been open to Canada. We could never aspire to be a great power. Our population and economy are too small. The choices of conquest, or of empire have never been open to Canada. Nor has it ever been open to us to act unilaterally or alone. On all important issues, success for Canada has meant cooperation with others. Look at economics. We are a country of traders. We depend on the international economy as do few others. We need clear rules, open access, stable markets. That means we pursue our economic interests with others. So we have pursued a policy of more open trade through cooperation with other traders.[10]

Though Canada has been ranked with the world's highest standards of living, and though it has a high GNP, there are still a number of factors which limit its ability to be anything other than a middle power.

Canada is the world's second largest state in geographical terms and it is abundant with natural resources. However, a number of factors negate its potential to be a great power. Its proximity between two superpowers, with the United States immediately on its southern border, undermines its ability to be a regional leader. With a population under 35 million, it is unable to defend its southern border, should the need arise, and relies on its amicable relations with the United States for its security. It has been its limited population that also hinders Canada from exploiting its own natural resources.

In the 1950's, Canada went through its process of industrialization and this was known as its "Golden Decade". Prior to this, Canada had a successful agrarian society, and was contributing to the re-development of Europe after the Second World War. Canada, untouched by the ravages of war but with its need for industrial technology, was pushed in a direction to develop its own economy. With the greater proportion of its population located in central Canada (Ontario and Quebec), the time was right for this process. However, the majority of Canadian industry and its GNP was still dependent on its primary resources. Eastern Canada, known as the Maritime Provinces, relied heavily upon its fisheries, and the West on agriculture, forestry products, and later oil. The northern sector of Canada, situated on the Canadian Shield, mined minerals and ores. Canada's economy was based on primary industry and this continues today. It is these factors which have limited Canada's ability to play a dominant role in its own geographic region, and explained why Canada used international fora to express itself on the world stage.

The Commonwealth is one forum in which Canada has played a role as a middle power leader, acting as a catalyst, facilitator, and manager on issue-specific themes within this organization. Using entrepreneurial and technical skills, as well as its economic resources, Canada has played a continuing role which has shaped the Commonwealth. Its intercession on the Rhodesian matter at the 1964 London CHOGM, set the way for the creation of the Commonwealth Secretariat, and through continued political and economic support for this agency allowed the Secretariat to grow and develop into and international organization. Leading this development of the Commonwealth was Arnold Smith, a senior Canadian civil servant. Canada continued to shape this organization through its introduction of the Commonwealth Fund for Technical Cooperation and the Commonwealth Youth Programme at the Singapore CHOGM in 1971. These programmes, 40 per cent of their budgets funded by Canada, were designed to give new purpose to the Commonwealth and to protect this organization from the dissolution it faced over the crises in southern Africa. Thus Canada, through innovative ideas, managed to preserve the Commonwealth.

The Commonwealth also served Canadian foreign policy by providing it with the means to deliver bilateral aid to various regions of the globe. In 1950, the Colombo Plan, launched through the Commonwealth, was designed to provide aid to India, Pakistan, and Sri Lanka that had recently gained their independence from Britain. This, which was soon expanded to other South-East Asian states, was joined by two other Commonwealth bilateral aid programmes the Commonwealth Caribbean Aid Programme in 1958 and the Special Commonwealth African Aid Programme introduced in 1960. These programmes helped foster Canada's relations with its Commonwealth partners.

In 1975, Pierre Trudeau's call for more trade between First and the Third World preceded a similar *reveillez* by Sonny Ramphal, the Commonwealth's new Secretary-General. Moralistically supportive of the need to enhance the economic well-being of the Third World, Canada took a rhetorical stand toward the cause. However, in other fora, most notably the United Nations Conferences on Trade and Development, Canada could not support the introduction of preferential trade programmes for Third World states, as it too dealt mainly in commodities and such preferences would undermine its own economy. This demonstrates the precarious position of Canada economically within the international system. Though it may have been financially supportive of its Commonwealth partners in the third World, Canada could not afford to instigate the changes that it had called for in 1975.[11]

Finally, Canada played an important role in managing the Commonwealth throughout the two crises in southern Africa which continually taxed this organization from 1961 to 1987. Bridging the rift between the "old" members and the "new" members of the Commonwealth, Canada played a mediating role, offering solutions to circumvent the problems that arose at the Head of Government meetings. In 1970, these matters peaked with Britain's announcement that it would once again sell arms to South Africa. A number of African states, after breaking diplomatic relations with Britain, also threatened to leave the Commonwealth should Britain proceed with its sales. Pierre Trudeau, and his personal advisor, Ivan Head, worked to resolve this conflict through personal assurances, and to alleviate the problems temporarily. At the following CHOGM in Ottawa, 1973, Trudeau used the opportunity as chairman to introduce the summit retreat as a means of pre-empting any further unrest on this matter.[12] Canada had successfully managed these crises to prevent the dissolution of this organization, and under the Prime Ministership of Brian Mulroney, Canada took a new direction leading the Commonwealth in an attack on *apartheid*.[13]

As a middle power state, Canada used its entrepreneurial and technical skills to avert the problems that faced the Commonwealth, and contributed to its development into an international organization. Using the skills that it developed in other international fora, and through which it had developed in its own growth as a state, Canada was able to offer leadership to the Commonwealth when it was necessary to do so. To a limited extent, Canada also utilized its economic resources to alter the face of the Commonwealth. This demonstration of leadership will be explored in more detail in the chapters that follow.

Divided into five chapters this book will develop the argument that Canada acted as a middle power leader within the Commonwealth. The first two chapters present the foundation on which the rest of the argument is set. Laying out this groundwork, Chapter one describes the Commonwealth as an international organization, and focuses on three of the functions that it performs: an economic and political function, as well as the binding role it plays drawing together former British colonies. Overall, this chapter describes how the Commonwealth can be used as a conduit for a state to express its foreign policy goals.

Chapter two describes Canada's use of the Commonwealth between 1931 and 1991. The Commonwealth has served Canada by acting as a conduit for it to express its trade, aid and human rights ambitions. This chapter serves also to describe the factors that affect Canada's foreign policy decisions. Split into two groups, the domestic and external factors that affect Canada's foreign policy decisions towards the Commonwealth are explored. This Chapter helps to develop a general understanding of Canada's foreign policy ambitions within the Commonwealth, which become implicit in the subsequent chapters.

Chapters three, four, and five, then explore three case studies that become the heart of this book. Chapter three examines the structural contributions that Canada made to build and shape the modern Commonwealth. The evidence is given chronologically and relates Canada's contributions to building the Commonwealth Secretariat and the divisions and programmes within it. Chapter four then describes Canada's economic role as a Commonwealth member, giving economic assistance to its Commonwealth partners through bilateral and multilateral programmes. Finally, chapter five describes Canada's role in building cohesion within the Commonwealth when the crises in southern Africa threatened its very existence.

In the conclusion, the information presented in chapters three, four, and five will be examined through the theory of middle power leadership. Drawing upon this evidence this book will show that Canada has exhibited technical and entrepreneurial leadership skills within the Commonwealth. Moreover, these skills helped to shape and give purpose to this organization. This book will conclude that Canada has acted as a middle power leader within the Commonwealth.

Chapter One

The Commonwealth as a Conduit for Foreign Policy

The value of the Commonwealth lies in its use as an instrument assisting and facilitating the promotion of certain policies and ideals, and the stimulation of practical co-operation between members.
Department of Foreign Affairs and International Trade[14]

As AN INTERNATIONAL organization, the Commonwealth is concerned with cooperation and consultation amongst its members, uniting many regions into a single forum that works for the betterment of its membership.[15] Yet, as so many writers have stated,[16] the Commonwealth defies accurate description. As Arnold Smith wrote in 1966, "the Commonwealth has always been harder to describe than to operate, even though the latter may not always be simple."[17] Some writers, such as KC Wheare,[18] declared that the Commonwealth was not constitutionally based and thus not an international organization, but rather an international association.[19] Margaret Ball and Nicholas Mansergh called it a "fraternal association"[20] or a "purely functional association."[21] JN Kinnas declared that the Commonwealth fell within this classification of international associations because of the remnant structure of the British Empire and the transactional nature of Britain with its former colonies.[22] Other writers, such as Sir William Dale, have claimed that there is an implicit constitution found within the principles adopted by the Commonwealth membership, and that the Commonwealth fulfils the requirement of an international organization as outlined by Clive Archer below.[23] Finally, there are those writers, such as AJR Groom, who do not distinguish between an "association" and "organization" but still believe that the Commonwealth is *sui generis* and does not have a constitution.[24]

Finding a starting point from which to present the Commonwealth, therefore, involves some difficulties, for the first question always asked is "what is it?" The second question is "what does it do?" The third that should be asked is "how does it perform its functions?" This book defines the Commonwealth as an international organization that is concerned with cooperation and consultation amongst its membership, and which provides a functional or practical purpose.

An international organization can be defined, in general terms, as a multinational body that is constructed upon a constitutional format; it has a Secretariat, or other central agency to assist in the decision-making processes, and that the Secretariat is "a permanent secretariat with a permanent headquarters arrangement and which performs ongoing tasks";[25] encourages the participation of all of its membership, and works towards the expressed aims of that membership,[26] and that these aims should be the desires of the whole, or at least the majority, and not just the expressed wishes of one state.[27] There should also be regular meetings held between the parties, and all members must have full voting rights. Furthermore, an international organization is based upon a constitutional structure, as founded by a Charter or a treaty. The United Nations, as do many of its Specialized Agencies, falls within these criteria because of the way they are formed and structured. A constitution gives direction to the aims and goals of the organization as well as the decision-making procedures that are necessary in order to establish quorum.

An alternative definition for an international organization is given by AJR Groom, who, in his work on international cooperation, gives a functional definition for an international organization. He states:

> By international organization we mean the growth of a structure that enables world transactions to take place, be they economic, political, social or cultural. Such a structure must be able to fulfil four functions, at least to a minimal level. It must have the means to receive and impart communications both endogenously and exogenously; it must be able to integrate its subunits; it must

have some conception of loyalty to the whole—a notion what constitutes "we"; and, finally, it must have enough self-knowledge, and therefore some form of collective memory about shared values and common interpretation of experiences, to be able to set goals. Without these it will not be able to sustain itself.[28]

This definition sets out general criteria for an international organization that can be applied to the Commonwealth.

The Commonwealth as an International Organization

Through the Statute of Westminster, 1931, the Commonwealth was created, and over the years it would develop and evolve into the international personality that it is now recognized as today.[29] Historically, the Commonwealth's roots extend further back than 1931. After the "Canadian experiment" in granting this former colony its independence,[30] Britain, under Prime Minister Benjamin Disraeli, sought to recapture the grandeur of its old Empire. This was achieved through the use of the Colonial Conferences that would become the Imperial Conference System of the Commonwealth, and later into the Commonwealth Head of Government meetings (CHOGM). These meetings, along with the structure of the relationships between Britain and its former colonies, were indicative of an effort to maintain control in a changing world. Before the Commonwealth was formed, the Colonial Conferences were used by Britain to maintain its old empire. When this dominant-subordinate relationship between Britain and its Colonies evolved into the Commonwealth, Britain was still at the centre of the Commonwealth and maintained this position through the Commonwealth Relations Office (CRO). Many of the norms of the Commonwealth were premised upon economic, democratic, and legalistic standards as set down by Britain through colonialism. The Commonwealth was premised upon three implicit principles. In the words of Margaret Ball:

These include in the first instance the principle of equality of states within the Commonwealth, with its correlative obligation of non-interference in the internal affairs of other members. On a par with equality in today's Commonwealth is racial non-discrimination.

Other principles regarded as fundamental include the rule of law, "due process," and, at least in theory, popular control.[31]

This is important to understand as it defines the Commonwealth's structure and purpose. As an international organization, there are two primary issues to explain with regard to the Commonwealth, its constitutionality and its functions.

Many writers believe that the Commonwealth is not an international organization for the very reason that it lacks constitutionality.[32] It is rather a *sui generis* body of states that are linked to one another through a traditional association based upon the old British Empire, and they maintain this association through a sense of sentimentality and self-interest.[33] A major document that gives any loose sense of structure to the Commonwealth is the Statute of Westminster, 1931. The Commonwealth is, therefore, solely based upon Common Law practice and its historical sense of being.[34]

Margaret Ball, however, put forward the argument that the Commonwealth could be considered to have a constitutional structure because it operates as an international subsystem.[35] She argues that its actual functions, and the mechanisms that allow these functions to occur, entitle it to be considered as an international organization.[36] She goes on to say:

> The primary function of the Commonwealth, as we are repeatedly told, is consultation—consultation undertaken not with a view to decision-making but in anticipation of enhanced understanding which leaves the members free to do as they like, and to cooperate with one another to the extent that they may find it mutually acceptable or desirable to do so.[37]

Ball then goes on to describe that the basis of the Commonwealth is premised upon three principles that lend themselves to its functionalism.[38]

Sir William Dale has taken this view further and, combined with the conception of English Common Law, developed a Commonwealth constitution from declaratory principles made at Head of Government Meetings (CHOGMs). The main source for Dale's principles came from the 1971 Singapore CHOGM. The Declaration of Principles formulated at Singapore built upon the sentiments of the growing Commonwealth. As new states were gaining their independence, the Commonwealth membership was growing. Many of these states were from the Third World, and the growing collective opinion was changing towards economic equality and anti-racial beliefs.[39] The 1971 Declaration reflected these values, adding to those already mentioned by MM Ball. Subsequent CHOGM's have reduced the generality of these original principles by giving more weight to each one of the six principles found in the declaration.[40] At the London Summit, 1971, and in 1979, at the Lusaka Summit, a stand against *apartheid* in sport (Gleneagles) and further definitions as to what constitutes racism were put forward.[41] Furthermore, the Melbourne CHOGM, 1981, and the New Delhi Summit, 1983, developed the principle of improving international economic conditions.[42]

Additional CHOGM's developed upon the remaining principles held within the Declaration, but the gist of all of these advancements is the increasing formalization of this organization. The 1971 CHOGM set out criteria to which the membership was expected to adhere. Though some of the earlier principles discouraged internal interference within a member state, the Declaration developed a generalized set of standards on which the Commonwealth was to be based.

Further developments upon the constitutional structure of the Commonwealth are more implicit in nature. Whereas the development of principles for the Commonwealth can be traced through documentation, other constitutional characteristics are more obvious through the procedural practices of the participants. The decision-making procedures of the Commonwealth are based upon consensus at biennial meetings of the Heads of Government (CHOGM's) of its membership. Unlike the meetings of other international organizations, the meetings of the Commonwealth are of an informal nature with no planned speeches. Customarily these fora have lasted a week. This was the standard set during the times of the crises that faced the Commonwealth over the South African and the Zimbabwean issues. Lately, however, due to the diminishing urgency of issues affecting Commonwealth states, and improved systems of communication, these meetings have been reduced to five days only. There are also meetings in between the CHOGM's that are for the Finance Ministers, and other high officials, of each state. These are once again of an informal nature and allow member states to consult over issues of financial concern.

The importance of these meetings is to allow member states to collaborate on issues of concern. The theme of each meeting is usually decided at the previous CHOGM. Decisions are made upon a consensual basis, but they have no binding effect upon the membership. In other words, though the principles give the Commonwealth constitutional direction, they are not legally binding. An example of this occurrence in Commonwealth history is the 1987 Vancouver CHOGM in which the general consensus of the members was to endorse sanctions against South Africa to encourage an end to *apartheid* in that country. Britain, however, did not subscribe to this policy for reasons of its own, one being, its economic ties to South Africa. Consensus of all the members was not obtained yet the Commonwealth still endorsed this action. Because of the nature of this organization, however, no actions were taken towards Britain to ensure its compliance.

Two points become apparent. First, the need for unanimity has changed with the precedent being set at the 1987 CHOGM; and second, the lack of legally binding, decisions by the Commonwealth leads one to question whether there is a true constitution/charter as set out in international law, or whether the constitution of the Commonwealth is truly *sui generis*. Suffice it to say that there is a loose constitutional structure that lends some credence to the Commonwealth being an international organization.

The next criterion of an international organization is the possession of a centralized agency that assists in the decision-making process and in organizing the institution. Within the Commonwealth this is represented by the Secretariat, which was established in 1965. Though the Commonwealth is a flexible institution that is premised upon meeting human needs through a transactional means of intercourse, the Commonwealth Secretariat itself imparts a sense of constitutional structure upon this international organization that enables it thereby to fulfil its functions of organizing the other various functions of this multilateral institution. To understand this service that it performs, a brief survey of this organ will be made.

The Commonwealth Secretariat was established in 1965 replacing the Commonwealth Relations Office (CRO), which was part of the United Kingdom's government structure. With the introduction of the Secretariat the whole persona of this international organization was transformed from the old Commonwealth system founded from the British Empire to one with a new structure, function and image.[43] Though there was initial resistance to this innovation by many of the leading states of the Commonwealth, the changing structure of membership due to the process of decolonization implied that such change was inevitable:[44] a more centralized and unbiased body was needed to remove the image of colonization that was harboured in the former structure of the Commonwealth. The Commonwealth Secretariat was headquartered in Marlborough House in London and was responsible for the operations of this international organization.

Unlike some Secretariats, the Commonwealth Secretariat has been structured in such a way that limits the power of this office.[45] As Margaret Doxey explained, "[I]t has none of the authority or influence which the UN Security Council and General Assembly can bring to bear bring if consensus is present",[46] nor may it interfere or comment upon the internal affairs of member states.[47] The primary function of the Secretary-General, and the sub-offices of the Assistant and Deputy Secretaries-general, is to manage and oversee the various functions of this organization. "In broad terms, a Secretary-General's job has three dimensions: administrative, representational, and political."[48] Many of the functions that fall under the authority of the Secretariat shall be explored when looking at the economic, political and the unifying purposes served by the Commonwealth, but for now they may be stated briefly. The Secretary-General acts mainly as a manager to help organize the biennial meetings of the Commonwealth; maintains the relations of the Commonwealth, both internally amongst its own membership and externally with other non-member states and international institutions; helps organize finances and their distribution to various projects; and fosters the development of the Commonwealth as an institution. In order to assist the Secretary-General in these tasks there are two Deputy Secretaries-General, one looking after political affairs[49] and the other charged with the economic affairs of the Secretariat.[50] Furthermore, there are two Assistant Secretaries-General that help manage the Commonwealth Fund for Technical Cooperation (CFTC), the Commonwealth Youth Programme (CYP), the Commonwealth Science Council (CSC), and a host of other functions that are designed to assist member states in their own development.

The above descriptions of constitutionality and the office of the Secretary-General help to demonstrate that the Commonwealth meets the definition above of what constitutes an international organization. The

Commonwealth is based upon a semi-formalized agreement indicating its principles and goals, with a centralized agency that assists in the decision-making process. The next issue to be examined is that of the Commonwealth's function.

All international organizations serve a purpose, and the Commonwealth is no exception. The definition of an international organization,[51] set out at the beginning of this chapter, gives a general overview of the purpose of an institution which can be applied to the Commonwealth. There are many issues that the Commonwealth works on behalf of its membership through cooperation and consultation. Through these two forms of collaboration, the Commonwealth attempts to improve the social, economic, and political situations of its members. One of the Commonwealth's earliest efforts in this area was at the Ottawa Conference, 1932, where Commonwealth members unified their efforts to combat trade barriers set up in the United States through the Smoot-Hawley Bill, 1930. At this same conference, directions were given to Dr. OD Skelton to seek other economic means in which member states could improve their domestic economic situations. Skelton came up with seven proposed specialized agencies that were presented at a Committee meeting in London the following year.[52] This set the ground work for establishing sub-agencies of the Commonwealth. Today there are over two hundred such agencies that deal with a variety of issue areas.[53] These range from issues on human rights to matters of educational development.

In dealing with these various issues, whether they are economic, social, or political in nature, member states are responsible for their own research and development, and assume the costs of the various projects. Thus the structure of this organization is state-centric. The information is then shared to allow each state to learn from their "cousins".[54] Furthermore, exchanges of experts between member states facilitate the training of experts and trading of information.

The cost of such cooperation has been accepted by the individual member states. The only cooperative efforts in which a budget was subscribed to was for the overseeing committees which helped to facilitate these transactions. They were given a semi-autonomous status through their own limited budgets. Once again, however, there was state representation upon these committees that indicates the state-centric nature of this organization.[55] The principle behind cooperation and consultation, therefore, was self-interested collective activity that assisted in the benefit of member states. Anomalies to this structure developed in 1950 with the Colombo plan where Commonwealth states worked together to assist in developing the economies and social conditions in fellow member states through direct contributions to these states. This was further developed in 1971 with the creation of the Commonwealth Fund for Technical Cooperation (CFTC), which was a plan to generate the developmental capabilities of the Commonwealth.[56]

What becomes apparent when looking at the functions of the Commonwealth as an international organization is its evolution from an association of states, bound by a common heritage, to that of an association of states working together for the betterment of all. Through the maturation of this body, a functional organization has grown that is, though still reflective of state self-interests, concerned with a greater welfare of its membership and those associated members of the Commonwealth.

The Functions and the Sub-Regimes of the Commonwealth

The Commonwealth serves an economic role, a political role, and one not easily qualified, called "its binding community ties." These functions of the Commonwealth can easily be explained through the school of functionalism set out by David Mitrany in 1946,[57] and indeed some writers do explain it in these terms. In its economic role, its political role, and in the manner in which the Commonwealth creates a binding community, it is apparent that the Commonwealth is a forum through which states exercise their influence upon specific issues. As an international organization, therefore, the Commonwealth serves as a conduit for national and collective foreign policy goals of its membership. All international organizations are used for such purposes, and the Commonwealth is no exception[58] as it allows for "communication, status, prestige and for the legitimization of policy."[59] The Commonwealth is a flexible institution that allows for the management of change and influence in a large section of international society. For this reason, regime theory can be applied, in part, to explain the Commonwealth.

An international regime is a means through which states maintain control over a specific issue area,[60] and they involve "a set of implicit or explicit principles, norms rules and decision—making procedures around which actors' expectations converge in a given area of international relations."[61] Though an international organization is not necessarily a regime, because it may be based upon a multitude of issues, it can be if it acts to co-ordinate state expectation and "organize aspects of international behaviour in various issue-areas."[62]

For our purposes here, the Commonwealth will not be considered as a regime in itself, but instead as an agency used to coordinate a number of issue specific themes, which in themselves can be considered to be regimes. Thus, the Commonwealth is in essence the collection of a number of sub-regimes that deal with economic and political themes. Within the Commonwealth, states, such as Canada and Australia, use this forum as a means to express their foreign policy ambitions.[63] State actions executed through an international organization in this fashion allow for a sense of collective legitimization, and legalization, of the changing norms of international society.[64]

One: The Economic Relations of the Commonwealth

Economic issues were one of the earliest binding factors of the Commonwealth along with political issues. The Colonial Conference system (1872-1926) was partially concerned with trade between Britain and the Dominions, and it reflected Britain's desire to maintain contact and control over economic relations.[65] The structure of the trade patterns with these states was quite centralized with the majority of trade for the Dominions being continued with Britain. There was very little direct trade amongst the Dominions themselves,[66] and very little trade with other states outside of the Empire. Canada was the one exception with a high proportion of its trade, though by no means the majority of its trade, directed towards the United States.[67] The only economic aid that was offered to the former colonies was the preferential trade agreements for certain products that Britain desired.[68] Thus Britain was able to influence what products its former colonies could procure and export through the control of demand.

This demonstrates a classical version of a regime that is structured with a hegemonic state controlling an economic system: in this case trade amongst the colonies. With the advent of the Commonwealth in 1931 a new style of regime becomes apparent in the Commonwealth that is indicative of its economic uses. Through the utilization of collective behaviour, the Commonwealth has been able to deal with contentious issues that have been a threat to its members. The first instance of this occurring was again in the area of trade and the protection of Commonwealth members' economic interests. There are two examples of Commonwealth members coordinating their behaviour to control their international environments. This first occurred in 1932 with the Ottawa Conference, and the second occurred with the negotiations of the Lomé Conventions.[69]

When the Commonwealth came into existence in 1931, the world was in an economic depression, and this had lasting ramifications for the Commonwealth.[70] The United States in 1930, itself suffering from the depression, created the Smoot-Hawley Tariff limiting the import of products into the United States threatened its domestic industries.[71] Though Canada did not pose a direct threat to US industries, it was directly affected by the Tariff and demanded that Britain do something to rectify this economic situation. The result was the Ottawa Conference, 1932.[72]

The Ottawa Conference, 1932, set up retaliatory measures against the United States, and other countries by re-enforcing the Imperial Preference system. This meeting between the Dominions and Britain re-affirmed Britain's position in receiving imports from the former colonies and increased the quotas and number of products that the Dominions could export to Britain. The net effect upon the United States was for it to re-evaluate its tariffs.

Under the insistence of Cordell Hull, the United States began efforts to negotiate an agreement between Britain and Canada. It was not until 1934 that the Reciprocal Trade Agreements Act in the United States was signed, opening the way for trade agreements between Canada and the United States.[73] Even after that there were still trade difficulties between these states that lasted up until the Second World War.

The second example of the Commonwealth working collectively to enhance the bargaining position of its members was with the Lomé Conventions. Prior to Britain joining the European Economic Community (EEC) in 1973, there were fears that it was becoming less concerned with Commonwealth affairs.[74] This was a direct result of the loss of control sustained through the inauguration of the Commonwealth Secretariat. When Britain announced its intentions to join the EEC, many Commonwealth states were worried as Britain was their traditional market for export and they would be unable to compete with the EEC.[75] There were further fears of trade restrictions being placed upon Britain limiting its old Commonwealth alliances. One solution was the Yaounde

Conventions that gave preferential treatment to African states that were former colonies of France,[76] but this treaty still fostered the old colonial structure that was not acceptable to these states. Thus a new agreement needed to be sought and this was followed through with the Lomé Conventions.[77]

The Commonwealth Secretariat, using experts from throughout the Commonwealth, helped to negotiate the treaty between its members and the EEC.[78] In the end certain states were excluded from the treaty[79] because it was believed that they were industrially independent, but special concessions were made for other African, Caribbean, and Pacific (ACP) states. The gist of the Lomé Conventions is that it allows ACP states to export unfinished products to Europe as long as they are not in direct competition with European products. The point being made, however, is how the Commonwealth worked together to secure the best deal for the majority of its membership.

The first direct investment into the Commonwealth as an international entity was through the Colombo Plan (1950-1965).[80] In 1948, in Colombo, Ceylon, Commonwealth Foreign Ministers met and devised a strategy in which they would assist in the development of their new memberships.[81] The first recipients were South-East Asian states who had just received their independence,[82] and later extended to those states in the region that would gain their independence through the process of decolonization.[83] Direct financial and technological aid was given to these fledgling states to assist them in their developmental processes and the Commonwealth acted as a catalyst for instigating these procedures. Aid, however, was still given directly from one member state to another, but this carried on the process of an "international self" initially fostered through the Ottawa Conference, 1932. Of the international aid that Canada gave directly after the Second World War, the majority of this went to Commonwealth members. The next stage in Commonwealth development came with the creation of the Commonwealth Fund for Technical Cooperation (CFTC) in 1971.[84]

With the initiation of the Commonwealth Secretariat in 1965, a centralized body existed that allowed for development projects to be administered directly through a centralized agency. Such change was not without its political difficulties as control over the use of the contributed funds was lost.[85] However, the CFTC became a political reality in 1971. Associated with the CFTC is the Technical Assistance Group (TAG) that works closely with member states to develop their needs, whether these are in a social capacity or in an industrial/economic capacity, but, nevertheless, this is a further example of economic cooperation and consultation that provides benefits for the membership of the Commonwealth. Ever present are the original structural patterns of Commonwealth consultation as member states continue to contribute information and their expertise, but these specialized sub-agencies of the Commonwealth also work collectively to deal with particular concerns of each member state.

Another area of economic cooperation that has taken place within the Commonwealth has been closely linked to the North-South debate. On a number of issues, through the cooperative actions of the Commonwealth, the individual members have benefitted, though to what degree they have benefitted is questionable. In the first instance, the Commonwealth's work with UNCTAD, 1964,[86] helped to instigate development programmes for its less developed countries. More importantly, though, the issue of underdevelopment was brought to the attention of Western eyes. Later, in 1973, when the Oil Crisis arose with OPEC states and the call for a New International Economic Order, 1974, the Commonwealth was supportive of this position, and the Singapore CHOGM, 1971, reflected this earlier concern through adopting economic development as one of the Commonwealth's principles.[87]

The political influence of the Commonwealth cannot be ignored at this point, because the majority of its members were also a party to the Group of 77. The G-77 was instrumental in calling for the NIEO in 1974 due to economic disparities between the North and the South. The Commonwealth has pursued efforts to assuage these differences through the multitude of economic development programmes that it encourages, and it also has assisted through cooperative meetings of Finance Ministers and the sharing of economic strategies. However, from the end of the Second World War such institutions as the GATT have discouraged such preferential trading arrangements as the Imperial Preference system. One area where Commonwealth cooperation has been present is in the negotiations of the Lomé Conventions, where the Secretariat used its influence to protect the interests of its members.

One point that has remained consistent, however, is the source of funding for these projects. The majority of the Commonwealth's funding is still obtained from Western states, with Canada vying with Britain for the position of top contributor.[88] As the majority of Commonwealth states are members of the Southern hemisphere, they are relatively poor and thus their contributions, proportional to their GDP, are nominal. This can lead one to question the validity of the Western states actions, and whether or not the majority of states in the Commonwealth are acting as "free riders".[89] If the Commonwealth is an international regime, then the matter of "free riders" is relevant. Are these Western states operating at a cost in the short term in order to reap long term benefits, or are they operating solely in a virtuous fashion for the benefit of all states?

What has become apparent is that the Commonwealth serves three economic functions. It works as a collective bargaining tool; it serves as an economic development body lending assistance to its members; and it serves as a forum for sharing economic information and ideals. Though its original form was that of a trade bloc, it now serves this function in an ancillary fashion. The gist of all these measures is that the Commonwealth works collectively to benefit its membership.

Two: The Political Relations of the Commonwealth

As with the economic relationships of the Commonwealth, the political associations are interconnected with the other domains being examined. There are a multitude of issues that have taken place within the Commonwealth's history that have been of a political nature and have had consequences in shaping this international organization. To look at all of these issues would be a futile endeavour, and though they would be interesting in their own right they do not help in fostering the theme of how the Commonwealth serves as a conduit for foreign policy.

The political history of the Commonwealth dates back to the first Colonial Conference in 1872, though in some respects the history of the British Empire is also relevant. These Conferences had political ramifications. Though some countries were starting to strive for their independence, such as Canada that gained its independence in 1867, the Conferences were an attempt by Disraeli to recapture the glory of the waning Empire.[90] Britain, through the constitutional structures given to the former colonies, and through the Conference system maintained political control over the former colonies through a legal capacity, through foreign policy, and through the economic relations (trade and aid) that the former colonies were dependent.[91] It would not be until 1931 with the Statute of Westminster that these former colonies would become slightly more independent.

Up until 1929, Britain had always remained largely responsible for the foreign policy of its former and current colonies.[92] Even in a situation between Canada and the United States, Britain was responsible for the foreign relations. The best example of the control that Britain had over the foreign affairs of its former colonies was with the League of Nations in which the former colonies were represented by it. Some states, such as Australia and New Zealand, were quite happy to leave these matters to Britain. The first steps taken to remove this position of control, however, arose through the legal capability of former colonies to enter into bilateral trade with other states. The first incident of this occurring was between Canada and the United States in 1923.[93] By 1927, Canada had established its first diplomatic mission in Washington, DC, though, as already stated, some states were eager to leave this area of politics to their old imperial master, others were not so keen, and the Statute of Westminster was the first confirmation in these former colonies of legal sovereignty.

The Statute of Westminster, 1931, created the Commonwealth, forming an association that consisted of five member states, including Britain and four of its former colonies—Australia, Canada, New Zealand, and South Africa. For Canada's part the Commonwealth became an important facility for developing a foreign policy. When Canada was granted its independence on July 1, 1867, under the British North America Act, it was primarily to assert the distinction between Canada and the United States of America.[94] Though Canada was now formally an independent state, there were, however, strong constitutional ties to its former imperial ruler Great Britain. Though Canada participated in many international fora, it did so under the skirt of the British Empire.[95]

With sovereignty being sought, mainly by Canada, the power to decide one's own foreign policies was important. When the Commonwealth was created, a suggestion of a Commonwealth Foreign Policy was put forward. This idea was supported by Australia and New Zealand, though rejected strongly by Canada that wanted to be able to control its own destiny.[96] It is ironic that in 1932, Canada needed the support of its Commonwealth partners to protect its export markets into the United States. However, the end result of this matter was that Canada obtained this sovereignty over its foreign relations and this was demonstrated by Canada's delay in declaring war against Germany in 1939, and by Canada's reactions to an Imperial War Council.[97] The issue of a collective foreign policy was raised once again in 1949 by Churchill,[98] but this idea was once again rejected.[99]

A minor political issue that arose within the Commonwealth, but was demonstrative of the political will for independence amongst the former colonies was the issue of citizenship and immigration policies. In 1948, persons of all Commonwealth countries were recognized as subjects of the Crown.[100] This implied the ability of persons to move freely around Commonwealth states.[101] However, in 1946 Canada established a citizenship policy[102] that negated the ability of persons of the Commonwealth to enter freely into Canada and they were thereafter required to apply for residence permission if they wished to move to this state. This was followed by other states soon after, though Britain left its borders open the longest until 1972.

An important political issue arose in the Commonwealth as former colonies became independent republics. The first case was India in 1949, which declared itself a republic and chose not to recognize the Crown as the Head of State. This removed an already weakening political device, the Governor-General's office, from its constitution that in some Commonwealth countries still carried political weight responsible to the British Government. The question of whether India should have been allowed to maintain its membership within the Commonwealth became pertinent, as the Monarch was seen to be the head of this organization. However, Britain wanted India to stay and the Commonwealth, with the consent all the other members, allowed for states to be republics within the organization.[103]

The next issue of political significance to the Commonwealth was the inauguration of the Secretariat. From the genesis of the Commonwealth, Britain had been responsible for the coordination of Commonwealth affairs through the CRO. At the outset of the Commonwealth there had been a suggestion for a Secretariat, but this was initially rejected.[104] At the 1964 Ministers meeting this matter was again raised. The difference this time was that the face of the Commonwealth had changed due to decolonization, and that many of the former colonies were skeptical of the fact the Commonwealth came under the direct control of the same department of the British Government that had controlled them prior to their independence. Something needed to change and having an independent agency coordinating Commonwealth affairs was a viable solution. Initially there was strong resentment to this plan by the original members of the Commonwealth, but soon Canada supported this plan when it realized its inevitability.[105] The structure of the Secretariat has been mentioned in the last section, and so no reiteration is needed, but the political significance of this structural change is very relevant and needs some explanation.

The inauguration of the Commonwealth Secretariat marked the beginning of Britain's waning interest in this organization.[106] Though the process of decolonization led to the visual change in membership, this structural change had ramifications for the balance of power within this organization. Some states feared that the Commonwealth would become a forum for African concerns alone. Reluctantly, Britain acquiesced to the demands of the other members for the Secretariat.[107] The Duncan report, 1969, indicated to the British Parliament the declining interest that the Commonwealth offered, and Britain's lack of interest culminated in the 1971 Singapore CHOGM where Britain's Prime Minister, Edward Heath, personified Britain's growing apathy to the new Commonwealth. This raised fears amongst the rest of the membership that the Commonwealth would soon dissolve without Britain.[108]

Canada, Tanzania, and Singapore reacted to this internalized fear through the application of diplomatic skills that brought Britain back to the bargaining table. The subject being discussed at this time was The Declaration of Commonwealth Principles, which included the principles of Anti-racism and Economic Development for Commonwealth members. It was these issues that created further problems for Britain eroding more of the foundations of its former empire.[109]

More specifically, though, was that the Commonwealth was beginning to exude collective pressure upon a member state to change its internal policy. This was in contravention to one of the Commonwealth's initial principles.[110] The only means with which such issues could be discussed is with the consent of the party/parties concerned, as Trudeau did in 1973 at the Ottawa CHOGM. The result of the 1971 CHOGM, however, was to water down the original Declaration in order to meet a compromise amongst the membership,[111] but the Commonwealth became a forum for expressing political concerns on South Africa.

The initial problems regarding South Africa find their roots back in 1957, when South Africa disputed Ghana's claim for independence,[112] which was the first state in black Africa to actually obtain its independence. Because of the changing international sentiments towards decolonization, and because of the fact that South Africa was to be labeled a rogue state with regard to its "protectorate" status over South West Africa, there was much resentment by South Africa to the decolonization process. This led to accusations by the Diefenbaker Government in Canada of racism that was declared in the Commonwealth meeting approving Ghana's enlistment into this organization as a republic. Adding fuel to this matter, in 1961 when South Africa declared itself a republic, it believed that it would rejoin the Commonwealth under its new status. Canada, however, as did others, objected to the entrance of the Republic of South Africa because of the constitutional structure of *apartheid* in this country and, with the need for consensus amongst its membership, the Commonwealth could not accept South Africa back into the Commonwealth. The result was that South Africa withdrew its application for membership.

Similar problems arose in the Commonwealth during the decolonization process, the Rhodesian crisis being one of them, the Nigerian War a second, and the Amin Government in Uganda another. None, however, was as traumatic as the issue of South Africa. This was an issue that plagued and strengthened Commonwealth ties for years to come. With regard to the changing face of the Commonwealth, and its power structures implicitly helped, it was to further erode Britain's control and position as a leading state in the Commonwealth. The next phase of political deterioration for Britain with regard to the Commonwealth took place in 1987 with the Vancouver CHOGM.

This meeting discussed the imposition of economic sanctions by Commonwealth members against South Africa in an attempt to encourage decolonization in South West Africa, and to encourage the dismantling of *apartheid*. Britain had close political and economic ties with South Africa and stood against such action, but the majority of members[113] voted in favour of sanctions. Once again through a cooperative means of collective action the Commonwealth was seeking to influence international opinion and change.[114] The most significant result of this meeting was that the Commonwealth members acted without the consensus of all of its members for the first time in its history. Britain usually acquiesced to the demands of the majority but not on this occasion. This established a constitutional precedent for this organization, but the decision was not binding and Britain was free to continue relations with South Africa.

What becomes apparent in this section is the changing political structure of the Commonwealth. In the beginning the Commonwealth was an implement of British foreign policy. However, as the structure of the Commonwealth changed, its political uses changed. Today the

Commonwealth acts as a forum for collective decisions that are non-binding upon its membership, and which are implemented on a voluntary basis. Through these collective decisions the Commonwealth can be used as a political device to place pressure upon other states, as with South Africa, to force change.

Three: The Binding Community Ties of the Commonwealth

The political and economic issues confronted in the Commonwealth at times have been troublesome and have nearly led to the demise of the organization. However, the original premise of the Commonwealth has always been cooperation and consultation on matters of mutual concern to its membership. These matters in themselves have created a unifying effect for this international organization as it overcame its difficulties, emphasizing the common heritage left to all Commonwealth members through the old British Empire. These include a common legal system; a common language; the parliamentary governmental system; and at one time the common allegiance to the Crown. Most important of all are the principles on which the Commonwealth is based.

Summary

The Commonwealth is based upon the goal of ameliorating the status of its members through cooperation and consultation. It covers many issues of interest to its membership, but these are mainly economic and political themes, and thus the multitude of agencies that reflect those concerns of the Commonwealth have been based upon members' self-interests. Such self-interest has taken many forms that have shaped the direction the Commonwealth has taken, and its structure has changed over time in deference to these concerns. The Commonwealth has evolved from a British institution, reflecting Britain's influence over its former colonies, to an institution reflecting the concerns of all its members. The Commonwealth has developed from an introverted organization, based solely upon the betterment of its members' economic standing and development, to an institution that has a political personality which has been influential in international affairs, especially regarding Southern Africa.

What has become apparent in this assessment of the Commonwealth is that the organization is a conduit for foreign policy. The modern Commonwealth reflects the desires of its members, both on economic and on political themes. Through assessing the structure of this organization and the constitutional principles on which it rests, one can see that through the behaviour of cooperation and consultation, the Commonwealth has become an agency capable of coordinating, its actions in order to deal with issues, whether they be economic or political, that are aversive, as well as advantageous, to its membership. Thus, as an organ of foreign policy ambitions, it has become an implement for managing change over its international environment, if only to a minor degree, as demonstrated in the preceding sections looking into the economic and political uses of the Commonwealth.

Chapter Two

Canada and the Commonwealth: An Overview: 1931-1991

"We didn't impose our views on the Commonwealth, but stood by the people."

Joe Clark, at Lusaka, 1979[115]

As CANADA'S OLDEST means for pursuing its interests outside of North America, the Commonwealth has continued to be of significance in Canada's international relations since its development.[116] The Commonwealth has provided Canada with a number of benefits. It has offered Canada an avenue to distinguish itself from the United States, which has always overshadowed Canada in other international fora, by providing it with a forum in which the United States is not a party. The Commonwealth allows Canada to maintain links with its historical roots, while providing Canada contact to many sources of its current multicultural identity. Finally, the Commonwealth has provided Canada with an economical means of access to five continents, allowing it to foster relations with various regions of the globe.

To help understand the role that the Commonwealth has played in Canada's international relations this chapter has been divided into two parts. The first part provides a basis for understanding the determining factors in the development of a state's foreign policy. This section argues that a state's foreign policies are not made within a vacuum, distinct from other areas of politics, both domestically and internationally. Building on this, the second section of this chapter provides a thematic description of how Canada's foreign policy objectives have varied over sixty years of Commonwealth history. The reader will be shown that the main areas in which Canada played a role, which will be elaborated in subsequent chapters.

Foreign Policy Determinants

A state's foreign policy resembles the twenty seconds of media attention that it receives on the evening news. Separated from the other segments of daily news items, international events traditionally have developed the aura of disassociation from the domestic affairs of a state. To the "man on the Trans-Canada Highway" international events are estranged from his daily existence. Only in recent years has this perception started to fade. Through the eyes of historians and political analysts, the interrelatedness of political happenings has shed light on the continuity of a state's foreign policy. In analyzing a state's foreign policy it is important to understand the many factors that affect its outcome and direction. These can be grouped into two general categories: domestic and international.[117]

Domestically, Canadian foreign policy strategies have been influenced by a number of factors. These include its media, pressure groups, and the structure of its government. The media can convey information to a state's population in a very short time. Through television, daily newspapers and, more recently, the internet, Canadians can be informed of global events at regular intervals. Such information can cause shifts in public opinion that influence the Government of Canada to take certain foreign policy positions to appease its electorate.[118] Examples of this are seen in Canada's response to the natural disasters aired on the media, in the past decade—the Tsunami, Haiti, and, most recently, the flooding in Pakistan. The Government of Canada, aware of these events, but through its publication in the media, the public sentiment generated by images transmitted on television impels the government to send aid.

The impact of the media on Canadian foreign strategies towards the Commonwealth, however, has been limited. On only two occasions, it has been deemed to have had an affect. The first was the 1969 Biafran conflict in Nigeria. The CBC had broadcast reports of the massacre of Biafrans by the Nigerian army in 1969 soon after Pierre Trudeau's election to Prime

Minister. Following the broadcast, when questioned by the media as to Canada's response, Trudeau responded by questioning what relevance Nigeria and these events had to Canada. These comments were made in jest only, but they generated a negative response in the public. Public outcry forced the Government of Canada to investigate the atrocities to discover that many of the images displayed had been staged by one of the warring factions within Nigeria. It turned out that the government did not have to act, as it discredited the media on this occasion, but the fact remains that the government was forced to take some form of action.[119]

The second media event that influenced Canada's foreign policy towards the Commonwealth took place in 1985. Soon after the election of Brian Mulroney as Canada's new prime minister the media displayed scenes from the Sharpeville massacre, and other political events from South Africa in the 1970's, which generated public sympathy for black Africans in South Africa. More important was the influence these reports had on the Prime Minister himself.[120] South Africa had been an issue in the Commonwealth since 1961, but Canada had never taken a firm stance on this matter. In 1985, however, these scenes broadcast on the CBC encouraged the government to take a stand as public awareness increased. As Kim Richard Nossal stated:

> "Awareness" of *apartheid* followed this pattern: in July 1985, a full 52 per cent of Canadians polled claimed that they had not heard about South Africa's racial policies. By September, that had dropped to 34 per cent. In June 1986, the number of "unaware" Canadians had risen to 39 per cent. It is interesting, however, that over this period, the policy preferences of "aware" Canadians hardened. In June 1985, 19 per cent favoured cutting all ties with South Africa. This figure climbed to 26 per cent in September and 35 per cent by June 1986.[121]

The net result of the influence of the media on public opinion, and more so on Mulroney was to compel Canada to take a stand at the Nassau CHOGM in 1985.

Pressure groups can also influence a state's foreign policy. Through lobbying and exploiting the media, these groups can encourage, or discourage, the foreign policy decisions of a government. In Canada many of these groups are culturally based, reflecting its multicultural constituency.[122] The influence that pressure groups have had on Canada's relations with the Commonwealth is reflected in its aid programmes that it offers the regions with which it maintains cultural ties. Other pressure groups have influenced aid relations, the most notable of these being Canada's business sector, which in 1974 demanded greater accountability and the tying of Canadian aid to trade.[123]

For the most part, however, Canadian pressure groups have been unsuccessful in changing Canada's foreign policy towards the Commonwealth. In the 1960's, with the rise of the Rhodesian and South African crises, certain groups, namely academics, the media, and churchmen, voiced concerns on these matters. In 1967, Cranford Pratt, a renowned academic, and Clyde Sanger, a journalist with *The Globe and Mail,* sent a letter to Canada's Prime Minister, Lester Pearson, and to the Department of External Affairs asking the Government to become more involved.[124] Though Pearson received the letter, he tried to disregard these requests and to committing Canada to another CHOGM. His reasoning was that the CHOGM's were acrimonious conferences, which at this time could threaten to dissolve the Commonwealth, and this was not in Canada's interest. Though there were similar requests from other groups, Canada maintained its position on these crises until 1985, when Mulroney took Canadian foreign policy in a new direction.

The final factor that reflects Canadian strategies in foreign policies are the domestic influences, and these are broken into three main groups: the Executive, Parliament, and the bureaucracy. Traditionally foreign policy was the prerogative of the Prime Minister, who derived this power from the British monarchy. On gaining its sovereignty from Britain, Canadian foreign policy making continued to be centralized in the executive. In the initial years, Canada's foreign relations were limited to a few states, and were administered easily by a small staff responsible to the Prime Minister. As Canada's foreign relations expanded, there was a need for Department of External Affairs and a Minister to oversee this portfolio. As time progressed, it was also necessary to expand the Department of External Affairs, which increased the number of persons who could influence foreign policy.[125]

An important role of the Prime Minister of Canada is to act as the figurehead of the nation.[126] In the Commonwealth, Canada is represented at biennial meetings by the Prime Minister. Though another representative can be sent in lieu of the Prime Minister, to date Canada has always been represented by this top post.[127] This is partially indicative of the importance that this organization holds in Canadian foreign affairs, and also reflects the personal characteristics of successive Prime Ministers.[128] Within the timeframe of this book, 1963 to 1987, Canada's Prime Ministers have had their own interests in the Commonwealth. Lester Pearson, once a diplomat, was used to being involved in foreign exchanges and enjoyed the opportunity to continue to be involved in international politics. Pierre Trudeau, his successor, enjoyed the intellectual exchange of ideas with his peers, and he saw the CHOGMs as a beneficial forum for dialogue amongst a broad spectrum of the world's leaders, lending insight into future global issues.[129] Finally, Mulroney saw the Commonwealth as an international political forum in which he could shine, and he use it to propagate his personal stand for human rights.

Successive Prime Ministers have also fashioned the direction of Canadian foreign policy over specific issues within the Commonwealth. Pearson, for example, decided that, after the two acrimonious meetings of the Commonwealth in 1966, Canada would not attend another CHOGM until the rancorous matter of Rhodesia was resolved. His actions also set the tempo for Canadian foreign policy regarding southern Africa for the next twenty years, and he acted as conciliator in subsequent CHOGMs to resolve conflicts.[130] Trudeau committed Canada to a strategy of international assistance because of his concern for Third World issues. Mulroney, whose foreign strategies for Canada concentrated on continentalism, nevertheless saw the value of the Commonwealth as a forum for projecting Canadian concerns.

The Canadian bureaucracy can also influence the direction of Canadian foreign policy. The bureaucracy in the Department of External Affairs collects information that is gathered by Canada's Embassies and High Commissions. In Ottawa, it is processed by regional desks. By the time this information reaches the Secretary of State for External Affairs, the information has been distilled and only that information that has been deemed to be important by the Department is passed on. The implications of this are that the Department of External Affairs implicitly influences the direction of Canadian foreign policy. Mitchell Sharp, a senior civil servant under Diefenbaker in the Department of Trade and Commerce, was quoted as saying: "Civil servants do not make policy, all rumour to the contrary notwithstanding—it is the prerogative of the elected representative of the people. But in this day and age civil servants do have a profound influence on the making of policy."[131] Kim Nossal in *The Politics of Canadian Foreign Policy* indicated the negative control that the bureaucracy placed upon a minister.[132] Flora MacDonald, Secretary of State for External Affairs, from 1979 to 1980, complained to *The Globe and Mail* about the unfair control of civil servants, which gave her very little choice or time in urgent, long-winded memos.[133]

The bureaucracy in Canada has had the ability to influence Canadian foreign policy. However, with regard to the Commonwealth this control has been limited. The Commonwealth was overseen more by the executive than the bureaucracy. After the creation of the Secretariat in 1965, this became more evident. Arnold Smith and Shridath Ramphal, both Secretaries-General of the Commonwealth, were always more inclined to communicate personally with the Prime Minister or the Secretary of State for External Affairs on Commonwealth matters rather than going through the Canadian High Commission as a channel to Ottawa. This personal contact with the executive continually frustrated the Commonwealth Division in the Department of External Affairs. Trudeau also distrusted the bureaucracy and brought in his own foreign policy advisor, Ivan Head. Through his own research in the Prime Minister's Office, Head was able to keep abreast of information provided by the Department of External Affairs to balance their reports.

The final area of government that has influence on the development of Canadian foreign policy is Parliament. Its power is limited for it is concerned mainly with domestic matters that affect Members' constituents. However, it has pressured the executive to explain Canada's foreign relations. Nossal called this influence "educational" as members of the political opposition normally ask foreign policy questions for the benefit of the media, knowing that this information would be broadcast to the country. In 1966, the Conservatives, as opposition, raised questions regarding sanctions and Rhodesia. Pearson and Paul Martin, the Secretary of State for External Affairs, were asked for Canada's position on the Rhodesian crisis. The objective was to raise the issue rather than to know the answer. In one incident, Diefenbaker asked Pearson if he would attend the CHOGM in London in September that same year. The subject of this meeting would be the Rhodesian crisis, following on from the Lagos meeting in January. Pearson, facing rail strikes and other domestic concerns, stated that he would like to attend but needed to resolve these domestic matters first.

Diefenbaker replied that it would be in Canada's interest for Pearson to attend the second CHOGM.[134] On 2nd September, three days prior to Pearson's departure to London, Diefenbaker then questioned the viability of this visit.[135] The nature of this questioning reflects little concern for the international events but more the domestic politics involved. The Conservatives always had been strong Commonwealth supporters, with many of their party being of British descent. The matter gave them the opportunity, however, to question the government and to force it to defend its actions. Parliament was used, therefore, as a political tool. It has not had a direct influence on Canadian policy.[136]

International factors also influence the development of Canadian foreign policy strategies. There are four main factors that need to be considered in Canada's relationship with the Commonwealth: its economic relations; its geographical location; its treaty relations; and finally, the limitations of Canada's capabilities in foreign relations.

In general terms the economic relations of a state reflect its international relations with other states. The majority of Canada's trade always has been with Britain and the United States. This is for both historical and geographical reasons. Canada was traditionally a primary producer, supplying Britain with much needed raw materials. Though Canada was both an Atlantic and Pacific country, its main political, and economic, ties remained with Europe. This was due to the historical and cultural influences in Canada. It is for this reason that as late as 1970 Canada still favoured the "Third Option", a proposal for closer links to Europe. Many of its economic roots were still founded in Europe, with Britain and the European Community being its second and third largest trading partners.

However, Canada's geographic location has also dictated its trade relations. Canada is the only state on the northern border of the United States, and 90 per cent of Canada's population lives within 100 kilometres of the 49th Parallel. This has made the United States Canada's largest trading partner. This proximity to the world's superpower, and Canada's dependence upon the United States for its trade, influence its foreign policy strategies. In 1981, Rodney deC. Grey declared that "foreign policy should, in major part, be trade relations policy"[137] for Canada's trade is so inextricably bound to the United States that its foreign policy strategies must take into account this economic fact when devising policy.[138] In 1988, after over a century of Canada looking outside of the North American continent to Europe, its foreign policy strategy looked decisively to the United States and culminated in the Canada-United States Free Trade Agreement. This Agreement was later extended to incorporate Mexico in the North America Free Trade Agreement (NAFTA) in 1993.

These economic and geographic factors have influenced Canada's relations with the Commonwealth by structuring its foreign policy towards this organization.[139] Canada's trade interests always rested outside of the Commonwealth thus limiting this organization's role in Canadian trade relations. Britain is, of course, a Commonwealth country, but it was only in the Commonwealth's initial years that this organization served any practical economic role for Canada. Following the Smoot-Hawley Act, 1930, bloc pressure by the Commonwealth resulted in the US passage of the Reciprocal Trade Agreement Act, 1934. On the basis of this, trade liberalising agreements were concluded between Britain, Canada, and the United States in 1935 and 1938.[140] This is the only instance in Canadian history where the Commonwealth served a trade function.

Canada's international treaty obligations also effect its foreign policy strategies. In the post-war years, Canada's international relations expanded into many of the new international organizations being founded. Its support for the United Nations, the General Agreement on Tariffs and Trade (GATT), and the North Atlantic Treaty Organization (NATO), effected how it acted in the Commonwealth. These new international organizations offered Canada an opportunity to expand its foreign relations, which the Commonwealth at this time did not. With these new fora, however, came new obligations. The United Nations had the greatest effect upon Canadian foreign policy for its Charter brought forth legal obligations. Its concern to have a voice in this organization, which it did not have under the League of Nations, meant that Canada focused its attention on the United Nations for its international ambitions. Its greatest achievement within the United Nations was in 1957 when Lester Pearson and Dag Hammarskjuld introduced the concept of peacekeeping. This became Canada's greatest contribution to the United Nations and Canada subsequently became involved in many peacekeeping missions.

Closely entwined with peacekeeping was the United Nations position on self-determination, which had a strong influence on the decolonization process. As part of the United Nations Charter, self-determination led to the creation of many new states, but this had many negative consequences. Many of these states were too poor to sustain themselves, needing assistance from western states. Decolonization also brought with it many conflicts in which Canada interceded as both a peacekeeper and mediator. The United Nations became, therefore, a central forum in Canadian foreign policy. Decolonization was also a divide between the East and the West, which became a proxy battle ground for the Cold War. Canada's geographic location, and its alliance and commitment to NATO, allied Canada to the United States and Western Europe in the battle between the superpowers. These international fora detracted attention from the Commonwealth. However, the Commonwealth did offer Canada, after the process of decolonization, contact with various regions of the globe, and it was this contact that served as the Commonwealth's redeeming feature. Many of these new states were poor, and because of Canada's fears of communist expansion into these newly independent states, the Commonwealth became a forum for delivering aid. The result, however, of Canada's international relations in the post-war years was the devaluing of the Commonwealth as a forum for projecting Canada's national interest.

Finally, Canada's limited capabilities as a middle power state influenced how it approached its foreign policy objectives. Canada has chosen to use a multilateral strategy when formulating its foreign policy. As a middle power, Canada does not possess the resources needed to establish its own regimes, and, therefore, it must use those that are already in place.[141] Multilateral diplomacy has allowed Canada to export its influence to all corners of the globe.[142] Multilateral diplomacy can be defined as "the conduct of relations and their adjustment among several states within the framework of an international organization."[143] Robert Keohane further describes multilateral diplomacy as "the practice of co-ordinating national policies in groups of three or more states, through ad hoc arrangements or by means of institutions."[144] John Ruggie shows that multilateral diplomacy serves a function of ordering the position of states.[145] Thus the use of international institutions is not an uncommon practice in international relations and can form an important catalyst for forging unity and cohesion among states. This foreign policy stratagy has helped to foster Canada's global social consciousness and has allowed Canada to pursue its foreign policy objectives.

Canada's Commonwealth Policies

As one of the original members of the Commonwealth, Canada consistently has played a part in this organization, though the focus of this role has fluctuated from 1931 to 1991. Since its inception, the Commonwealth has served Canada as a tool to enhance its trade, aid, and human rights policies. These policies have varied throughout Canada's relationship with the Commonwealth, with each alternatively becoming its primary objective.

The Commonwealth's first function for Canada was in trade. The advent of the "Great Depression" in 1929, would place strain upon Canada—United States trade relations, and in 1930 the Smoot-Hawley Bill would place tariffs upon all products entering the United States. This threatened the Canadian economy as many of Canada's goods were destined for markets within the United States, and Canada was relatively powerless to do anything about this matter on its own. The creation of the Commonwealth in 1931 gave Canada a vehicle through which to challenge the Smoot-Hawly Bill. In 1932 Robert Bennett immediately called for the Ottawa Conference. The objective of this meeting of the Commonwealth was to counter the United States tariffs by placing reciprocal tariffs upon American products throughout the Commonwealth to pressure the American government to change its policies. A second objective was to obtain the assurance from Britain that it would allow for greater import quotas from its former colonies. Prior to the establishment of the Commonwealth, Britain guaranteed a certain market to its former colonies to assist in their development. This became policy after economic problems arose in 1872 with the first "debt crisis", and became known as the "Commonwealth System of Imperial Trade Preferences."

The result of these actions by the Commonwealth was to place economic pressure on the United States. In 1934, upon the advice of Cordell Hull and as part of the Reciprocal Trade Agreement Act, the United States agreed to reverse its policy. The Imperial Trade Preferences continued until after the Second World War, but more importantly from Canada's perspective was the increase in trade between itself, Britain, and the United States with the North Atlantic Free Trade Agreements of 1935 and 1938. Canadian trade increased between these two parties as a direct result of the leverage brought to bear upon Britain and the United States through the Ottawa Conference.

Trade diminished as a Canadian objective within the Commonwealth after the Second World War. In 1947, it became one of the original members of GATT that precluded the use of trade preferences. Canada's trade relations also centred upon its relations with Britain and, more so, with the United States. Eighty per cent of Canada's trade was between these two countries and these relations dictated Canada's economic policy decisions. In a bid to revive Commonwealth trade in Canadian foreign policy in 1957, John Diefenbaker asked the Department of Trade and Commerce for a paper investigating the possibility of increased trade amongst Canada and its Commonwealth partners. According to Mitchell Sharp, then a member of this Department, this inquiry was met with skepticism but was pursued nonetheless. The end result, however, was that trade no longer became a Canadian foreign policy objective within the Commonwealth.[146]

In the post-Second World War years, the character and the face of the Commonwealth changed, and with this change so did Canada's strategies within it. The process of decolonization began within the Commonwealth with the independence of the Indian subcontinent in 1947. This marked the beginning of the Commonwealth's transformation from association status to that of an international organization. More importantly, the process of decolonization would create a new class of state that needed to be addressed.

Decolonization had a significant influence on the international environment. Since the inauguration of the United Nations Organization in 1946 there have been nearly one hundred and fifty new states which have emerged upon the global scene. After the Second World War, the principle of decolonization became codified within the United Nations Charter. Articles 1, 2(7), and 73, dealt with such issues as "self-determination", "sovereignty" and the right of noninterference in domestic matters of a state, and the right of "self-government" respectively. Furthermore, Chapter XI of the Charter enforced upon colonial powers the responsibility of these states to report upon the progress of their wardships.[147] The United Nations was already administering the Trusteeship system, which was a remnant of the old League of Nations Mandate system. The Trusteeship system was designed to administer the independence of those territories placed voluntarily under its control, and it included "existing colonies, ex-enemy territories occupied by the Allies during the war, and former mandated territories."[148] Under the review of the Trusteeship

Council that was responsible to the General Assembly, this body would evaluate the "political, economic, social and educational advancement of the inhabitants of each territory and their progressive development towards self-government."[149] When a state was deemed to be ready for independence, it would be granted this right and admitted to the General Assembly of the United Nations. By the mid 1960's only a few territories remained under trusteeship.[150]

In spite of these positive actions in the United Nations Special Committee and General Assembly, the decolonization process in the Trusteeship Council was slow. Due to the bureaucratic backlog of processing information, many states came forth for review only every three years.[151] The Special Committee also concerned itself with general issues that were to be applied to all territories. The net result of these actions was the delay of the decolonization process, which by 1960 stimulated a furor within the General Assembly. Control of a state's domestic situation still rested with the colonial power. The ensuing decolonization process, however, caused many problems. The first was the economic burden placed upon the United Nations and its membership. This has taken many forms, but relates mainly to the administration costs in overseeing the decolonization process, and the costs of technical and economic assistance programmes. There have also been increased threats to international peace and security that have arisen through the premature granting of independence to some states. In some cases these new states were ill-prepared for self-government, or there were still many internal boundary, social, or ethical problems that needed to be ironed out. Whatever the cause of these problems, it has been necessary for other states to become involved in their internal affairs.[152]

Canada, itself a former colony, had a very strained position in formulating its response to decolonization. Its first position was a moral one, which can be seen by its position held within the General Assembly decisions made with regard to anti-colonial issues, and with its stand within the Commonwealth Head of Government meetings. In both of these fora Canada had taken a pro-decolonization position, or, alternatively viewed, an anti-racial viewpoint. Canada's second position, with regard to the subjects of decolonization and anti-racism, was one of self-interest. Canada was trying to balance its relations between its NATO allies and traditional economic trading partners with that of its moral viewpoint shown above. In short, though within the multilateral fora Canada was seen to fight alongside the anti-colonial bloc, in its bilateral relations it continued to be neutral.[153]

Though Canada had been made a Dominion in 1867, it was still struggling to maintain this independence in this epoch of decolonization. Britain, as a colonial power, was still trying to retain its course of Empire established under Disraeli, of which it tried to subject states through the British Commonwealth. Through the early post-war years Canada did not take any position against colonialism, as it was trying to fortify its own character. With its new alignments with NATO, and its membership within the Commonwealth, Canada was trying to maintain an individualistic position between the United States and the United Kingdom, and this was not an easy task. Increasingly, its autonomy was being eroded through its NATO commitments that increasingly saw Canada's external affairs being placed under American influence.[154] With the Suez Crisis, 1956, Canada would again assert its independence from the United Kingdom.

Since the end of the Second World War, Canada has continued to preserve its distinct, though newly formed, identity from Britain. As a Commonwealth member it was the only state not within the Sterling bloc. Furthermore, Canada continued to protest, or at least sidestep, the suggestion of an Imperial foreign policy for the Commonwealth. It did, however, rely upon Britain as an avenue of trade, as mentioned above. In 1956, though, with the Suez Crisis, Canada chose not to side with its Commonwealth partner, but instead to align itself with the United States. In this instance, Canada distinguished itself as an independent state. It was for this very reason, combined with the fact that Canada had never been a colonial power, that Canada was accepted as a peacekeeper. In the following year, with the new Prime Ministership of John G Diefenbaker, Canada began to take a stand against South Africa and its *apartheid* policy.

Canada's position with regard to decolonization began to be accentuated both in the United Nations and the Commonwealth after the election of Diefenbaker in 1957, which corresponds to the rise in interest in the decolonization issue. Up until 1959, Canada's position with regards to the anti-colonial bloc lacked substance: it was in this year, along with Ireland, that it aligned itself with the anti-colonial bloc.[155] Prior to this, Canada had played an important role in allowing Republics to join the Commonwealth, but it did very little else after the

London Declaration, 1949. After 1959, however, Canada sided with the anti-colonial bloc with regard to General Assembly resolutions. Later in 1961, because of South Africa's *apartheid* policies, its quasi-colonial position in South West Africa,[156] Canada would not accept its application to the Commonwealth as a republic, suggesting, instead that South Africa did not apply.

Throughout this period of history, Canada aligned itself in this multilateral environment with the anti-colonial bloc. It participated in peacekeeping missions that arose because of security issues directly linked to decolonization, and Canada participated in, and contributed financially to, the number of development agencies that arose. Its efforts were not to be restricted to this decade alone, as Canada persisted in its stand against *apartheid*. Its levels of intensity, however, fluctuated with the various Prime Ministerships that ensued. Furthermore, within the multilateral association *La Francophonie,* Canada initiated efforts to overcome the hurdles of decolonization perpetuated by France.[157]

This being said, Canada was also in a difficult position as two of its closest allies, the United States and Britain, were both colonial powers. With regards to these two states, and even South Africa, Canada took no direct action and continued with its bilateral relations with these countries. Consequently, even though Canada publicly supported the anti-colonial position, its political and economic interests could be seen to undermine this position: within Canadian foreign policy there has always been the desire to press forth Canadian interests, however detrimental they might be to international society as a whole.

The main avenues of Canadian foreign policy, the international institutions of which it was a member of, served Canadian interests. The Commonwealth, and later *La Francophonie,* gave Canada a vehicle for foreign policy that was not constricted by American continentalism. Yet both of these institutions had ulterior motives for their purposeful associations. The Commonwealth gave Canada a market for its industries outside of the United States, and *La Francophonie* was always based upon the objective of quelling domestic problems at home. This attitude is emphasized when the Commonwealth changed directions from being solely an economic institution to that of a cultural-development one in the late 1960's. In 1963, when the first preliminary changes of the Commonwealth took place with the call for a Commonwealth Secretariat,

Canada supported its African counterparts to protect its own international image.[158]

The political changes that were occurring within the world, but more particularly within the Commonwealth, were reflected in Canadian foreign policy strategies. The Commonwealth had diminished from being Canada's primary medium on the world stage, underscored by the United Nations and NATO, but it still presented Canada with an avenue to many parts of the globe. The issue of decolonization brought forth its own problems to the world which needed to be addressed as many of these new states were struggling to survive. Economic assistance was the response to the culmination of these issues, and became Canada's new foreign policy objectives within the Commonwealth.

The Commonwealth was the first channel that Canada used to give aid to the Third World. The Colombo Plan, which originated from the Finance Ministers' meeting in 1948, set out a strategy for Commonwealth members to give bilateral assistance to newly independent states in South-East Asia, the first recipients being India, Pakistan and Ceylon.[159] In 1958 and 1960, similar programmes were created for the Caribbean Commonwealth and the African Commonwealth respectively. The motivation behind these programmes reflected the changes occurring within the Commonwealth and the United Nations, as well as with Canada's continued fears of Communism.[160]

In the 1970's, with the advent of the Group of 77 (G-77), a lobbying bloc of Third World states, more pressures were brought to bear upon the affluent First World to offer new alternatives to economic aid. In 1974 there was a proposal for a New International Economic Order (NIEO) that was a call by the G-77 for a restructuring of the international economic system. Many of these states, though independent from their former imperial masters, still felt that they were under-advantaged economically and were exploited by many of the Western states. Under the influence of a new Secretary-General the Commonwealth took a new direction in Third World issues reflecting these demands. In 1970, Canadian foreign policy took a new direction. As part of its strategy, international development was one of Canada's new objectives.[161] In 1975, Pierre Trudeau indicated Canada's continued support for the Third World in his Mansion House speech that called for more trade with the Third World as well as aid. This sentiment for the need of more international development would continue to be Canada's vision of the Commonwealth.

The transition from the Commonwealth being used as a facility for distributing aid to a forum for Canadian concerns on human rights took place in 1981. The Commonwealth continued to be a forum for distributing international development assistance, but Canada's policies incorporated a new direction as well. In 1981 the Commonwealth Secretariat created a division to look at Women's issues in development and this division was initiated by Canada. After the UNCTAD conference in Cancun, 1981, development lessened as a primary concern for Trudeau. This was due to the constitutional debates that resounded across Canada, focusing his attentions to home. Despite these domestic concerns, Trudeau brought forth his new international agenda item, the "peace initiative" in 1983.[162] It was not until the new Conservative government took power in 1984 that Canadian foreign policy took a new direction under the leadership of Brian Mulroney.

In 1984, the Government of Canada called for a revision of its foreign policy objectives. Canada, realizing its geographical and economic situation, pushed towards a policy of Continentalism. Under previous administrations, Canadian foreign policy had looked to Europe as a means of distinguishing Canada from the United States.[163] Mulroney, however, brought Canada closer to the United States with the 1988 Free Trade Agreement that was subsequently revised with the North American Free Trade Agreement (NAFTA) in 1993. In the review of its foreign policy, however, human rights also became an important issue. The question, however, was how to project these policies. The Senate Committee on International Relations in 1985 came forth with the suggestion of utilizing the Commonwealth as a vehicle to launch this new Canadian objective. The Commonwealth presented an advantage in that the first issue Canada took a position on was *apartheid* in South Africa, a subject that had been before the Commonwealth since 1961. Canada always played down this matter within the Commonwealth, preferring to mediate to preserve the organization, but in 1985 Mulroney chose to take a firm stand against *apartheid*.[164] This eventually led to a global stance that isolated South Africa. This resulted in the independence of Namibia in 1989, and eventually the collapse of *apartheid* in 1993.

Canada supported the Human Rights Initiative, 1987, which was a policy proposal put forth by Richard Bourne of the University of London's Commonwealth Studies Centre and Derek Ingram, a journalist, who was a strong proponent of the Commonwealth.[165] The first chairperson of this association was Flora MacDonald, a former Minister of Foreign Affairs for Canada. The Human Rights Initiative was eventually incorporated into the Commonwealth's political agenda as the Harare Declaration in 1991, which was strongly supported by Canada.[166]

Summary

The purpose of this chapter has been to give a general overview of Canadian foreign policy towards the Commonwealth, 1931 to 1991. It has demonstrated how the Commonwealth served as an instrument in Canadian foreign policy, giving Canada a forum to express its trade, aid, and human rights ambitions. This chapter also presented an overview of the domestic and international factors that influenced Canada's foreign policy toward the Commonwealth. Foreign policy is not made in a hermetic environment, distinct from other aspects of politics, and this is important to remember. Canada's Commonwealth policies have been affected by Canada's economic and political relations with the United States and Britain, through its responsibilities in the United Nations and NATO, and through the domestic elements that influence public opinion and the Government.

All of these factors influenced how Canada employed the Commonwealth and must be taken into account when reading the subsequent chapters of this book. These will explore Canada's relationship with the Commonwealth Secretariat, its struggle to maintain the organization throughout the crises in southern Africa, and its aid relations with its Commonwealth partners. Implicit in these chapters are the struggles that ensued between Canada's bureaucracy and the Secretariat and its attempts to balance its moral obligations while protecting its own economic interests.

Chapter Three

Building the Modern Commonwealth:

There will be a natural tendency for the Secretariat to expand its operations as it monitors and participates in Commonwealth activities. While this is understandable and necessary as a response to identified Commonwealth needs and its growing programmes, we do not wish the Secretariat to swell to the point where it becomes a cumbersome factor in the association of the Commonwealth. We must, however, recognize that by the virtue of its role, the Secretariat will figure prominently in any consideration of Commonwealth activities, a consideration which demands that we maintain a closer continuing contact with it and its operation.

Department of Foreign Affairs and
International Trade, August 15, 1973.[167]

CANADA HAS ALWAYS been a supporter of the Commonwealth and its sub-organizations, and its contributions have taken two primary forms: the economic and political patronage that Canada lends this organization. The former is self explanatory. The latter takes the shape of Canada's backing of and influence in the development of these organizations. For clarity of structure, this chapter examines Canada's contribution to the central organ of the Commonwealth, the Secretariat, and, *inters alia,* the development of the functional bodies that have been created. These include the Commonwealth Fund for Technical Cooperation (CFTC) and the Commonwealth Youth Programme (CYP), among others.

Canada served the Commonwealth through its political and economic support that influenced the development of this organization, but Canada did not bring an overbearing presence in the Commonwealth by pressing its own interests. Rather, it adopted a detached presence that served to moderate the development of the Commonwealth and to maintain its objectives of cooperation and consultation. It was because of Canada's awareness of its own "middle power" status that it operated in the Commonwealth in this fashion.

As Canada's story unfolds chronologically, three themes will become apparent. The creation of the Commonwealth Secretariat, 1965, gave Canada the opportunity to shape this organization to reflect its interests. One interest was to create a cost efficient Secretariat that did not duplicate the activities of other international fora, and the other objective of Canada was to shape the Commonwealth to reflect the interests of its membership, limiting the influence of Britain and the powers of the Secretary-General. Canada also helped to shape this organization through introducing and opposing new programmes. Through Canada's participation in the development of the Commonwealth Secretariat it, therefore, moulded the Commonwealth to reflect Canadian values.

"In the Beginning . . ."

At the Heads of Government meeting in London, 1964, the suggestion for the creation of a centralized body to oversee Commonwealth actives was put forward. It was the result of the changing face of the Commonwealth that had expanded to 33 states from its original 5 in 1931. The majority of these states had recently gained their independence from Britain and the proposal for a Commonwealth Secretariat was the next step in removing British control over the affairs of the then loose Commonwealth association. Prior to the establishment of the Secretariat, its functions were performed by the British government. At the following Heads of Government meeting in London, 1965, the Commonwealth Secretariat was established under the principles set out in the *Agreed Memorandum.* This document set out the structure and function of the Commonwealth Secretariat.

Under the *Agreed Memorandum,* the Commonwealth Secretariat was responsible for the administration and coordination of Commonwealth meetings later to be known as CHOGMs; for coordinating the bilateral aid programmes established under the Commonwealth; and for coordinating political affairs concerning Commonwealth members. In short, the Commonwealth Secretariat was to be an international body established to facilitate the cooperation of international events for its membership. The Commonwealth Secretariat was, therefore, an international bureaucracy managed by senior bureaucrats from member countries. In establishing this Secretariat it was realized that skilled persons from the member states' civil services would need to be seconded to the Commonwealth Secretariat.

The Commonwealth Secretariat was made up of nationals from its various members states. The "old" members of the Commonwealth were wary of this new body and wished to see restraint and a limited set of functions for the Secretariat.[168] The "new" members of the Commonwealth, however, wished to see the end of "an old boys' club" that reflected the era of imperialism. The compromise was the selection of a Canadian, Arnold Smith, as the first Secretary-General of the Commonwealth. His nomination was based upon Canada's initial support for the Commonwealth Secretariat that appeased the "new" member faction, namely Afro-Caribbean states, as well as the "old" member faction of which Canada was a member. The task of establishing, the Commonwealth Secretariat fell upon Smith's shoulders.[169]

Arnold Cantwell Smith was a career Diplomat who had worked in Canada's Department of External Affairs since the 1930s. Professional in every sense of the word, he endeavoured to create a Commonwealth Secretariat that was uncompromised by national preferences. His first task was to organize the Commonwealth Secretariat to meet the mandate established under the *Agreed Memorandum* and to staff this organization on a limited budget. The Commonwealth Secretariat would be located in London, as most member governments had High Commissions in that city, which offered the necessary communication infrastructures. The British government offered the new Secretariat Marlborough House as its headquarters without charge.

Through consultations with the High Commissioners in London, Smith nominated his two Deputy Secretaries-General which reflected further the two factions of the Commonwealth. From Ghana, Smith chose Mr. A.L. Abu who formerly had been Ghana's Permanent Secretary of the Ministry of External Affairs, and the secretary to the Cabinet and Head of Ghanian Civil Service. This position helped to represent the Afro-Caribbean bloc within the Commonwealth and was quite appropriate considering that it was Ghana's President, Nkrumah, who had put forward the proposal for the Commonwealth Secretariat. Smith's second Deputy was from Sri Lanka, Mr. T.E. Gooneratne who was seconded from Sri Lanka's Treasury Department. This post gave representation to the "old" member faction of the Commonwealth. In later years, Smith surrounded himself with persons from Australia and New Zealand, with which Canada had strong relations, but in 1965 these two countries, along with Britain, were not strong proponents of the Commonwealth Secretariat.

A further nine senior diplomatic officers were seconded to the Commonwealth along with 30 support staff, and these persons represented the regional distribution of the Commonwealth's membership. These persons worked within four divisions: Administration, Conference Services, Economic Affairs, and International Relations that had seven Director-level positions staffed by persons from Australia, New Zealand, Britain, India, Pakistan, Nigeria and Jamaica. It is interesting to note that of these 10 senior positions within the Commonwealth, only three were held by "new" member states. The reason for this was simply because of the need for trained senior Civil Servants capable of performing the functions of the Secretariat.[170]

When considering the financial contributions of member states to the Commonwealth Secretariat, Britain gave the largest proportion, 30%, of the Secretariat's annual budget. This was followed by Canada, which gave 20%, then Australia and New Zealand, which gave approximately 15% each. The remainder was divided amongst the rest of the Commonwealth members according to their capability to pay. In these cases, they gave token amounts. Thus, in principle every member state gave to the Secretariat, but the brunt of the costs was shouldered by the developed members. These figures remained relatively constant throughout the period from 1965 to 1987,[171] with slight variations in contributions from India, Sri Lanka, and Nigeria, whose economic status fluctuated.[172] Britain and Canada remained the two foremost contributors to the Commonwealth Secretariat.

Canada saw the role of the Commonwealth Secretariat as an organization of senior civil servants coordinating Commonwealth activities but recognized initially a political function in defusing the situation that had arisen over Southern Rhodesia, between Britain and the Afro-Caribbean members of the Commonwealth. It was never Canada's intention to create an organization to develop policies, but only to coordinate cooperation between Commonwealth countries. Canada also saw in the Commonwealth Secretariat an organization that would be sufficiently flexible to fulfil its functions of administering and coordinating economic and political affairs, unlike the United Nations, which had become bureaucratically cumbersome. For this reason Canada preferred a small organization, though it was expected to expand in time.

After the first year, plans were drawn up by the Commonwealth Secretary-General to create a new legal division within the Secretariat. This idea was first presented at the Commonwealth Law Ministers meeting in April 1966 and this division was to assist many of the smaller member states in constitutional as well as international legal matters that as new states they could not perform for themselves.[173] Expansion of the Secretariat was expected, but it was never foreseen that this would occur as quickly as it did. From Canada's perspective this was an unwelcomed development for two reasons. First Canada regarded the creation of a legal division both as redundant and as a threat to the flexible nature of the Commonwealth Secretariat through the adoption of unwanted structures.[174] The second issue was the increase in budgetary costs that such a new division would create. Canada did not want to see the Commonwealth develop into an expensive venture that would exact a large annual cost from it.[175] Canada's solution was to offer assistance to these newly independent states from its own and other Commonwealth members' legal departments.

Unfortunately for Canada, this proposal was supported by its Commonwealth partners, most notably Australia. Australia had been one of those Commonwealth countries that questioned the creation of the Commonwealth Secretariat in 1964, supporting the development of a Secretariat that had minimal powers. Thus, Australia's support for the proposal for a legal division was much to Canada's surprise. This was illustrated by a letter from AG Campbell, Head of the Commonwealth Division in the Department of External Affairs to AR Menzies, Canada's High Commissioner in Canberra:

> Our reaction to Australian unwillingness to stall the establishment of a Commonwealth Secretariat Legal Section was to wonder why

the Australians should favour a Legal Section when they had been opposed to enlarging the Secretariat. I was therefore amused to find from your letter of July 15 that your reaction from "down under" to our position has been to wonder why we should have opposed a Legal Section when we had taken a favourable attitude to the Secretariat.[176]

Canada's efforts to stall this development of the Commonwealth Secretariat were thwarted, and it acquiesced to the wishes of its Commonwealth partners.[177]

Canada also became concerned about the rising costs when subsequent proposals for the expansion of the Commonwealth Secretariat were made. In the Finance Committee meetings Canada tried to limit the indiscriminate hiring practices of permanent staff by the Commonwealth Secretariat. Finance Committee meetings were used by Commonwealth members to manage the budget. On the suggestion of Canada, all member states were represented at the regular Committee meetings by their High Commissioners in London.[178] Canada, wishing to curb the spending of the Commonwealth Secretariat suggested that member states second support staff to the Secretariat until a later time when more appropriate and permanent staff could be hired. This was emphasized in an internal memo that dealt with this subject:

> The finance sub-committee, on which the Canadian member has played a leading role, has attempted to restrain the Secretariat from hiring indiscriminately and proposed that until suitable permanent staff can be found, governments should help meet the Secretariat's staff shortage by seconding employees on a temporary basis.[179]

This was a stalling tactic used by the Canadian government to curtail the expansion of the Secretariat, but it also had the effect of keeping a heterogeneous work force within the Secretariat, reflecting the multicultural nature of the Commonwealth. Though Smith tried to have as many Commonwealth nationalities represented within the organization, this was difficult as the Secretariat did not have the funds to cover the costs of moving these people.[180]

The problems of cost and the expansion of the Commonwealth Secretariat were just one problem that Canada faced. Another issue was the question of what powers the Commonwealth Secretariat should hold. When the concept of the Commonwealth Secretariat was brought forward in 1964 it was decided at that Heads of Government meeting that the Secretariat would not be a body for creating Commonwealth policy, but rather a clearing house for political and economic issues that the Secretariat could appraise but was duty bound not to intervene in the political relations between High Commissions.[181] However, the *Agreed Memorandum* was vague on the duties and powers of the Commonwealth Secretariat, and it appears that liberal definitions were applied by the Secretary-General to define his own role and powers. As early as December 1965, Britain expressed concerns to Prime Minister Lester Pearson that Arnold Smith sided too closely with African concerns when dealing with Rhodesia.[182] Other concerns developed as well in the first year of this new organization. In a letter from AR Menzies, Canada's High Commissioner in Canberra, to the head of the Commonwealth Division in the Department of External Affairs,[183] it was mentioned that Australia had also expressed concerns that Smith had exceeded the mandate for Secretary-General when he chose to sponsor new members to the Commonwealth. As a state gained its independence through decolonization, Smith proposed that it should be welcomed into the Commonwealth. Australia believed that this should be Britain's prerogative. Further concerns were raised about the Secretary-General chairing Committee meetings of the Commonwealth that might call upon the Secretary-General to reprimand a High Commissioner.[184] In the eyes of these Commonwealth countries, the Secretary-General held the status of a senior civil servant only.

This question of the status of the Secretariat was aggravated further when Britain suggested awarding the title of "His Excellency," a title given to Ambassadors and other international Secretariats, to the Commonwealth Secretariat.[185] This title in itself would imply a higher standing for the Commonwealth Secretary-General than just a senior civil servant. When Canada was asked for its position on this matter it told Britain that it did not agree with this title being applied to the Commonwealth Secretary-General, partly because he was a Canadian and because it would change the mandate of the organization. Once again, however, Canada acquiesced to the wishes of the majority on this matter.[186]

Further evidence of this concern of the Secretariat exceeding its mandate was raised in a report reviewing the Secretary-General's role, which was presented at the London Heads of Government meeting in September, 1966. In this confidential report drafted from a meeting of High Commissioners in London, an African government expressed these views:

> However, on a number of occasions the Secretary-General has found himself at cross-purposes with the British Government and with some High Commissioners in London . . . This is particularly the case because the Secretary-General envisages an active role and substantial political functions for himself and appears determined to create precedents and assert claims . . . [W]ith respect to substantive and especially political functions the Secretary-General appears to have tried to move too far too fast . . . [187]

In this same document, the British government, which believed the Secretary-General to be overly sympathetic to African concerns expressed this view:

> At the present stage discussions along such lines could lead to a serious curtailment of the Secretary-General's role and limit the future potential of the office. It would therefore appear desirable to try to head off any suggestions that the powers and functions of the suggestion be reviewed at this meeting. [188]

Canada had its own problems with Smith. In April of this same year, Lionel Chevrier, Canada's High Commissioner in London, wrote a personal letter to Pearson complaining that Smith did not utilize the proper channels when liaising with the Government of Canada. This complaint arose after Smith had gone directly to Canada's Minister of Finance, Mitchell Sharp, to see if Canada would mind hosting that year's Finance Ministers meeting.[189] He stated:

> I do not wish to be misunderstood on this point but there is some risk, I fear that incidents of this kind if they should become

too frequent could undermine and whittle away the status and authority of the High Commissioners in London.[190]

Pearson responded to this letter by allaying Chevrier's concerns after he discussed the matter with Paul Martin, the Minister for External Affairs.[191] Pearson had expressed similar concerns to Julius Nyerere and Kenneth Kaunda, by letter, accusing Smith of "empire building."[192]

In his own defence, Arnold Smith gave his account of his role as Secretary-General. He acknowledged this complaint, but stated that "I did not arrogate executive functions' to the Secretariat, in contravention of the Agreed Memorandum, but was straightforwardly asked to undertake them."[193] This misunderstanding could have developed from the ambiguity presented in the *Agreed Memorandum* itself. Clyde Sanger, who had worked closely with Arnold Smith, defended his actions by describing Smith as a professional and consummate diplomat.[194]

In the first year of the Secretariat's history, Canada played a cautionary role. In a draft of an article prepared for Pearson by the Department of External Affairs, Canada saw the new Commonwealth Secretariat as an experiment of the Commonwealth Association and its endeavours for peace. Its birth was a challenge to the "balance of power", demonstrating that states could work together peacefully to achieve common goals through voluntary associations. This was different from the United Nations that was based on contractual liabilities and acted as an extension to the Cold War politics in the international system.[195] The beauty of the Secretariat, to Canada, was its flexibility incurred through a small and efficient organization. It was this philosophy that directed Canada's attitudes in the first year, but these would vary with the advent of a new administration.

A Need to Expand

While the Pearson Administration was cautious towards the expansion of the Commonwealth Secretariat, the Trudeau Administration promoted it. In Trudeau's first term of office, the Commonwealth adopted a number of new divisions and organizations under the Commonwealth Secretariat. Canada now realized the need for the Secretariat to adopt these roles formerly undertaken by the British government, and Canada found a new use for the Commonwealth Secretariat.

In 1967, Derek Ingram, on behalf of the Nudge Committee in the Royal Commonwealth Society, wrote a letter to Pearson appealing to Canada to support an Information Division within the Commonwealth Secretariat.[196] This letter was prompted by an announcement by the British Government that it would no longer support this service of the Commonwealth. Britain, in reaction to its failing Empire,[197] wished to shed much of its Commonwealth responsibilities, and the Secretariat offered it a means for sharing its costs.[198] At this stage the Royal Commonwealth Society only was petitioning to have a conference on this matter and wanted Canada to sponsor it. Pearson did not want another Commonwealth conference at this time for fear of the acrimony that would arise over the Rhodesian issue. Pearson was also wary of the costs that an Information division would entail. It was soon realized that these former responsibilities of the British government would soon be assumed by the Secretariat because of the needs of its smaller members. As Britain's old role was increasingly transferred to the Secretariat, its duties would expand to assist its smaller members that did not have enough resources to look after their own interests. Thus, the need for the Secretariat to expand was inevitable.

At around this same time Mr. G.G. Serkau, a Canadian citizen, wrote a letter to Pearson suggesting that Canada should use the Commonwealth to push certain values. In his letter he stated:

> I myself am not seeking employment. On the other hand, I would very much like to work with others, if possible, in persuading the new nations of the Commonwealth to accept the proper spirit of guidance and assistance to the end that the peaceful democratic way of life is in their best interests and can be obtained.[199]

This was supported by other comments emanating from the Department of External Affairs, the Commonwealth Division, to Maurice Strong, the Director of the External Aid office, suggesting that Canada was no longer aware of the changes occurring in the Commonwealth.[200] Ten days prior to this letter being drafted, the Minister of External Affairs, Paul Martin, made a speech to the Imperial Defence College dismissing the common clichés that surrounded the Commonwealth—"a common civilization, a common heritage, parliamentary institutions; the rule of law; and allegiance to the Crown"—by stating "you can't use them anymore." The Commonwealth had become a framework designed solely to give aid to the Third World.[201] Through the process of decolonization, the Commonwealth had expanded, leaving behind the traditions on which it was founded. A further complaint commonly uttered in the first year of the Secretariat was that the organization concentrated upon its political functions too much and not enough on its other duties of administration and economic cooperation. These actions duplicated the problems in other international fora, negating the functional purposes of the Commonwealth. Here was an opportunity for Canada to redress this balance.[202]

The Commonwealth had been the catalyst for the creation of Canada's bilateral aid programmes. In 1948, the creation of the Colombo Plan, in its initial stage, dealt solely with Commonwealth countries in Asia and South-East Asia. Later, in 1958, the Commonwealth Caribbean Assistance Programme was created, followed by the Special Commonwealth African Assistance Programme in 1960. These were all bilateral aid programmes where the affluent states gave aid and assistance to the poorer states in the South. The Commonwealth Secretariat offered an opportunity for the poor Southern hemispheric states to help each other through programmes created in the Commonwealth. Though the Commonwealth's bilateral aid programmes persisted, potential for South-South assistance had not yet been realized. Instead, the Commonwealth perpetuated the political problems of aid programmes in other international fora.

Canada's expansionist push within the Commonwealth Secretariat began in March, 1967. In a meeting, of High Commissioners in London, one of the regular meetings held to manage the Secretariat known as the Review Committee on Intra-Commonwealth Organisations,[203] Canada suggested that the Economic Advisory Committee, along with the Finance Committee and the Commonwealth Educational Liaison Unit, be established as a permanent and formal feature of the Commonwealth Secretariat, and furthermore, that a High Commissioner and not the Secretary-General chair these committees. This suggestion was a direct result of the complaints of Britain and Australia about having the Secretary-General chair such meetings.[204] Arnold Smith immediately opposed these changes as unnecessary and proclaimed that the purposes of these Committees were already being performed by frequent meetings of the High Commissioners. This could be increased if it was deemed necessary. Canada persisted in its position and further indicated that it should only be the High Commissioners representing their countries and no other persons.[205]

In making these suggestions, Canada sought two goals. First, it wanted to make the Secretariat more efficient by performing the functions that it was mandated to do. Second, it sought to limit the powers of the Secretary-General. The Secretariat was intended to be an agency designed to coordinate Commonwealth activities with its members. The heart of the power in the Commonwealth was supposed to remain, therefore, with its members. In reality, however, the Secretariat was able to control Commonwealth events because of its centrality in these affairs. By reasserting that the members states were to control Commonwealth affairs through their High Commissioners chairing these various committee, Canada was attempting to reassert the members' control of the Commonwealth. After 28 meetings of the Review Committee, the Committees suggested by Canada became regular features of the Commonwealth Secretariat that winter.[206]

In December 1967, the Commonwealth Scientific Committee (CSC) was made a ward of the Commonwealth Secretariat, later to become a part of it in the following year. There were many specialized agencies and organizations that fell under the shadow of the Commonwealth, but they were too specialized to be adopted by the Secretariat.[207] The CSC, however, was sufficiently general in its projects that it could be of service to the Commonwealth members. The projects of the CSC were general schemes dealing with agriculture, clean water production and so forth, which were of value to a number of the Commonwealth's members. Through integrating this agency into the Secretariat, many of the Commonwealth's members were able to benefit from the information that it produced.

Canada's position on this matter is very interesting. Though Canada on average contributes approximately 25% of the CSC's annual budget, and the first Scientific Advisor to the Secretariat was a Canadian, Dr. Richard Glen, the Department of External Affairs did not seek this post. Dr. Glen was a senior civil servant from Canada's Department of Agriculture and already had done some work with the Commonwealth Secretariat the previous year advising on Agricultural policies. He was well educated and experienced in administrative tasks and had served the Commonwealth Secretariat well. It was because of these factors that the Secretariat nominated him for the post. As was customary with the secondment of Canadians to the Commonwealth, the government usually "topped up" their salaries to maintain the Canadian standards of living, but in this instance the Department of External Affairs was reluctant to do so. This implies two telltale facts: the first, because of the Department of External Affairs reluctance to "topping up" Dr. Glen's salary, he was not a nomination put forward by the Canadian government; the second was that the Department of External Affairs did not hold this post in high esteem as it offered Canada very little benefit.[208] Canada, therefore, seemed to have reluctantly accepted this post. Implicit in this action by the Department of External Affairs was its desire to seek more influential positions within the Secretariat rather than posts that served only an administrative function. This remained the case even when Canada was the primary benefactor to Commonwealth programmes.

There were further developments in Commonwealth aid in 1968. A new Division was created a year earlier, for Development, Aid and Planning, and the first Director of this post was a Canadian, Mr Gordon Goundrey.[209] Once again the Department of External Affairs was reluctant to top up Mr Goundrey's salary as it did not serve Canadian interests.[210] Aid, however, was becoming a large part of Canada's foreign policy and the new Administration under Trudeau was in the process of setting up the Canadian International Development Agency (CIDA) as a Crown Corporation under the Presidency of Maurice Strong. In these early days of CIDA, Strong and Smith met a number of times to discuss the issue of Commonwealth Aid. Aid was becoming an important facet of the Commonwealth Secretariat.[211] In later meetings Smith proposed the creation of the Commonwealth Technical Assistance Scheme, which needed and received Canadian support. The political support for this came from R. Gordon Robertson, from the Privy Council Office, and Maurice Strong, who had made freedom of action one of his conditions for leaving the private sector to help set up CIDA.[212] These two gentlemen saw the advantage that this Commonwealth scheme would have for Canada, making its own aid programmes more efficient. Smith used these allies to by-pass the chain communication through External Affairs by going straight to the top of the Canadian government. External Affairs was reluctant to support the Aid project as it was not one of its initiatives, as it would not have much influence over it.

The result of this meeting was the granting of funds to the Commonwealth Technical Assistance Programme that would become the forerunner to the Commonwealth Fund for Technical Cooperation. The Commonwealth Technical Assistance Scheme was:

> Basically the plan would be to allocate funds to the Secretariat for use primarily in the smaller Commonwealth countries. As Mr. Strong saw it the areas would be those which under Canadian bilateral programme policy were identified as areas of non-concentration. This would have the advantage of providing some measure of Canadian technical assistance for these areas but would relieve the Aid Office of administrative details for small programmes . . . Mr. Smith urged that the initiative should be Canadian and should not be conditional on contributions by other Commonwealth countries. Mr. R.G. Robertson could see political advantages in a strictly Canadian initiative. Mr. Strong had indicated that his paper would cover such matters as objectives, degree and method of control, and guidelines for the Secretariat.[213]

It was also noted at this meeting that CIDA did not want to staff such a project but that financial accountability was important. "At the beginning there would need to be separate accounting for Canadian funds, and also for any others, if other governments decided to participate. Later perhaps it might be possible to fuse them."[214]

Arnold Smith wanted to keep a close Secretariat overview of this project. He believed:

> . . . that for different types of activity, the resources of different Divisions of the Secretariat could be called on, but there would have to be key personnel involved exclusively in financial control to enable an accurate accounting to be made of all funds provided.[215]

At this same meeting a question was raised as to the type of projects to be financed by the Commonwealth Technical Assistance Scheme. The question directly referred to preferences over agricultural assistance to that of educational assistance, both being a type of assistance that Canada gave in its bilateral programmes. "Mr. Smith hoped there would be no limitations of this kind." He then went on to proclaim that "the Secretariat would take over some C.I.D.A. projects and contracts and in developing new ones would apply the same standards as for C.I.D.A. programmes."[216]

What becomes apparent with the development of the Commonwealth Technical Assistance scheme is the bifurcation of Canadian bureaucratic interests in the Commonwealth Secretariat. From a bureaucratic position the Commonwealth Division within the Department of External Affairs and CIDA, a Crown Corporation that is associated to this same department, see the Secretariat from different perspectives. The Commonwealth Division maintained that the Secretariat should remain a flexible organization. CIDA, on the other hand, believed that the Secretariat's potential was not very well understood by Canada and had started to develop its own inroads into this organization. These positions were indicated in a letter from Mr. D.M. Cornett, from External Affairs, to Maurice Strong of CIDA. This letter was in response to a number of questions raised by Strong in an earlier letter. Cornett wrote, in response to Strong's question of strengthening the Commonwealth: "On the first point I think that our answer should be couched to indicate that the problem is not so much one of strengthening and building up the Commonwealth as preventing its disintegration."[217] Cornett then went on to re-emphasize that to Canada the Commonwealth's value was in its consultative functions. He then went on to discuss the development of a formalized Secretariat and what problems this might create from Canada's perspective. Cornett wrote:

> Moreover, we have had some reservations about the role of the Secretariat as the focus of the consultative process . . . As we see it, there is considerable risk that if the Commonwealth becomes too formalized and too institutionalized, with a large active Secretariat vigorously pursuing specific programmes, the centrifugal forces at work arising from the divergent interests of members may cause it to fly apart. This danger would appear particularly acute if the Commonwealth were to turn into yet another forum where the less developed countries exert even stronger pressure than at present for development assistance.[218]

In trying to define what role Canada should play within the Commonwealth, External Affairs was very concerned to limit the powers of the Secretariat. In developing an aid agency within the Commonwealth, it was important that Canada maintain some control over the finances that it spent upon such programmes. The Commonwealth Technical Assistance Scheme, though it reported on Canada's donations separately, still left control of these funds under the Secretariat, which heavily favoured Third World causes. It is this concern that led to the development of the Commonwealth Fund for Technical Cooperation (CFTC). Canada was looking for a way to utilize the Commonwealth as a forum to deliver aid, but not to concede control of this programme. The move to create the CFTC would accomplish both of these concerns of the Commonwealth Division, while following the objectives of CIDA, through the establishment of a new international agency.

The CFTC was established at the Singapore CHOGM in 1971, but details for this organization were developed at the Finance Ministers meeting in Barbados, 1970. It was at this meeting that Canada pledged to fund 40% of the CFTC's annual budget, and this commitment was re-iterated by Trudeau at the 1971 CHOGM. What was established in the CFTC was an anomalous Commonwealth organization that was separate from the Secretariat. The CFTC had its own Economic Review Board that was distinct from the Finance Committee, which reviewed the Secretariat's budget. The Secretariat, however, was responsible for the administrative duties revolving around the CFTC. This included the hiring of personnel and the Chairmanship of the Economic Review Board meetings, which were chaired by the Assistant Secretary-General in charge of Economic Affairs.[219] The other representatives at these meetings were the Director of the CFTC as well as representatives from the contributing member states. The Secretary-General was often present at these meetings, though more in an advisory capacity rather than in a decision-making function. Establishing the CFTC in this fashion was part of Canada's campaign to create a functional organization that would deal with the needs of its Southern partners. The ambition of the CFTC was to encourage the South to assist the South.[220] It was also "Canada's agenda to keep the development side free of political influences."[221]

Ironically, there was also a political purpose behind the creation of the CFTC. According to Ivan Head, the CFTC served as a gesture from Canada to the African states of its commitment to Third World concerns. In an effort to maintain the Commonwealth, after the concerns raised by the Afro-Asian states over Britain's plan to renew arms sales to South Africa, Canada intervened in this matter. Its position was to uphold

Britain's right to determine its own trade and foreign policies without the interference of its Commonwealth partners.[222] Fearing that this position would create the impression that Canada was now siding with Britain against the Afro-Asian caucus of the Commonwealth, Canada initiated the CFTC. Its aim was to bolster African confidence in Canada's support for their concerns.[223] The creation of the CFTC also served to notify its African members of the value that the Commonwealth presented to them. In the controversy that arose over British arms sales to South Africa, many African states indicated that they would leave the Commonwealth should Britain not change its position. The creation of the CFTC was a reminder to these states that they in fact needed the Commonwealth to assist in their development.

At the Ottawa CHOGM, 1973, Trudeau pledged to give two dollars for every dollar of contributions given by Third World members up to the limit of 40% of the CFTC's budget. The reasoning behind this commitment was twofold. The first was to encourage Third World participation in this scheme to remove the stigma that these countries always "received" rather than "gave" to multilateral aid projects. The second reason was to secure Canada's influence within the structure of the CFTC. Canada maintained a dominant presence in the CFTC by committing itself to 40% of its budget. This allowed Canada to control this new organization, which gained it the first Managing Directorship of the CFTC.[224] The CFTC became one of Canada's primary interests within the Commonwealth thereafter.

It was one of Canada's concerns to keep development assistance and politics divorced from each other within the Commonwealth context, and the responsibility for this fell upon the shoulders of George Kidd. This objective of Canada also created immediate tensions between Arnold Smith and Kidd that would be echoed in later Secretariat/CFTC affairs. In the initial Commonwealth Technical Assistance Scheme, the Secretary-General had a large say in the direction of development projects. Many of these were influenced by political processes rather than practical needs or concerns. In establishing the CFTC, Kidd modeled its policies upon establishing those found within CIDA, the agency from which he was seconded. More importantly, Kidd maintained a distance between the CFTC and the Secretariat to remove political influences. This separation of power led to controversy for Canada regarding the Secretariat and the CFTC.[225]

Canada's position towards the Commonwealth Secretariat evolved during the first term of the Trudeau Administration. Under Pearson, Canada's policies towards the Secretariat continually tried to maintain a small flexible agency designed to promote functional consultation, and this was a policy that was maintained by the Department of External Affairs. However, CIDA, one of Trudeau's initiatives, saw that the Commonwealth had prospects for Canada, and encouraged Canadian support for Commonwealth aid programmes. This led to the expansion of the Secretariat. More so, it increased Canada's influence in the Secretariat, which was beginning to reflect Canadian values.

An Age of Dissent

The Commonwealth embarked upon a new course with the new Secretary-General, Shridath Ramphal in 1975. He led the Commonwealth in a direction primarily concerned with Third World issues. Canada's relations with the Secretariat changed in this period due to the division of its interests: the executive, namely the Prime Minister's Office, had a differing view on the Secretariat than that of its bureaucracies. This bifurcation of interests affected Canada's attitudes toward Commonwealth affairs. The root cause of this division of interests came from the Secretary-General's own perspective of his role within the Commonwealth. Ramphal had been Guyana's Minister of Foreign Affairs prior to becoming Secretary-General and had enjoyed personal relations with many countries. He saw the Commonwealth as a Heads of Government club, which led him to by-pass the formal channels of communication through the High Commissions. Ramphal also liked to maintain personal control over the Secretariat's activities, surrounding himself with a core of approximately six individuals.[226] An example of this was presented in an External Affairs report that documented an informal meeting between CJ Small, who was the Deputy Secretary-General in 1978, and the Director of the Commonwealth Division in External Affairs. John Small reported that he found it difficult to do his job as Ramphal had excluded him from his inner circle.[227] It was these characteristics of Ramphal's tenancy as Secretary-General that influenced much of Canada's actions towards the Secretariat.

After the Ottawa CHOGM, 1973, Canada continued to support some aspects of the Secretariat's expansions, but to a lesser degree. At the Singapore CHOGM, 1971, Canada supported plans to create the Commonwealth Youth Programme (CYP), which came into being at the Ottawa CHOGM. The CYP was established in an effort to coordinate a number of various youth programmes of Commonwealth countries, as well as to highlight specific issues of importance to children,[228] and was largely the result of a Canadian initiative.[229] As an example, Mulroney pledged $25 million at the Nassau CHOGM, 1985, to deal especially with this matter.[230] Canada supported the CYP because it did reflect Canadian moral concerns, and in its first years Canada contributed 40% of the CYP's budget. Within its first year of operations, however, concerns would be raised within Canada as to the effectiveness of this organization, and because of Canada's large contribution it felt that the CYP should become more productive. Canada also made suggestions that the CYP, as a youth programme, should have the Youth of the Commonwealth become more active within the organization itself, as with similar programmes within Canada.[231]

In 1976, India proposed the creation of the Jubilee Fund in honour of Queen Elizabeth's Silver Jubilee the following year. The purpose of this fund was to help children within the Commonwealth. Though such a cause was consistent with Canadian moral values, the Government of Canada did not support this proposal. It saw this fund as inefficient, duplicating the objectives of the CYP, and for this reason would not contribute to it. Canada once again reiterated its concerns on the inefficiencies of the CYP and believed that such matters would be best dealt with by not creating a new fund but by making the CYP more proficient. This was to become a common complaint by Canadian officials toward Commonwealth programmes that would almost stigmatize Canada's role within the Commonwealth.[232] Canada wanted to see the Commonwealth Secretariat run cost effectively reflecting Canadian social values.

Another Canadian initiative was the creation of a new division for women's issues within the Secretariat. The impetus for this again came from Canadian social values. Women's issues had been a fundamental part of Canadian society for more than a decade, and, as it gained prominence in international society, the Commonwealth became a favourable forum for Canada to use.[233] The division of Women's Issues and Development was established within the Secretariat in 1981, and a Canadian, Dorienne Wilson-Smillie, became its first director.[234] The importance of this new division was that it was the first to be created in any international organization to deal specifically with women's issues. This was important from a Canadian perspective as it did not duplicate activities in other international fora and was, therefore, cost efficient for Canada. To emphasize this subject as important to Canada, Mulroney sent a letter to Ramphal prior to the Nassau CHOGM, 1985, emphasizing the importance that Women's issues should have on the Commonwealth Heads of Government meeting agenda. The letter states:

> The Conference of Commonwealth Ministers responsible for Women's Affairs in conjunction with the UN meeting at Nairobi this month will be making recommendations that we must take seriously at Nassau. Only when Heads of Government recognize and act on the necessity to integrate women fully into the development process can the process move forward—until that happens it is severely hobbled and we must all overcome traditional reluctance to be able to accept that indisputable fact. Given its importance, I would like to see this item dealt with as part of the economic discussions rather than (this time at least) under the functional cooperation heading.[235]

This comment was made in response to the lack of reception that this matter had at the Commonwealth Ministers meeting earlier that year.[236]

The final area of expansion that Canada supported was the creation of the Commonwealth of Learning in 1989. The idea for this organization arose in 1987 at the Vancouver CHOGM and its purpose and functions were designed to:

> Create and widen access to opportunities for learning, by promoting co-operation between universities, colleges and other educational institutions throughout the Commonwealth, making use of the potential offered by distance education and by the application of communication technologies to education. The Agency's activities will aim to strengthen member countries' capacities to develop the human resources required for their economic and social development, and will give priority to those developmental needs to which Commonwealth co-operation can be applied. *The Agency will work in a flexible manner and be capable of responding effectively, to changing needs.* It will serve the

interests of Commonwealth agencies and educational institutions and doing so in a way that is consistent with the principles that have guided the Commonwealth. In performing its functions the Agency will seek to ensure the appropriateness of programmes and of distance education techniques and technologies to the particular requirements of member countries.[237]

Prior to the Vancouver CHOGM the suggestion for a Commonwealth University, similar to the Open University in Britain, had been made by Ramphal. The idea was not well supported by External Affairs because of costs. Support did, however come by Flora MacDonald who was Minister of Communications in Canada, and it was sponsored from this department.

Canada became the largest contributor to the Commonwealth of Learning, with India as the second largest contributor. Britain, however, was not as supportive as it did not seem to reflect its interests. In response, therefore it offered an over-inflated cost estimate of access to the Open University's Internet as its contribution. For Canada's part, it was the largest contributor and gave the necessary support to establish the Commonwealth of Learning.[238] The first Presidency was given to an Indian, Professor James Maraj.[239]

For Canada, this organization had great significance for a number of reasons, the most being that it was the first formal Commonwealth organization to be located outside of Britain. Canada had been pressing for decentralization of the Commonwealth through a process of not supporting the expansion of the Secretariat, or similar programmes, unless they were located outside of Britain.[240] A position it had taken since 1974. It was known inside External Affairs that Britain still controlled a number of Commonwealth activities,[241] which was disconcerting to Canada.[242] Furthermore, studies of other international organizations had shown that the geographic location of an international institution gave the host state significant influence over that organization. Canada got its wish in the Commonwealth of Learning with a Commonwealth organization premised upon the principle of flexibility being located outside of Britain.

At the same time that Canada initiated programmes within the Commonwealth Secretariat it was not entirely happy with this organization in the latter years of this study. The problem stemmed from External Affairs' relations with the Secretariat, reminiscent of the relations found earlier in the Secretariat's history. The Canadian bureaucracy did not like the way the Secretary-General, at this time Sonny Ramphal, by-passed the channels of communication initially set out in the *Agreed Memorandum*. Ramphal saw the Secretary-General's position on the equal footing with that of the heads of Commonwealth countries, not as the role of a senior bureaucrat. This led to much consternation from External Affairs.[243]

The second issue that worried this department was that of costs. An issue that, again, was present from the foundation of the Secretariat. The reason for this was based in the way the Canadian Government allotted its budgets for each department. The Commonwealth Division was a minor section within External Affairs that could not afford the liberal ambitions of Ramphal, thus it protested against many of his ideas.

In March 1976, External Affairs in Ottawa received a telex from its London High Commission explaining Ramphal's desire for the Commonwealth to have a permanent representative at the United Nations. This was presented to Canada by the Secretariat in the hope that Canada would co-sponsor this idea.[244] The Commonwealth had long had observer status at the United Nations because of its association with the Rhodesian Crisis, but Ramphal wanted to take this one step further, and Chief Emeka Anyaoku, the Assistant Secretary-General, was sent to New York to discuss this matter with Kurt Waldheim, the United Nations Secretary-General, who was quite receptive to this idea.[245] Canada, however, was not so supportive and an internal memo discussing this proposal was not accepted in External Affairs. The memo stated "would it not be preferable to continue the present arrangement, which is more flexible and in keeping with Commonwealth practice?"[246] The second paragraph of this memo then went on to express that Canada did not consider the Commonwealth as an organization but rather an association: "it would not be in keeping with the concept of the Commonwealth as an "association" to be given observer status (sic) and equated with other international "organizations"."[247] It was Canada's intention to curtail the power that it believed the Secretary-General was trying to usurp.[248]

This matter initiated a small "battle" between External Affairs and the Secretariat where Canada continued to assert that the Commonwealth should remain an "association." As mentioned above, the reason for this was that the Secretariat was by-passing the Department of External Affairs and going directly to the Prime Minister or the Minister of External Affairs. This then generated "top-down" pressure upon the department, which was never appreciated.[249] In a letter from External Affairs to the Governor General's office, this distinction between an "association" and an "organization" was put forward, emphasizing Canada's position as supporting the Commonwealth "association." "One of the distinct aspects of the Commonwealth . . ." it was written, "is that, unlike international organizations or other groupings, it provides for no regular meetings of ministers of External Affairs."[250] What was most interesting about this statement was its irrelevance to the subject matter of the letter, Canada's position on the Silver Jubilee Appeal. The Department of External Affairs was trying to win political support from Canada's Governor General, its representative with the Queen who was head of the Commonwealth. Through pleading their case to the Governor General, External Affairs was hoping to win influence over the Secretary-General and its executive.

In this same letter, External Affairs went on to emphasize the proper channel of communications that should be used when the Commonwealth Secretary-General wanted to contact Canada. He should direct his concerns through the High Commission in London. The reason for this was to emphasize the "practical reasons essential in the interests of speed, control, and co-ordination."[251] The letter then went on to explain that the Canadian High Commissioner was more aware of Commonwealth matters, as he sat on Management Boards for the CFTC, the CYP, the Finance Committee and the Commonwealth Sanctions Committee.[252] Through encouraging support for the Secretariat to use the proper channels of communication, External Affairs was hoping to re-assert its control over Commonwealth affairs.

This loss of control that External Affairs was trying to regain was indicative of a greater struggle growing between Canada and the Secretariat. External Affairs was trying to bring the Governor General on side for the department as a means of counter-balancing the pressures being placed upon them from above, as Ramphal continued to go directly to Canada's executive, by-passing External Affairs. External Affairs also saw the Secretary-General assume more power for himself and his office, in contravention to the *Agreed Memorandum*.[253] This was accented in an informal conversation between John Small, the newly appointed Assistant Secretary-General and the Director of the Commonwealth Division on a visit to London. Small made comments on the control that Ramphal had within the Secretariat, using only a close circle of persons for its affairs. By acting in this fashion, Ramphal created an inner-core within the Secretariat that seemed to operate independent of the wishes of its members. Gordon Fairweather accentuated this point in a critical report he wrote on the Secretariat after the Zimbabwe elections. The report expressed a number of concerns regarding the Secretariat's interference in these elections. More relevant to this chapter was the Secretariat's exclusion of "developed" countries at a meeting where a letter was drafted to Robert Mugabe congratulating him on his election victory.[254] Ramphal brushed this off as an "oversight" but this concern that Ramphal was too enthusiastic in Third World affairs worried Canada's Department of External Affairs. The report went on to state:

> General trends in the Commonwealth Committee on Southern Africa—our High Commission reports that the value of the Committee is deteriorating because of its increased use by LDC's to "establish a phoney consensus" rather than on exchanging views and ideas informally and frankly.[255]

The report ends by stating that Ramphal was trying to create an independent organization of the Commonwealth Secretariat and states, "As you know, the above points are not untypical of dealing with the Secretariat—either now or in the earlier years."[256]

This report was drafted to reflect a number of concerns that had arisen over the year regarding the Commonwealth Secretary-General's actions. It was apparent to External affairs that Ramphal was building his own empire through the Secretariat. When Ramphal became the Secretary-General in 1975, he was sponsored by Canada on the condition that he held this office for no more than five years. However, even though "Ramphal was the darling of Canadian politicians"[257] there was, nevertheless, much concern when he was re-elected to serve for another five years. With the Liberals defeated in the 1979 elections, Ramphal quickly seized the opportunity to be re-elected.[258] Due to the animosity that existed between Ramphal and External Affairs, this news was not very pleasing to Canada's civil servants. A follow-up report on the Lusaka CHOGM, 1979, made this point: "He is now in place probably for another five years and our job is to work with him."[259] A further memo sent from Ottawa to London that same year again emphasized the dislike that External Affairs had for Ramphal. After the Iranian Hostage crisis, 1979, the sarcastically phrased memo asked:

Will the Commonwealth Secretary General or Secretariat as a matter of routine transmit text of statement to Iranian Embassy in London, or will Iranians have to content themselves with reading it in *The Times* like everyone else? (Or in the *Guardian* if they are true revolutionaries.)[260]

Finally in March 1980, in a memo from Ottawa to the Canberra High Commission, concern was raised over the abdication of Queen Elizabeth II. These were thoughts proposed by Ramphal to Australia, asking whether Prince Charles would become the immediate Head of the Commonwealth "Association", or would he need to go through a process of acceptance from the Commonwealth members as a whole. In penned notes at the bottom of this memo a question was asked as to whether Ramphal was challenging the Crown to become head of the organization, as set out in the London Declaration, 1949.[261] The gist of these comments was that they emphasized External Affairs' concern over Ramphal's empire-building, which was one way for this department to vent its frustrations in being by-passed by the Secretariat over the majority of Commonwealth Affairs. External Affairs' continued complaints over Ramphal's attempts to change the Commonwealth into an organization from its flexible "association" roots were well-founded, however misguided were their intentions.

The costs of running and managing the Commonwealth Secretariat were a second concern to the Canadian bureaucracy. From the very beginning of the Secretariat's history, issues of cost were important to Canada. This would not change throughout this period of study. Canada continued to have concerns about the extravagance, the under-employment of Canadians, and the duplication of services taking place in the Secretariat.

Canadian bureaucrats often accused the Secretary-General, Sonny Ramphal, of extravagant displays during his tenure. John Small in his informal report on the Secretariat mentioned this complaint. The issue revolved around a meeting held for the leaders of the Commonwealth's Third World members where they drafted a letter of congratulations to Robert Mugabe. Small's complaint was that this meeting was lavishly catered for unnecessarily.[262] Other examples cited by Small were the choice of hotels Ramphal chose when visiting countries either in an official or unofficial capacity.[263] John Harker remarked upon a similar event where Ramphal spent a week in a top hotel in Ottawa, waiting to see the Minister of External Affairs.[264]

In partial defence of Ramphal's actions, it is important for the Secretary-General to have comfortable accommodation when visiting countries to entertain persons if necessary. This is similar to most countries when the Head of State goes on official business that suitable accommodation be found to project an image of the country, but External Affairs did see some abuse by Ramphal, and there needed to be a watchdog. Canada had given the Secretariat £10, 000 for such travel purposes where £6, 000 was to be used by the Secretary-General and the remaining £4, 000 to be used by the Assistant Secretary-General's when on official visits. John Small, however, recounted that this did not occur, and Ramphal used these funds for himself.[265]

The second issue of concern was the matter of salaries for Canadian employees of the Secretariat. The roots of this problem went as far back as 1965 when the Secretariat was founded. Initially personnel were seconded to the Secretariat from member states. This was not intended to be a permanent arrangement but rather a temporary one where the Secretariat employed these persons and paid their salaries from its budget. What had become the practice for Canadians seconded from Canada's Public Service was that the government department they left covered the depreciation in salary that occurred when they joined the Secretariat. Under Government Employment Regulations, however, this arrangement then placed the onus upon the Canadian government to hire these persons back after their term was completed with the Secretariat. The Canadian government preferred to give persons working for the Secretariat a leave of absence from government service, negating their legal responsibilities under Canadian Public Service employment regulations.

For the Secretariat, this placed pressure upon the hiring of Canadian personnel, as they could not attract competent persons for the job. In the cases of Goundrey, de Laet, and Clyde Sanger, all Canadians who worked for the Commonwealth Secretariat, they came from other sectors of industry and were approached by the Secretariat specifically for their posts.[266] The Secretariat then approached External Affairs asking the Canadian government to "top up" their salaries as a means of encouraging Canadian representation. External Affairs was reluctant to do this for the very reasons mentioned above.

Ironically, in 1979 the Secretary-General became concerned that some employees of the Secretariat had two "paymasters", which he felt was unsuitable for fear of generating insufficient loyalty to the

Commonwealth.[267] This change was favourable to the Canadian government as it no longer needed to "top up" the salaries of Canadians working for this organization. The other side of the coin, however, was that many Canadians would not accept the lower employment conditions offered by the Secretariat. It would, therefore, become more difficult to have Canada represented in the Secretariat. As a compromise, member governments were allowed to grant their citizens a living allowance when working for the Secretariat.[268]

Finally, one of Canada's concerns regarding the Secretariat was that it duplicated some of the functions of the United Nations. The Commonwealth's attraction to Canada was that it supplemented the role of the United Nations in its endeavour to create peace and not to copy this organization. It was for this reason that Canada did not support the creation of a Commonwealth Emergency Force when it was called for on two separate occasions. Canada had continually pressed this matter of not duplicating functions in an effort to improve efficiency and limit costs. This perspective was stressed in a "post-mortem" prepared by External Affairs after the Lusaka CHOGM, 1979. It stated:

> The Commonwealth seems likely to decrease in importance in proportion as it initiates or duplicates UN practices, procedures and programs. Mr. Ramphal risks this tendency. Moreover, it is not the best forum for North/South dialogue as far as Canada is concerned, given the small proportion of developed countries.[269]

In 1981, however, a bifurcation in goals would ensue between External Affairs and CIDA over the structure and management of the CFTC as External Affairs pressed to make the Secretariat more efficient.

The CFTC, along with the CYP, and the Commonwealth Foundation were all financed through voluntary contributions made by member states. The Secretariat's budget, on the other hand, was financed through assessed contributions of its member.[270] For Canada, the funds paid to the Secretariat came from the budget allotted to External Affairs, but the funds given to the CFTC were donated by CIDA. The problem arises within this relationship over the reporting procedures required by the two Canadian departments. CIDA was responsible for reporting to the Treasury all funds given to multilateral agencies. It was also a requirement of CIDA that it was able to oversee all multilateral projects supported by

Canadian funds and that CIDA standards were to be applied to these projects.[271] Unfortunately, in the late 1970's some of the Secretariats projects, mainly Agricultural and Educational ones, were financed through CFTC funds, thus invariably through CIDA. This raised concern within this Crown corporation, as they were unable properly to supervise these projects. This problem became compounded in the 1980's when the Secretariat wanted to amalgamate CFTC into itself.

The Secretariat had limited budgets that precluded it from performing a number of the tasks that Ramphal had envisioned. The CFTC, however, was well financed by Canada and could provide the Secretariat with funds that it desired. External Affairs supported this merger upon the principle that it would remove the duplication of services and make both the Secretariat and the CFTC more efficient. CIDA, however, opposed any such convergence as it was pandering to the whims of many Third World states.

Because of its large contributions into the CFTC, Canada had a moderating influence within this organization. Of all of the Commonwealth organizations this was the one institution in which it had the most interest. Canada saw the CFTC as a practical tool, facilitating Canadian foreign policy, and it was for this reason that it chose to ensure the separation of politics from the CFTC when it was established. Through the integration of the CFTC and the Secretariat, this policy of removing politics from aid would be negated. It was known that many of the supporters for this merger were the Afro-Caribbean states that coveted the funds found in the CFTC for projects that would not be supported by Canada.[272] It was no secret that Canada attended the management board meetings of the CFTC "with calculators" in accordance with CIDA policies for efficiency and integrity.[273] If these funds were under the Secretariat's control CIDA would have less influence in the allocation of CFTC funds.

External Affairs supported this merger for practical reasons, those of cost and efficiency, but it was opposed by CIDA because of its ambitions to separate politics from aid. CIDA also needed to maintain the integrity of its aid policies that included its reporting procedures and the need to maintain CIDA standards in all multilateral projects that it supported.[274] For this reason Canada insisted upon an "evaluation" process that would continue to maintain its overview of technical assistance projects. This sparked resentment from Ramphal as he considered this as "spying" by

Canada.[275] Robert McLaren, as an Assistant Secretary-General interacting with External Affairs, tried to explain to Ramphal that this was not the case and that this evaluation was a "management technique." It was the gravity of this situation that led McLaren to interact with the government for if Canada, or more to the point CIDA, was not happy with its ability to maintain Canadian standards upon the CFTC/Secretariat projects that it would remove its funding from this programme. It was under this realization that Ramphal acquiesced to this evaluation process, for the Secretariat was still dependent upon Canadian support and contributions.

One final issue must be examined before this chapter can be concluded, and that is of Canadian personnel working for the Commonwealth Organizations. Canada has been a substantial contributor to the Commonwealth's various organizations. In the Secretariat, it has on average given 20% of that institution's budget; in the CFTC it has given 40% of the budget; in the CYP it gave on average 23% to 30% of the budget; and to the Commonwealth Foundation, which was established in 1965, Canada has given 25% of the operating budget.[276] It has been the case in other international fora that when a state gives heavily to an international institution it gains a proportionate number of administrative places in appreciation. In the Commonwealth, however, this has not been the case for Canada, which, even Ramphal acknowledged, was sorely under-represented.[277] From 1963 to 1987, Canada has held only 18 Director level positions or above.[278] To put this in perspective there have been approximately 167 positions at Director level or above available in this same timeframe. This information is skewed when one takes into account that a number of the Secretariat's personnel held their office for more than the three years initially prescribed,[279] but the point being made demonstrates that Canada has not used its economic contributions to influence the Secretariat through the over-abundance of Canadian personnel. The one institution where Canada does require a Canadian presence is in the CFTC.

Canada has had a number of persons in the CFTC representing its interests. This was mainly to ensure that CIDA policies were adhered to in formulating many of the CFTC's projects. In doing so, however, Canada earned a poor reputation for over-scrutinizing proposed CFTC projects to the point that Canada was perceived in a "miserly" light. As John Small stated, however, "it is a shame that this behaviour stigmatizes Canada's benevolent character for it is never mentioned that it gives the most to those projects accepted."[280] In fact in many of the projects sponsored by the CFTC, the personnel used for these tasks come from LDC's, perpetuating South-South policies.[281] Canadians were only used in those technical projects where they alone possessed the desired skills.[282]

Another question of influence that arises when analyzing an international organization is that of the loyalty of personnel. In the words of Inis Claude:

> . . . the identity of every organization . . . tends to be lodged in its professional staff. Members, stockholders, or citizens may control the organization, but they cannot be it; the staff, in a fundamental sense, *is* the organization . . . the invention of the international secretariat may be described as the real beginning of international organization.[283]

The question however is whether these persons can divorce themselves from their own national interests? This has always been one of the dangers of an international organization and the Commonwealth has not been immune from such problems.

For Canada's part it has always tried to maintain impartial personnel in the Secretariat. As early as 1967, Marcel Cadieux in his role as Under Secretary of State for External Affairs sent a memo to all of Canada's High Commissions cautioning them about allowing Arnold Smith to utilize Canadian communication facilities. He wrote that "Canadian posts should reserve the granting of hospitalities to Canadians working with the Secretariat in order to preserve the Commonwealth Secretariat's image of service to all Commonwealth countries."[284] He went on to state that "Mr.Smith is particularly anxious to appear as a Commonwealth Servant and not as a Canadian representative when visiting Commonwealth countries."[285] This internal memo was released in response to the actions of Mr. St. John Chadwick, the Chairperson of the Commonwealth Foundation, who used the British High Commission for Foundation business. This conveyed an impression that the Foundation was under the aegis of the British government, and this was something that Canada did not want to happen with regard to the Secretariat.[286] It was important to Canada, therefore, to protect its own integrity, as well as that of the Commonwealth's organizations.

It is known, however, that on a number of occasions Canadians working within the Commonwealth Secretariat reported upon conditions, morale, and other internal matters occurring within the Commonwealth Secretariat.[287] Mr JC Best conveyed Ramphal's perspective on Canada's role within the Secretariat;[288] John Small mentioned the problems that he faced with Ramphal and his inner circle within the Secretariat;[289] and Arnold Smith, on leaving his post as Secretary-General, gave informal debriefings to External Affairs personnel.[290] In a memo prepared for Mr. Morgan from External Affairs, prior to a visit to the Commonwealth Secretariat, it was stated that:

> There are many meetings on Secretariat business involving EA personnel and they have been pretty well covered—at least those we know about and on which we require reports. We are not, of course, as well informed on meetings not involving EA, but we would like to think that they are covered too, since the various aspects of Secretariat operations are meant to reinforce the political dimension, which is our concern.[291]

Most persons interviewed, however, denied relaying information or reporting to the Canadian government. Robert McLaren stated that during his term as Deputy Secretary-General he only reported to External Affairs when it was in the Secretariat's interest to do so.[292] John Harker mentioned, however, that most persons working for the Secretariat were anxious to maintain a good rapport with External Affairs to protect their interests of returning to a suitable post on leaving the Secretariat.[293] It is perhaps for this reason that Ramphal wished to remove the matter of "topping-up" of the salaries of Canadians employed by the Secretariat.[294]

Summary

In reviewing, this chapter its theme focused almost explicitly with Canada's relations with the Commonwealth Secretariat, as this was the central agency of the Commonwealth after 1965. In assessing its relationship with this central Commonwealth organization, along with the peripheral agencies such as the CFTC, the CYP, and the CSC, Canada played a "moderating" role. It used its influence to temper some of the extreme ambitions of the Secretariat and the Commonwealth's members in an effort to shape the Commonwealth into a practical association for its membership. In applying its influence, however, it never did so "at the expense at the freedom or independence of small states."[295] The cost was always upon Canada, which it served responsibly. Faced with overwhelming support for certain matters, Canada acquiesced to the wishes of the majority on two noted occasions: the creation of the legal division within the Secretariat and the bestowing of the title of "His Excellency" on the office of the Secretary-General.

However, Canada also used its wealth to expand the philanthropic endeavours of the Commonwealth through the creation of the CFTC and the CYP. These agencies did serve Canadian foreign policy interests by assisting in the administration of smaller projects that its own agency, CIDA, would not undertake, but they also served the greater interests of the Commonwealth's members. Canada, in many agencies, was the largest contributor, yet it was not over-represented in these agencies. The CFTC was the one agency that Canada demanded the right to oversee projects, but this was because of its own national accounting procedures, as established within Canadian Government policies and CIDA's constitutional mandate. If it appeared parsimonious, it was only because it had high standards for its aid programmes and that it should never be forgotten that Canada was the largest financial contributor to the CFTC. Canada's objective by these actions was to encourage the efficient use of funds to produce benefits. The liberal expenditure desired by some states would have only bankrupt the CFTC to the disadvantage of the Commonwealth. Thus Canada acted as a moderator rather than a "Scrooge". Through its actions in the creation of these agencies Canada was able to insert its own values into the Secretariat.

With regard to the political expansion of the Secretariat's activities and its desire to make the Commonwealth an international actor on the stage with the United Nations, Canada also served to curb these ambitions of the Secretary-General. From Canada's perspective such measures as the introduction of a Commonwealth Emergency Force or Permanent Representation within the United Nations would negate the Commonwealth's true international advantage: its effectiveness through flexibility. The status of Permanent Representative within the United Nations would have increased the audience for Commonwealth concerns, but it would diminish the political effect that the Commonwealth's informality served. This position would have taxed the manpower and resources of the Commonwealth and deflected from its ability to serve members. Through its campaign to maintain the Commonwealth's status as an "association", Canada facilitated in the moderating of the Secretary-General's ambitions. Such an effort was not entirely altruistic, for the Department of External Affairs was at odds with Ramphal for his circumvention of the channels of communication, but the concerns of External Affairs reflected practical needs.

Through Canada's participation within the Commonwealth, it helped to establish and shape the agencies of this association. Its participation, however, was not through overbearance but rather through solid support for the principles upon which the Commonwealth was premised: cooperation and consultation. Through its moderating behaviour Canada served its own interests through a detached presence. JC Best said it well when he paraphrased Ramphal: "it was not a question of the number and level of Canadians at the Secretariat, but whether that body was aware of Canadian views and operations. He believed that the Secretariat was definitely aware of Canada in this sense."[296] It is safe to say, therefore, that Canada had influence within the Commonwealth, and this influence was present in the values that Canada emphasized within the programmes that it initiated. These actions by Canada helped to shape the Commonwealth, redirecting its development into a functional organization.

Chapter Four

Developing the Commonwealth

The role of leadership today is to encourage the embrace of a global ethic. An ethic that abhors the present imbalance in the basic human condition—an imbalance in access to health care, to a nutritious diet, to shelter, to education. An ethic that extends to all men, to all space, and through all time. An ethic that is based on confidence in one's fellow man. Confidence that wit imagination and discipline the operation of the present world economic structure can be revived to reflect more accurately the needs of today and tomorrow. Confidence that these factors which have the effect of discriminating, against the developing countries can be removed from the world's trading and monetary systems. Confidence that we can create a trading order which is truly universal and not confined to or favouring groups defined along geographic or linguistic or ideological or religious or any other lines. Confidence that access to liquidity for trade and for development will not be restricted by factors other than those accepted by all as necessary in order to contribute to the health of the entire world system.

Pierre Trudeau. London 1975[297]

IN THE POST-WAR years, the primary function of the Commonwealth was to deliver bilateral aid to its Third World members, which served Canada's purposes. This is the reason why Canada strove to maintain this organization.[298] Administered through the Canadian International Development Agency (CIDA), Canadian aid to the Third World has taken many forms. The majority of Canadian aid to Commonwealth states has taken the form of bilateral grants and loans used to develop the economic and social infrastructures of the recipient states, allocated to states according to their assessed needs. Canada has also offered technical assistance, usually in the form of educational and agricultural aid, to many Commonwealth countries to supplement the development of the economic and social infrastructures of these states. Finally, Canada has made financial contributions to the Commonwealth's multilateral aid programmes, which were dispersed to recipient countries on Canada's behalf.

The majority of Canadian aid was directed towards Commonwealth countries for a number of reasons. The initial one being that Canada had stronger ties with the members of this organization. With biennial meetings of the heads of state and a number of other conferences held for social concerns each year, Canada was better able to understand the needs of its Commonwealth partners. As this organization already had established its own programmes for supplying bilateral aid to many Third World countries, a further increase in Canada's Commonwealth commitment was a practical option. The Commonwealth, however, also dictated the style of Canada's foreign aid budget. The majority of Canadian assistance to the LDCs of the Commonwealth took the form of educational assistance. At the 1956 Prime Minister's meeting, it was decided that "the Commonwealth Governments will strive for a progressive improvement in the standards of life of their own peoples and will assist in similar efforts in other parts of the world."[299] In 1959, the Commonwealth held its first conference on education, and the Commonwealth Education Liaison Committee was established this same year. Education became a "cooperative" concern of the Commonwealth and found its way onto its economic agenda. With the requests of many of the LDCs within the various regional aid programmes available for educational assistance, this was the type of aid that Canada gave in response to these demands.[300] To truly develop an understanding of Canada's role within the Commonwealth, however, proves difficult, as Canada does not differentiate the aid given to Commonwealth and non-Commonwealth states. Rather it groups its aid packages into regions.[301]

To better understand Canada's economic relations with its Commonwealth partners, the three primary regions in which Canadian aid to the Commonwealth has been delivered will be examined. These areas are Asia and South-East Asia, the Commonwealth Caribbean, and Commonwealth Africa. The text will then go on to explore Canada's multilateral aid that has been given to Commonwealth members through the various regional banks and the Commonwealth Fund for Technical Cooperation (CFTC). Finally, this chapter will argue that the economic support that Canada has given to its Commonwealth partners was rhetorically based, and though Canada did help these states, its efforts were limited.

Development Assistance

When the Liberal government was returned to power in 1963, under the leadership of Lester B. Pearson, it reintroduced a sense of "internationalism" into Canadian foreign policy. Pearson was committed to a multilateralist foreign policy agenda, as were his predecessors Mackenzie-King and St. Laurent, and he believed that this policy would help to establish Canada's international identity. The Commonwealth played an important role in the initial stages of Pearson's foreign policy. This is demonstrated by the fact that 90% of Canadian aid between the years of 1950 to 1965 went to Commonwealth countries.[302] This percentile diminished as more states outside of the Commonwealth required assistance and Canada's international responsibilities widened. The distribution of Canada's foreign assistance programmes handled through the External Aid Office, established in 1950. Though there was an office of Commonwealth Affairs within the Department of External Affairs, the majority of Canada's aid to Commonwealth countries fell into three regional categories mentioned above.

Asia and South-East Asia

Canada's first aid programme gave bilateral aid to Asia and South-East Asia. Promoted through growing fears of Communism in this region by Australia and New Zealand, the Colombo Plan, from 1948 to the 1970's, was designed to offer economic support to this area of the world. The initial members of the Colombo Plan were India, Pakistan, and Sri Lanka (Ceylon),[303] but as the process of decolonization occurred, its membership grew. By 1968, there were 22 states covered by the Colombo Plan, the majority of which were not Commonwealth members. The main

Commonwealth states that received aid from Canada were those mentioned above, along with Malaysia, which gained its independence in 1957, and Singapore, which gained its independence from Malaysia in 1965.

Canada's participation in the Colombo Plan initially was motivated by fears of Communism and also a sense of social responsibility to the Commonwealth. As Pearson stated:

> . . . it seemed to all of us at the conference that if the tide of totalitarian expansion should flow over this general area, not only will the new nations lose the national independence which they have secured so recently, but the forces of the free world will have been driven off all but a relatively small bit of the great Eurasian land mass . . . If southeast Asia and South Asia are not to be conquered by communism, we of the free democratic world . . . must demonstrate that it is we and not the Russians who stand for national liberation and economic and social progress.[304]

Aid was a tool used by Western states to challenge the expansion of Communism, as indicated by Pearson's statement. Canadian aid programmes throughout the 1950's and 1960's were, therefore, motivated by its fears of Communism.

At the Commonwealth Finance Minister's Meeting in 1948, Canada also believed that economic and social cooperation would help these newly independent states, and this was still the case in 1963. There was no evolutionary blueprint set up for the development of these states, as the Commonwealth was premised upon a principle of non-interference within the internal politics of another member state,[305] though a consultative committee was established to discuss the economic problems facing South-East Asia. This committee met annually to assess the changing needs of the recipient states, and bilateral aid was given to the specific state through the form of grants and loans or technical assistance.[306]

Canadian aid within the Colombo Plan consisted of technical aid on a variety of projects, at the beginning of Pearson's term. In Pakistan, it was the construction of a transmission lines project that continued throughout the Pearson Administration, along with a hardboard-development project.[307] In India, Canada offered continuing assistance on the third stage of the Kundah Hydroelectric project,[308] and in Sri Lanka, Canada continued to give assistance to various electrification projects.[309] Finally, in Malaya, Canada continued to assist in the Malayan East Coast Fisheries Project. Further projects commenced in 1963 consisted of "the Umtru Hydroelectric power plant and a cobalt-therapy unit in India; an expansion of the Sukkur thermal-electric power plant and a land-use study in Pakistan; the construction of facilities at the Kayunayake airport in Ceylon; and a hydroelectric engineering study of the Upper Perak River in Malaya."[310] All of this aid was directed towards developing the economic infrastructure of these countries. Canada also pledged further support to this region through access to industrial commodities. This allowed these states to overcome foreign exchange difficulties faced because of their weak currencies. Canada also sent 31 secondary school teachers and teacher trainers, along with seven university professors, to this region to assist in social development.[311]

In the following year, 1964, Canada increased its aid budget to, and continued to assist in, the Colombo Plan,[312] with aid directed towards industrial and educational development, and it maintained its assistance to the various projects stated above. The only new project in this year was the industrial aid given to Sri Lanka in the expansion of the Mutwal Refrigeration Plant. Canada did, however, increase its educational support to this region, and in 1964, 74 educational advisors were working in this region. Additionally, 1,351 students from South-East Asia were studying in Canada under the Commonwealth Scholarship and Fellowship Program.[313]

Throughout the remaining years of the Pearson Administration, industrial and educational support continued for this region through the Colombo Plan. In 1966, the most significant new project initiated was in Pakistan, where Canada assisted in a refugee housing project due to tension growing between India and Pakistan over the Kashmir territory, along with a nuclear-power generating plant. Canada also sent food aid to this region in the form of 66,000 tons of wheat to Pakistan and 1,000,000 tons to India.[314] The distribution of food aid continued on, and Sri Lanka also became a recipient in 1967.[315]

Canada again became involved with the need for supplying military aid to this region of the world in 1968. Earlier in the decade, 1963, Canada had given India a loan to purchase 16 Caribou aircraft, supporting India in its war against China.[316] In 1968, it was Malaysia that required military assistance. In 1967, Britain announced its withdrawal of military support from South-East Asia, and this affected Malaysia and Singapore, as well as Australia and New Zealand, which were dealing with issues of Communism, namely guerrilla activities, in the region.[317] Canada offered its support through military training to deal with this problem.[318]

The Commonwealth Caribbean

The first assistance programme for the Commonwealth Caribbean countries was started in 1958 with the Commonwealth Caribbean Assistance Programme. In later years, Canada developed strong ties with this region, but in 1963 its aid budget to the Caribbean was still quite minor compared to that given in the Colombo Plan. By 1968, the Caribbean received only $59 million in aid between 1958 and 1968, compared to the $980 million the Colombo Plan received between 1950 and 1968.[319] As with the Colombo Plan, the Commonwealth Caribbean Assistance Programme was a bilateral scheme based within the Commonwealth,[320] and the majority of aid that Canada offered this region was in the form of industrial and educational assistance. The majority of Canadian aid to the Caribbean revolved around social standards, and many of the projects in which Canada participated reflected this. In 1963, Canada helped to construct a number of schools and a university in Trinidad, as well as to develop fresh water wells and port handling facilities.[321] The most significant technical assistance that Canada sent to this region was 20 teachers and advisors to improve the educational facilities of this region. [322] In the following year, the aid programme to this region increased, and 26 more teachers and 11 advisors were sent to the Caribbean.[323] This was consistent with Canada's support and attendance of the Commonwealth Education Conference that same year, which promoted education as a means of advancing Third World development.[324] In 1965, Canada continued to support educational development in the Caribbean, but it also began further development projects to assist infra-structural development, such as the building of roads, bridges, and even airport facilities.[325]

This pattern of Canadian assistance continued throughout the Pearson Administration. The only significant change to be noted was the establishment of the Caribbean Free Trade zone that helped the local economies through internal markets. Canada had already strengthened its trading ties with this region in 1966 at a conference held in Ottawa,[326] and by 1968, Canada planned to offer financial assistance to the Caribbean Development Bank, though this did not become a reality until the following year under the Trudeau Administration.[327] Canada assisted its Commonwealth partners in the establishing of their economic independence and implemented trade relations with the emerging trade blocs around the world through its Commonwealth ties. Following the establishment of the Caribbean Free Trade zone in 1966, the Association of South—East Asian Nations (ASEAN) was established in 1967, establishing trade relations with its Commonwealth partners in this region as well.[328]

Commonwealth Africa

The first African state to gain its independence from Britain after the Second World War was Ghana in 1957. When it gained its independence Canada offered it support through military assistance, as well as economic and technical support. However, it was not until 1960 that the Commonwealth set up the bilateral aid programme for Africa, known as the Special Commonwealth African Aid Plan (SCAAP). As with the Colombo Plan and the Commonwealth Caribbean Aid Programme, SCAAP was a multilateral agreement amongst the affluent Commonwealth members to provide bilateral economic and social assistance to this region. Once again Canada concentrated on educational development, along with a variety of technical assistance programmes, and by 1968 Canada had given $59 million of aid to this region.[329] It was not until the Trudeau years that Canadian aid to Africa increased dramatically, but during the Pearson Administration all of Canada's assistance was sent solely to countries that had already gained their independence. The majority of Canadian aid was directed to East Africa and Nigeria.

Canada's foreign relations with developing countries during this Administration were dictated through its commitment to multilateralism. In 1963, when Pearson first took office, the OECD had brought forth a report stating the inadequacies of international development assistance. Canada gave only 0.3% of its Gross National Product (GNP) to development aid. In this same year, Canada's Minister of External Affairs, Paul Martin, announced that Canada would increase its foreign aid budget in correspondence with its OECD commitments that were aiming for aid budgets to reach 0.7% of their GNP.[330] The United Nations Conference on Trade and Development (UNCTAD), which sat for three months in 1964, reiterated the need for trade and aid increases to be made for LDC's. It was apparent that more assistance was needed for these countries to develop their economies. Canada, therefore, increased its aid contributions to the Third World.

It should be noted that, unlike the aid of many other industrial countries, Canada's aid did not have political strings attached in the form of conforming to Canada's human rights agenda or the purchasing of Canadian goods and services.[331] It was, however, a product of the Cold War. The initial impetus to foreign assistance strategies in the Colombo Plan was partially motivated by fears of Communism. These became a grave reality in the 1960's with the Vietnam War in South-East Asia, and with its military aid to India in 1963, and to Malaysia in 1967. Later within Africa, with this increase in decolonization and the advent of "proxy" competition between the West and the East, aid became an important bargaining chip for alignment purposes. Canada's aid policies at this time were dictated by a number of factors that explain its aid policies. Its proximity to the United States, and its economic position within the international system encouraged Canada to take an anti-Communist approach, and to support liberal economic theories. The Trudeau Administration tried to break this mould, and Canada strove to strike its own foreign policy chord.

Trudeau Administration (1968-1984)

When Pierre Eliot Trudeau took over as leader of the Liberal Party on Pearson's retirement in 1968, he initiated a re-evaluation of Canada's foreign policy objectives, with the Department of External Affairs bringing forth a six pamphlet report called *Foreign Policy for Canadians* that set out new objectives for Canada's foreign policy position in 1970. As with most foreign policy strategies, it reflected national self-interests, but it also sought to divest itself from the restraints that controlled Canada's foreign policy actions under the previous administrations.[332]

Canada's new aid strategy contained Canadian liberal social values, which were exported in its policies. Furthermore, Canada's foreign policy tried to distance itself from the anti-Communist influence of the United States and to make its own way in the international system. The Trudeau Government put forth a foreign policy strategy that changed the Canadian peoples' attitudes towards aid. Canada's economic assistance to the developing world under previous administrations was influenced by its commitment to a variety of other international fora, most notably UNCTAD and the OECD. The new policy was based upon a social principle of social justice. It was to generate an awareness of international problems in order to encourage Canadians to get involved in international development matters.

1970 to 1975

Canadian aid in this period was split into two categories: multilateral aid, which consisted of 25% of Canada's aid budget, and bilateral aid, which made up the remaining 75% of Canada's aid budget.[333] This aid was managed through the Canadian International Development Agency (CIDA), which replaced the External Aid Office in 1968. Again, Canada used Commonwealth programmes to deliver its aid.[334] The Colombo plan continued to receive the majority of Canada's bilateral aid budget, with approximately 55% of Canadian aid going to South-East Asian states. This percentage of Canadian aid decreased to approximately 49% in 1974 when aid to India was reduced due to political factors.[335] In that same year, aid to Africa increased because of the support for La Francophonie, and in the Commonwealth Caribbean, aid decreased in favour of private investment from Canada.[336] The majority of these funds went towards tertiary industries such as banking and tourism, though some funds were also invested in secondary manufacturing industry.[337] This, again, was one of the concerns of the 1970 policy paper, *Foreign Policy for Canadians: International Development*, which wanted to increase the amount of foreign investment by Canadian business into LDC's.[338]

The Colombo Plan

The form and structure of aid that Canada sent to Asia and South-east Asia between 1970 and 1975 did not change substantially. The most pressing political fact that should be mentioned is the hostilities which broke out in this region in 1971. In this year India invaded East Pakistan in a short and decisive war that led to the independence of Bangladesh. Though aid could have been used as a political tool for Western states to secure acquiescence to political demands in this region, under the advice of Maurice Strong, the president of CIDA, Canada maintained its aid programmes in an unbiased and humanitarian fashion.[339] The exception to this, however, was the pressure placed upon both India and Pakistan to deal with the refugees fleeing from this area, which was becoming a burden.[340] This problem was resolved in 1972 with the independence of Bangladesh, though this led to Pakistan leaving the Commonwealth for a period.

The successful detonation of a nuclear device by India in 1974 placed great strain upon its relations with Canada. In the 1950's, as part of the Colombo Plan, Canada had given India a CANDU Nuclear Reactor. The terms of this donation were that it only be used for peaceful means to generate electricity, and an agreement along these lines was signed. In 1972/3, Canada feared that India might breach this agreement and sought reconfirmation that was granted, but which India violated the following year, 1974, stunning the world with its detonation of a nuclear device. Whatever the reason was for India's actions, Canada's nuclear aid to India under the Colombo Plan ended.[341] Aid to India, in general, was reduced after this time, but this was because India was now regarded as a self-sufficient country, no longer in need of economic and social assistance. It did, however, stigmatize the relations between these two countries.

SCAAP

The percentage of Canada's bilateral aid to Commonwealth Africa doubled in 1971/72 from approximately 9% to just over 18% as compared to the other bilateral aid programmes to which Canada contributed.[342] By 1974, this percentage reached its peak at 22.3%,[343] though it would stabilize in the following years at approximately 18.5%. This growth in aid development was indicative of Canada's chancing attitude to developing countries. The first UNCTAD, 1964, indicated the need of the developed world to increase its aid support to the developing world. Initially, Canada protested against the need to increase its international aid budget on the grounds that it could not afford this increase. Furthermore, Canada stated that the monetary quantification of international aid did not take into consideration the qualitative value of economic assistance, which countries like Canada gave.[344] However, Trudeau's new policies realized the interdependence of international development and international affairs. Canada re-appraised its foreign assistance packages to take into account the needs and demands of the Third World.[345] The increase in Canada's aid in 1974 was reflective of Third World needs. In response to the 1973 Oil Crisis, Canadian foreign policy responded to the needs of LDC's, however, due to the beginning of an international recession, this slight increase in funding was short lived, and dropped to the previous level of 18% to Commonwealth Africa. This higher percentage of aid to African states, rather than Caribbean and Latin American states, was partially to off-set the minimal levels of trade with this region of the world. The majority of Canada's aid to these countries involved programmes to assist in educational development, and regional projects of economic concern.

In the 1970's, the Commonwealth African states that received the most Canadian aid were Nigeria,[346] which had recently emerged from a civil war, and Tanzania, Uganda, and Kenya.[347] In the early 1970's, Tanzania received Canada's favour due to the friendship between Trudeau and Julius Nyerere. As Commonwealth leaders, they befriended each other at the 1969 London CHOGM, which precipitated Canadian aid to Tanzania upon grounds of "social justice" and the Commonwealth link between these two countries.[348] Between 1968 and 1971, Canadian aid to Tanzania amounted to approximately $3 million annually in grants and loans. In 1972 and 1973, this amount doubled to $6 million, and in 1974 and 1975 the figures jumped up again to $17.67 million and $38.34 million.[349] These figures on Canadian aid to Tanzania are evidence of the special friendship fostered between Nyerere and Trudeau, but they also reflect something else—the crises in southern Africa.

The issue of South Africa had come to the foreground in 1970 over Britain's proposed deal with South Africa. Tanzania, standing against *apartheid,* threatened to leave the Commonwealth if this deal should have come to fruition, and there were fears within the Commonwealth that such a move would dissolve the organization as other African states left.[350] Tanzania, however, was not in an economic position to leave the Commonwealth, as the majority of its economic aid was obtained through its Commonwealth associations. Arnold Smith, the Commonwealth Secretary-General, and Trudeau realized this and efforts were made to reverse Nyerere's decision. The correlation between Canada's increased aid and Tanzania's changed direction in 1971 indicate that international development assistance was used to persuade Tanzania and the others to remain within the Commonwealth.[351]

Southern Africa was also growing in importance in Canadian foreign policy, and it received much aid and development assistance. Zimbabwe (formally known as Rhodesia), Zambia, and Lesotho, were among many of the states to receive special attention. A region of Africa plagued by problems, Southern African states received assistance in the form of food aid, education assistance, and loans and grants to develop their own economies and economic infrastructures. Canadian expertise was sent to this region. With regard to the Commonwealth specifically, South Africa attracted most of Canada's political attention. At the 1969 and 1971 CHOGMs, South Africa was a subject of concern to Commonwealth members. Compared to other African states, however, the nature of Canada's relations with South Africa was primarily based on trade. South Africa became Canada's largest trading partner in Africa. Its relations with other African states were primarily based on bilateral assistance programmes, and though some states did export primary goods to Canada, this percentage of trade was quite negligible.[352]

The Uganda crisis was another African issue that arose in this time frame. In 1972, Idi Amin seized power from the Obote Government in Uganda.[353] This led to a tyrannical regime that shocked the world and, in part, unified the Commonwealth.[354] Uganda was divided into many tribal groups, with a large Asian population that was mainly responsible for Uganda's tertiary industries.[355] Uganda passed new immigration laws and policies in 1967, nationalizing its domestic industries, and by 1972, approximately 200,000 Asians, holding British passports, were demanding that they be allowed to emigrate to Britain. The Wilson Government had passed new immigration legislation, 1968, to slow down this process, allowing only 1500 Asians to enter Britain per year through a voucher system.[356] At the end of 1972, however, the Amin Government expelled 60,000 Asian Ugandans. This created a problem and Britain was unable to deal with this situation alone.[357]

Amin tried to improve relations between Uganda and the rest of its Commonwealth partners in 1973 and 1974, but by 1976 the matter had degenerated further. A number of Ugandan citizens were reported to have disappeared, and it had been alleged that members of the Amin Government had also been executed. Uganda's position within the Commonwealth was quickly waning. At the 1977 London CHOGM, Britain declared Amin unwelcome at the conference.[358] At the London CHOGM, the Uganda crisis was discussed and a statement condemning the acts of this government published.

Initially, Canada gave support in this crisis by accepting a number of Asian refugees, 7000 in all, after appeals were made by the Heath Government in Britain and the Commonwealth Secretariat, 1972/3.[359] Its intentions were solely to alleviate the pressures on its Commonwealth partners. At the Ottawa CHOGM, 1973, though some Commonwealth members were upset that Uganda should be attending the conference, Trudeau ignored this fact, concentrating his attention on strengthening Commonwealth unity, which had suffered due to the crises in southern Africa. By 1976, however, Canada condemned the Amin Government and withdrew its bilateral aid support, falling back on its policies of international social justice. Canada could not support an inequitable regime like the Amin Government. This, along with the support of other Commonwealth nations, most notably Kenya, Tanzania, and Britain, created economic pressure, as well as military pressure, that saw the end of the Amin Government in 1979/80.

In *Foreign Policy for Canadians,* it was the aspiration of the Trudeau Administration to set new standards and goals for Canada's foreign policy. Motivated by a sense of individuality, Canada based its foreign assistance programmes upon the premise of expanding international social justice. This action earned Trudeau and Canada much valued support from the Third World, and it strengthened Canada's role within the Commonwealth. As the number of international organizations of which Canada was a member grew, there were beliefs that the Commonwealth would play less and less a role in Canada's foreign policy.[360] Never was this more the case in Africa, where Francophone Africa was competing directly with the Commonwealth for economic assistance dollars. Yet, Trudeau was a great proponent of the Commonwealth and of the Third World in general, and in 1975, when Canada's role in international development was reviewed,[361] it came as no surprise that its commitment to international social justice was heightened.

Strategy for International Development Cooperation: 1975-1980.

The 1970's began the third decade of Canada's international aid programmes. The initial intention of these programmes was to allow LDC's the ability to develop their own economies. By doing so, this would then create a "trickle down effect" of wealth generation that would alleviate international poverty. By the mid—1970's, however, it had become glaringly obvious that this was not the case. Tariff barriers and protectionism held back many Third World states. Droughts and other natural disasters played their part in decimating the agricultural sectors in these countries. Finally, the oil crisis of 1973/74 demonstrated further the economic disparity between oil rich and oil poor states. A new approach was needed if any headway was to be made into this global problem, and the *Strategy for International Development Cooperation* set out to do this for Canada. Based upon discussions presented at UNCTAD, the Commonwealth, the World Bank and the International Monetary Fund meetings, this document proposed an escalation of the *1970* foreign policy strategy as economic aid was just not enough.

Though Canada maintained its bilateral aid programmes to Commonwealth Africa and the Commonwealth Caribbean,[362] it sought other means to assist the developing world. One means was the further opening up of its markets to developing states through a generalized system of preferences.[363] Another means was to set up a commodity fund to allow for the stabilizing of prices for primary products. This was a cooperative effort with other developed states that eventually led to the Common Fund in 1979.[364] Along with Canada's traditional support of educational and technical assistance, it was hoped that such programmes would aid Third World states in developing into competitive markets.

This continued support for the Third World provided a blanket policy that would assist all developing states. After 1975, however, Canada would revise its bilateral aid programmes, offering economic assistance to the poorest of poor states. This was done in an effort to maximize the quality of economic aid that Canada could offer. Such policies covered a number of Commonwealth states from various regions of the globe in an indirect fashion, however, Canada still maintained direct assistance to the Commonwealth Caribbean and to Commonwealth Africa.

The Commonwealth Caribbean

Though the actual quantity of aid given to Caribbean states was far less than that given to other regions, the quantity *per capita* was at its greatest.[365] Canada had fostered a strong relationship with this region, as it was the nearest Commonwealth region to Canada. As with previous years, Canada contributed to various projects according to each island's need, and private investment also remained high. Many Caribbean states were suffering from high interest rates and inflation, and this problem was compounded by high unemployment levels. In 1975, Caribbean countries, along with African and Pacific states, entered into the Lome Agreement with the European Community. This same year Canada entered into discussions of a similar nature.[366] These were concluded in 1978, replacing "the 1912 and 1925 West Indies Agreement and the 1966 Protocol, which was no longer a suitable instrument to govern Canadian-Caribbean trade in view of CARICOM's adherence to the Lome Convention."[367] The majority of Canadian trade with this region was directed towards Trinidad and Tobago in the alumina, bauxite, sugar, and petroleum products, though Canada's exports to this region still exceeded the imports of these primary resources.[368] The Caribbean was a prominent recipient of Canadian support between 1975 and 1980. Though trade relations were improving, the balance was still in Canada's favour, and aid continued to remain the most important form of contact within this region. In 1978, due to accrued debts, Canada cancelled the repayment of loans which greatly aided this region of the Commonwealth.[369]

SCAAP

As a region, Commonwealth Africa had become an important area for Canada. The issue of Southern Africa had greatly affected Commonwealth relations, and it had raised this region to the forefront of Canada's development programmes. Trade with Commonwealth Africa, however, was limited to the stronger African states, such as Nigeria,[370] and the rest were aid recipients. The majority of Canada's aid to Commonwealth Africa was given for political reasons to support the front-line states affected by the struggles against *apartheid*. For this region, therefore, though political sentiments towards the Third World had changed, Canada's policy did not. Its economic relationship with Commonwealth Africa remained one based upon developmental assistance programmes. The majority of Canadian aid to this region was still directed towards Tanzania, averaging around $30 million in grants and loans annually.[371] In the early years of this period, from 1975 to 1977, Canadian aid to Nigeria was $10.2 million, $13.95 million, and $8.6 million consecutively. In 1978, however, this figure dropped to $3.17 million, and it declined further the following year to $0.56 million.[372] The reasons for this decrease in Canadian aid was that Nigeria had become economically stable and, within four years, it would begin to pay back some of its outstanding debts to Canada.

In summarizing the Trudeau years, 1975-1980, Canada's relationship with the Third World was still based upon it aid grants. The only exception to this, within the Commonwealth, was South-East Asia. In this region, covered by the Colombo Plan, many of the Commonwealth states were now finding their economic independence: Canadian aid to these states was, therefore, comparably lower than to other Commonwealth regions. The Newly Industrialized Countries (NICs), such as Malaysia and Singapore, were doing well and offered Canada contacts within the Association of South-East Asians Nations (ASEAN).[373] The Commonwealth Caribbean was also beginning to expand its trade relations with Canada, though it continued to import more from than it exported to Canada. Investments in this area were, however, improving. Africa, unfortunately, remained static with regard to improving trade relations with Canada.

The Final Years: 1980-1984

In the final years of the Trudeau Administration Canada's foreign policy outlook changed, and this was reflected in the restructuring of its Department of External Affairs. Though economics and foreign interests have always been closely linked, and even as early as the 1970 White Paper *Foreign Policy For Canadians*,[374] it was demonstrated that Canada's foreign policy was to be concerned with its own national self-interests, the Department of External Affairs was finally amalgamated with the Department of International Trade in 1982. As for the Third World, Trudeau maintained his position on LDC issues, but after the Cancun Conference in 1981, and the lack of support it received from Britain and the United States, this subject began to abate in Canadian rhetoric, as domestic issues, most notably the Constitutional debates, moved to the forefront. In this same time frame, Canada began to concentrate its efforts upon the new issues of human rights and environmentalism that would play a prominent role within the Mulroney Administration.[375] The ramification of this change in foreign policy strategy is the further tying of Canadian aid with the implications of ideological conditions.[376]

The Commonwealth Caribbean

Canada reviewed its relationship with the Commonwealth Caribbean in 1980, affirming its importance in Canadian foreign affairs. This region was growing in importance for Canadian trade and investments, as well as the political links within this region.[377] Canada also reviewed its aid strategy to the Commonwealth Caribbean, preferring to focus more upon bilateral than multilateral aid grants.[378] In 1981, "the Secretary of State for External Affairs announced that Canadian aid to the Commonwealth Caribbean would be doubled to $90 million by 1987" through bilateral grants.[379] This pattern would continue into the Mulroney Administration. The only significant change in Canadian-Commonwealth Caribbean relations was the decline in exports from 21% in 1981 to 15% in 1982/83. Canadian imports from this region remained constant in the form of primary resources.[380]

Africa and South-East Asia

The contrast between these two Commonwealth regions as regards to Canada's economic relations is startling. Africa continued to be a recipient of Canadian aid between the years of 1980 to 1984. The majority of this aid was focused on those front-lines states affected by the problems in Southern Africa. The most notable change occurred in 1980, when Zimbabwe was finally admitted to the Commonwealth. Canadian aid drastically increased from $400,000 to $5 million in order to assist in the development of the new government under Robert Mugabe.[381] As for Canada's economic relations with South-East Asia, these were mainly based upon trade with ASEAN countries. Canada's exports to this region were reaching in excess of $500 million annually.[382] Though some Commonwealth countries still received a high proportion of Canadian aid, Bangladesh being the greatest recipient, the majority of this aid was given in food and emergency relief. Only a small proportion was given to Commonwealth ASEAN states for the purpose of developing their economic infrastructures.[383]

In reviewing Canada's economic relations throughout the Trudeau Administration, one can see the transition in the support given to Third World countries. Within the three Commonwealth regions in which Canada concentrated its development strategies, trade relations were improved in the Colombo Plan catchment and within the Commonwealth Caribbean. In the latter portion of Trudeau's years in office, the growing support for the problems in Southern Africa was reflected in the aid given to front-line states. This was indicative of Canada's growing concern for human rights issues. Trade with this region, however, was not improved upon.

The Mulroney Years: 1984 to 1987

The foreign policy position of the Mulroney Administration guided Canada on a new course of action. Trudeau's Administration had been concerned with maintaining Canada's distinction from the United States, and had focused much of its attention on the "Third Option" and closer ties with Europe. Furthermore, Canada's foreign policy under Trudeau had maintained the internationalist traditions of previous administrations. In 1984, however, the Mulroney

Government concentrated on improving Canada's relations with the United States. Through a policy of "Bilateralism" that would come to fruition in 1988 with the Free Trade Agreement, Canada looked more and more into bilateral economic relations with the United States.[384] As for its policy towards the Third World, Canada continued on the course set in 1982 with more attention being paid to Canada's economic interest as well as human rights and environmental concerns. Progressively, however, Canada's relations with the Third World reflected Canada's ideological interests, and though Canada's aid budget increased to the LDC's, it was tied to conditions reflecting Canadian concerns.[385]

The Commonwealth continued to be of value to Canada, especially in the Caribbean. Canada's own economic interests were geo-politically tied to the North American continent, and the Commonwealth allowed Canada political access to its Caribbean neighbours. The investment initiatives encouraged under the Trudeau Administration allowed Canada much influence within this region, with Canadian multinational corporations making strong capital gains. Canada became responsible "for air transport, water resources, agriculture, and education programs in the Caribbean."[386] Trade with the Commonwealth Caribbean (included with this figure is trade for Latin America) reached $7.68 billion in 1984/85.[387] As for Africa, Canada's links with this Commonwealth region continued on from the Trudeau Administration.[388] Trade was minimal and consisted mainly of primary resources. In 1987/88 Canada announced that it would forgive $672 million of Official Development Assistance debt for 13 sub-Saharan Africa states.[389]

Canada's Multilateral Support of the Commonwealth

Canada maintains its relations with the Third World through a variety of channels, the Commonwealth being only one of them. From the Pearson Administration, Canadian support for such institutions as the World Bank, the International Bank of Regional Development (IBRD), the International Monetary Fund (IMF), the United Nations Development Program (UNDP), as well as UNCTAD, were just a few of the international institutions to which Canada contributed and which had a direct effect upon Commonwealth states. The most prominent multilateral support that Canada offers within the Commonwealth, however, is the support that Canada lends the Commonwealth Fund for Technical Cooperation (CFTC). Since its inception in 1971, Canada has contributed up to 40% of the CFTC's budget.[390]

Historically, the CFTC emerged from the Commonwealth Technical Assistance Programme (CTAP) which was established in 1966.[391] The function and purpose of this programme was to offer technical information on the needs of developing states that the appropriate assistance could be given. This multilateral effort resembles the bilateral assistance programmes of the Colombo Plan, the Commonwealth Caribbean Assistance Programme, and SCARP in many ways. All of these development schemes assess the needs of Third World states and then donors offer the assistance required. The difference with CTAP is that its studies were managed under the direction of the Secretariat. This programme also worked in conjunction with other development agencies, such as the UN Development Programme, sharing information.[392] However, this programme was never truly a multilateral venture as donor states still controlled which state received their assistance and through what means. In 1971, when the CFTC came to fruition, it was truly multilateral in that the funds pledged to this programme were managed by the Secretariat, and donor states no longer had direct control over the application of financial resources.

The CFTC has proven to be a forum that member states of the Commonwealth can contribute to the well-being of their association. Separate from other organs of the Commonwealth, the pledges to this fund are based upon members capabilities, which are paralleled to the dues paid to the Secretariat. This being said, some states, such as Nigeria, pledged more than their share, while others like Australia pledged less.[393] Canada is the largest contributor to the CFTC, pledging 40% of its total budget. When the CFTC came into being at the Singapore CHOGM, Trudeau pledged to double the donations made by other member states.[394]

This charitable act by Canada has had influence upon the Commonwealth and its members. The first Director of the CFTC was George Kidd, a Canadian who was working with CIDA, and he was appointed to this post by Arnold Smith because of Canada's donation.[395] This has implicit ramifications for the direction of the CFTC's progress and direction. Canada's foreign policy position had been re-evaluated, highlighting Canada's own national interests. In the white paper directed towards international development, Canada focused its aid support upon the propagation of social justice based upon its own intrinsic social values. The gratuitous pledge allowed the Commonwealth to assist further in development strategies, for, though monies were given freely, the CFTC's budget is still of a nominal sum.[396] In the initial years of the CFTC Canada gave $0.72 million, increasing this to $1 million the following year.[397] By 1976, this figure had increased to $4 million,[398] and in 1987 Canada's donations to the CFTC had totaled a sum of $18.53 million.[399] From a Canadian perspective, these sums are moderate and only form a minor portion of Canadian international development assistance. In 1987, the funds given to all multilateral development assistance programmes by Canada totaled $401.24 million.[400] The funds that Canada gave to the CFTC, therefore, equaled approximately 4.6 % of Canada's multilateral budget, serving as a vehicle through which to administer small loans to Commonwealth countries taking the administration burdens off of CIDA.

There are also a number of regional banks that Canada contributes to that offer direct assistance to Commonwealth countries. These include the Asian Development Bank, the African Development Bank and the Commonwealth Development Bank. These bodies perform similar functions to that of the World Bank and the IMF, lending money to Third World states for the purposes of infra-structural development projects. As mentioned above, Pearson committed Canada to a course of action assisting these organizations in the 1960's, but, by 1980, Trudeau was reducing these budgets and redirecting funds to bilateral programmes.

Canada's Economic Support for the Commonwealth

There were other avenues of economic support that Canada gave to the Third World, which fell outside of the Commonwealth but had ramifications for the majority of Commonwealth member states. Between the years 1963 to 1987, economic issues played a vital role in Commonwealth affairs. At the United Nations Conference on Trade and Development (UNCTAD) in 1964 the first rumblings of Third World unrest, regarding the international economic system, could be heard. By 1982, these economic concerns, which had culminated in the cry for a New International Economic Order (NIEO) in 1974, had collapsed and the World was facing another debt crisis.

For the Commonwealth these global events were of great concern. The majority of Commonwealth states fell under the title of LDC, concerned with their own economic progress within the world. As early as 1948, the Commonwealth had committed itself to assisting in the economic and social development of its newly independent members, and this had led to the creation of the three bilateral aid agreements. On top of these aid programmes, economic concerns were discussed at Commonwealth meetings and a Commonwealth Economic Committee had been established in 1956. Much of the work of this committee looked into developmental concerns of its member states.

The meetings of Finance Ministers, held annually since 1949, discussed many of the concerns of its members from the Third World. As economic concerns were being placed more and more on the international agendas, these meetings gained greater importance.[401] Many of the concerns voiced at UNCTAD had been expressed within Commonwealth meetings.[402] At the economic meeting in Port of Spain in 1967, Finance Ministers discussed "a review of the international economic position . . . trade developments, international monetary reform, the position of sterling, international indebtedness and the problem of interest rates."[403] These meetings, setting a precedent for other international conferences on the same subjects, allowed the Commonwealth states to sort out their own positions and to caucus upon matters of mutual concern. This procedure would continue throughout the 1970's and into the 1980's.

The 1973 Oil Crisis had an effect on Commonwealth affairs. The embargoes instigated by the OPEC Cartel had drastic repercussions for many Commonwealth countries. Already disadvantaged economically, the increase in oil prices diminished many of the LDC's own oil reserves. Already suffering from depressed economies, this event further inhibited their development. It was this event that sparked the proposal for the NIEO the following year.

Commonwealth reaction to this event was a renewed interest in trade and development issues at the Kingston CHOGM in 1975.[404] The main proposal that came forth from this meeting was the creation of a commodity agreement that allowed for the stabilization of pricing.[405] The theory behind this was that through commodity stabilization and price indexing linked to Western inflation rates, primary producers would be guaranteed a fixed income. Coupled with the Lome Convention signed in April this same year between the ACP states and the EEC, terms of trade were therefore shifting, toward the Third World. A further effort made at the 1975 CHOGM was to commission a report on the NIEO, which was submitted in 1977.[406]

The 1977 CHOGM saw a further report commissioned, the Campbell Report, on the Common Fund.[407] This report, initiated by Sonny Ramphal, was requested to facilitate the creation of a commodities agreement, as proposed at UNCTAD IV. The objective of the report was to reduce some of the skepticism growing within industrialized countries. This report, under guidance from the Commonwealth Secretariat, helped to coordinate Commonwealth member's actions as well as to assist in the promotion of Third World issues outside of this organization.[408] By 1982, twenty states had ratified this agreement. Further efforts, which had implications outside of the Commonwealth, were approached in 1979 with the drafting of another report "to investigate and report the structural change and sustained improvement in economic growth in both developed and developing countries,"[409] and in 1981, the Melbourne CHOGM was used as a testing ground for ideas that would be presented later that year at the Cancun Conference.

There are other issues that the Commonwealth Secretariat coordinated efforts with external agencies to encourage economic development: with the 1979, 1981 and 1983 meetings of the Food and Agriculture Organization (FAO), and with the UNDP, the Commonwealth Secretariat worked to encourage economic development.[410] The net result, however, was that economic issues, especially those regarding development issues, were a primary concern of the Commonwealth. It remains to look at Canada's involvement within these efforts. As an "old" and affluent member of this organization many of these issues had great bearing upon Canadian foreign policy and its relationship with the Third World.

Canada has been greatly affected by many of the concerns of the Third World. As a member of the OECD and an industrialized state, Canada had committed itself to assisting LDC's to develop economically. The philosophy behind such efforts was based upon long-term self-interest, as greater economic integration would help create peace and better economic markets. Further to this, international aid was a subtle means of fighting Communism, which was in Canada's benefit strategically. As a member of the Commonwealth, an organization dominated by Third World states, Canada has also needed to adapt to the changes that have affected this institution. The Commonwealth at one time served as the keystone to Canadian foreign policy, offering it a forum for expression that was not dominated by the United States. As the Commonwealth increased in size through decolonization, the Commonwealth gave it access to regions outside of North America. Most importantly, however, the Commonwealth is Canada's strongest tie with the Third World.

Canada's relations with the Third World have not varied drastically between the years of 1963 to 1987. Canada has stayed politically aligned with the industrialized states of the North. At UNCTAD in 1964, many LDC's were calling for a greater transfer of wealth from the North, and a proposal was put forward for an increase in the percentage of aid to be raised to 1 per cent of GNP.[411] This put quite a strain upon many organizations such as the Commonwealth, the OECD and the World Bank.[412] In 1963, Canada's contribution to economic development was 0.32 % of its GNP.[413] In 1964, Paul Martin, Canada's Minister for External Affairs, pledged to increase Canadian aid contributions, and these increased to 0.49 % of GNP in 1966. Throughout the next 22 years, Canadian aid contributions averaged around 0.47 % of GNP only peaking twice to 0.5% in 1974 and 1986.[414] Canada's response to the demands of the Third World was to vote against this proposal on two grounds: "the proposal did not allow a special position for industrial nations which are net capital importers, and . . . the Principle does not put enough emphasis on the quality rather than the quantity of aid."[415] Canada continued on this course, supporting the industrial North and maintaining its principles on the economic system.

By the early 1970's, aid to the developing world on the whole had reached its nadir,[416] and the Third World was now making more demands for a "fairer" economic system. As stated above, the Oil Crisis of 1973 reinvigorated the industrialized North into re-assessing their own positions, and the options available were straight forward: they could stand firm and challenge demands for change, or they could re-evaluate their positions and grant the Third World its demands. Canada's response was a compromise between these two choices:

> There seems to have been a shift toward a more subtle variant of *real-politik*—based response: one in which rhetoric alters significantly but the practice does not, in which pious declarations of intent continue to be confounded by a record which falls . . . further and further behind the agreed targets.[417]

The demands for a more just economic structure were pacified through minor adjustments to a General Preferential Tariff (GPT) set upon commodities that did not challenge traditional Canadian markets.[418] Trade between Canada and Third World states remained at a minimal level with the majority of Canadian trade directed towards the United States and Britain. National self-interest remained high upon Canada's foreign policy agenda.[419]

Pierre Trudeau, however, did support many of the Third World demands. As a well travelled person, through much of the Third World, he was sympathetic to their calls for restructuring the economic system, and this can be seen through his support within meetings. At the Mansion House (London) in 1975, he stated:

> . . . the developing countries . . . seek no piecemeal adjustments, but a comprehensive restructuring of all the components—fiscal, monetary, trade, transport and investment. The response of the developing countries can be no less well-prepared and no less comprehensive in scope . . . we must aim for nothing less than an acceptable distribution of the world's wealth.[420]

Later that year, Trudeau was supportive of Michael Manley's proposals at the Kingston CHOGM, 1975.[421]

Looking at the individual, Trudeau's support of Southern issues was important in that it helped bridge a gap between the "old" and the "new" members of the Commonwealth. This support reached its apex in 1981 at the Melbourne CHOGM and a few months later at the economic conference in Cancun, Mexico where Trudeau co-chaired the symposium. Collectively, however, Canada's foreign policy still favoured its national interests. As an industrialized state its support for the Common Fund was negligible.[422] Canada introduced the GPT on selected goods and introduced the STABEX scheme, similar to that of the Lomé Convention between the EEC and ACP's, but there were still restrictions within these programmes. For example, on manufactured products, there was a non-cumulative rules of origin clause that stated that 60% of a product being imported into Canada must originate from the country exporting the product.[423]

Canada's trade relations with the Third World remained consistently low.[424] There were a number of justifications for this. Geographical proximity dictates that Canada's largest trading partner would be the United States. Furthermore, Canada itself is a large producer of primary products, thus it is not in its own interest to reduce tariff barriers and open its markets to external competition. A final issue that should be mentioned is the economic benefits of trade. Though Canada's aid contributions have remained below stated goals, it does accrue some values for Canadians. As stated by the Winegard Committee in 1987, over 80% of Canadian aid was now tied to products manufactured within Canada.[425] Such a symbiotic relationship assists in inflating Canada's GNP as well as supporting Canadian businesses.[426] To reduce this hidden subsidization would not be in Canada's domestic interests.

To summarize, the economic issue of international development was at the heart of Commonwealth affairs from 1963 to 1981. With a majority of its membership falling under the heading of LDC's, the Commonwealth was greatly affected in the 1960's and the 1970' by the call for a New International Economic Order. Canada's response to this matter was, however, rhetorical.[427] Trudeau found the Commonwealth to be an excellent forum to express himself and his extroverted character, but Canada's foreign policy remained consistently aligned with the industrialized north and expressed its national self-interest. The Third World's call for a NIEO was never truly heeded and met resistance along the way from Canada and the rest of the North.[428]

Summary

Canada's relationship with its Commonwealth partners is invariably about its relations with the Third World. The influence that Canada has shown within the Commonwealth, therefore, has been concentrated upon its international development programmes. Initially through the External Aid Office, and then later on through CIDA, Canada has participated within many projects in the hope of improving the economic and social standards of its Commonwealth partners. Between the years of 1963 to 1987, Canada has given a considerable amount of aid to Commonwealth states. With the exception of South-East Asia, the majority of Canadian aid has found its way to Commonwealth members. Furthermore, within a multilateralist framework, Canada has been the largest contributor to the CFTC, an organ of the Commonwealth Secretariat designated to provide technical assistance to Commonwealth states.

Canada has also been a proponent of Third World issues. Under the Trudeau Administration, Canadian foreign policy took into account the needs and demands of the Third World. Directed by liberal economic principles, Canada encouraged trade and investment with the Third World as an alternative measure for improving the economic and social standards of the LDC's. These measures, coupled with Canadian international development assistance, have had an impact upon the Third World and in turn the Commonwealth. As mentioned at the beginning of this chapter, however, the implicit question underlying Canadian influence within the Commonwealth is the benefits that Canada derives from membership within this organization.

Some writers, such as Margaret Catley-Carlson, believe that because of Canada's lack of military and strategic interests within the Third World, Canada derives only the ancillary benefit of esteem from its participation in Third World issues.[429] As Kim Nossal points out, this can be a strong political motivator for individual politicians and for Canadians as a whole,[430] and such perceptions place Canada in good standing within the Third World. Others, however, believe that Canada has derived much more benefit from its contributions to development assistance strategies, and that in some cases, Canadian aid and support for Third World issues has been nothing more than rhetoric.

The initial impetus for Canada's involvement in Third World issues was its fear of Communist expansion. This was the main motivator for

Canada's actions within Asia and South-East Asia in the 1950's and 1960's. The same also rang true for Africa and to a lesser extend the Caribbean. Canadian participation within the Commonwealth is also viewed favourably from a domestic point of view, and this was again self-evident in a CIDA survey held in 1980 reviewing Canadians' view of international aid.

Canada also benefits directly from the tying of international development assistance. As stated above, 80% of Canadian aid is tied to products manufactured in Canada. This has the beneficial effect of inflating Canada's own exports and increasing its balance of payments. In 1975, while Trudeau was promoting better relations with the Third World, Canada was reducing its multilateral donations to development banks and similar agencies. The reason behind such strategies is that there is very little control over multilateral contributions, but there is a high level of control over bilateral contributions to Third World states. This allows the further tying of Canadian aid to Third World states.

Assessing the effectiveness of Canadian aid to Commonwealth states is difficult to quantify, but the general intention behind these programmes was to improve the economic and social standards of Commonwealth states. In Ralph Paragg's assessment of Canadian aid to the Commonwealth Caribbean he presented an overview of the objectives of international development. For such programmes to be beneficial they would need to develop the agricultural and industrial sectors of recipient states. There would also be a need to develop the economic infrastructures of these countries. Though Paragg stated that Canada had achieved this fact to a limited extent within the Caribbean, an example of this was the "confith" project improving the efficiency of the sugar industry,[431] on the whole Canada's assistance had been directed to those countries that it had trade interests, these being the larger Caribbean states such as Guyana, Jamaica, and Trinidad and Tobago. One area of industrial development that was deceptive as to its benefits given to Caribbean states was that of tourism. Canadian aid concentrated on developing this industry with the prospect of bringing wealth into this region. The majority of wealth, however, left this region, as foods and other goods required for these industries were imported from outside of the Caribbean.[432] The same is true for other regions, for example Canada's Wheat Agreement with Tanzania. Though Tanzania was in dire need of wheat resources to protect its livestock and peoples, very little was done to supplement agriculture in Africa.[433]

Another indication of the ineffectiveness of aid programmes in general to deal with Third World poverty were the calls in UNCTAD and the Commonwealth for increased trade and investment relations. Though Canada complied with the GPT in 1974,[434] Canada has only sustained trade relations with a few of its Commonwealth partners with the majority of its trade relations being with the First World.[435] The result of the high levels of bilateral aid given to Commonwealth states, mainly through grants and loans, has culminated in the accruement of huge debts. Though Canada dismissed these outstanding debts in the Caribbean in 1978, and also in Africa in 1986, it is indicative of the ineffectual capabilities of aid programmes.

In the mid 1970's, Canada responded to Third World demands for increased trade and investment into the various depressed regions as an alternative measure to improve the economic and social standards of these states. With those Commonwealth states that Canada does trade with, it is usually based on the need for specific primary resources. Within these same states Canadian industries and banks also invest into a variety of projects.

Canadian investment into the Commonwealth has been centred upon the Caribbean; the three main recipient states are Guyana, Jamaica, and Trinidad and Tobago. Though investment seemingly brings wealth into these states, and also assists in developing the domestic industries, it removes local control over development. Furthermore, the profits made within these industries are removed from the region. The result being a limited form of development as there is still no sharing of wealth.[436]

In concluding, Canada has benefited from its economic relations with the Commonwealth. Its aid programmes to Commonwealth countries, though quite limited in comparison to other First World states, offers Canadians many advantages. Inflated trade and investment interests are one area that Canada gains through its membership in this organization. More importantly, however, Canada maintains a diplomatic forum in which it can lead and compete with other First World states, and in which it is perceived to be a proponent of Third World issues. In return, Canada has offered aid to these countries as well as a voice in other international fora, highlighting the importance of Third World concerns. Thus the costs of membership within the Commonwealth are seemingly low, and have been in Canada's favour.

Chapter Five

Preserving the Commonwealth:

"The best policy . . . is slow, co-ordinated pressure by the West, step-by-step pressure . . . of course, not on our own, but moving forward, not marking time."

Linda Freeman on South Africa[437]

"You cannot simply order countries to behave . . . You have to cajole, persuade, do all sorts of things and quite often you have to try save their faces."

John W Holmes[438]

BETWEEN 1963 AND 1987, the Commonwealth faced a number of crises, including those in southern Africa (Rhodesia and South Africa), the India-Pakistan wars, the Nigerian civil war, and the problems in Uganda. In some instances these problems were so great that the question of the Commonwealth's continuance as an organization was raised. Though Canada was an active member in many other international fora, it could not afford to redefine its foreign policies to build new bridges and links to the Third World. In essence, the Commonwealth offered Canada the necessary links to the Third World, and it was in its interest to preserve this organization.

Through the examination of the two crises in southern Africa that occurred between 1963 and 1987, this chapter will show how Canada used its position to influence Commonwealth events to maintain the existence of this organization. These two matters will be the Southern Rhodesian crisis (1964-1980) and the South African crisis (1971-1987). Though both of these crises revolved around the issue of constitutional racism—*apartheid*—Canada took a minimalist approach to both matters, maintaining a middle ground between the two factions of "old" and "new" members of this organization. It was not until 1985 that Canada finally made a committed stand on these matters, taking a moralistic position firmly encamped within the "new" members' faction of the Commonwealth.

To present this chapter coherently, both of these matters will be taken chronologically. The justification for doing so is that in 1970/1 these matters overlap with the South African crisis overshadowing the Rhodesian problem. The Rhodesian affair then re-emerges in 1977/8 with the Commonwealth Secretariat and the Bingham reports on sanction-breaking, leading to the Lancaster House Conference, which resolved this matter in 1979/80. Finally, 1985 saw the South African issue resurface, but with a newfound strength within the Commonwealth initiatives. Furthermore, distinguishing itself from the structural influences that Canadians performed within the Commonwealth, this chapter looks at the influences of the Canadian governmental executive, as was present at and between Commonwealth meetings. Between 1964 and 1987, the Commonwealth Heads of Government met fourteen times to discuss matters of mutual concern, and how Canada acted within and towards these meetings is important in demonstrating its interests in these matters.

Assessing Canada's political actions will help to demonstrate how a middle power state used its structural position within the hierarchy of the Commonwealth to maintain this organization. It will show that Canada used two contrasting, yet similar approaches, with these crises. It took an initial lead in 1964 to 1966 with regard to the Rhodesian crisis, and again from 1970 to 1973 Canada played a significant role with regard to South Africa. On both occasions, however, Canada stood back to allow these problems to dissipate. This followed along with Canada's minimal cost approach that it favoured in the Commonwealth. Then in 1985, Canada took a leading role on the international stage challenging *apartheid*. These later involved greater costs to Canada that were compensated for by greater political returns within the Third World, but this was inconsistent with its earlier foreign policies.

The Rhodesian and South African Crises, 1963-1987

Between 1963 and 1987 the Rhodesian and South African crises were at the forefront of Commonwealth concerns. As two recurring issues centred on constitutional racism and decolonization, they appeared on the Commonwealth agenda almost consistently in this time frame. The actions of Canada towards these matters, however, varied with the different Administrations and according to which state was being considered. It was Canada's objective to maintain the Commonwealth and it did so through the role of bridge-builder between the two factions of the "old" and "new" members of this organization. At the same time, however, Canada tried to limit its costs of involvement for the charm of the Commonwealth in Canadian foreign policy strategies was its low level of cost and maintenance.

1964 to 1969

The Rhodesian and South African crises go back to 1946 when India and Pakistan petitioned for their independence from Britain. This marked the beginning of the Commonwealth's transformation into a multiracial institution. Prior to 1947, before India and Pakistan were admitted into the Commonwealth, the Commonwealth was White Anglo-Saxon in its composition. In the years that followed, as more of Britain's former colonies became independent and joined the Commonwealth as full members, its racial composition changed. By 1961, through the process of decolonization, the Commonwealth comprised of a majority of non-white states which strongly supported the end of British colonialism.[439]

This new visage of the Commonwealth, and its drive to secure independence for other British colonies, led to the problems that occurred in southern Africa. In 1961, South Africa changed its constitutional status from a Monarchy to a Republic and was to re-apply for admission to the Commonwealth. This was a precedent set by India in 1949. This event, however, created much controversy amongst the new members of the Commonwealth that were opposed to South Africa's minority white government and its constitutionalized racism. Canada's position, when the issue previously had been raised, was to remain neutral and to refuse to interfere with the domestic affairs of another state. By 1961, however, this approach was no longer suitable as there were fears that the well-being of the Commonwealth was being threatened. Canada's Prime Minister at the time, John F Diefenbaker, suggested to the South African government that it change its constitution so that it could be re-admitted into the Commonwealth as a Republic. Canada did not want South Africa to leave this organization, but it could not support *apartheid*, which threatened the integrity of the Commonwealth. This matter was temporarily resolved when South Africa withdrew its application to join the Commonwealth, and it would not re-surface as a Commonwealth concern again until 1971 at the Singapore CHOGM.

The Rhodesian crisis also found its roots in 1961. Through the process of decolonization, the Federation of Nyasaland, Northern and Southern Rhodesia had been created, but racial problems were inherent at the start of this process. Southern Rhodesia, which controlled the economic interests of this federation, was influenced by the white minority who refused to relinquish control to the black majority. Because of their economic advantages, they wanted to have a greater political say in the ruling of this state.[440] Canada remained neutral on these matters, as they were part of Britain's domestic affairs. By 1964, however, the Federation had dissolved and Malawi and Zambia gained their independence in July and October of that year. Southern Rhodesia was itself pressing for independence, but with a white minority government. This created fears within many of the newly independent states that Britain would grant it independence and that Southern Rhodesia would become another South Africa.

It had become obvious by 1964 that this problem of racism in Africa could lead to the downfall of the Commonwealth.[441] Many African state struggles for independence were based upon fighting white minority British governments in their countries, and there were strong fears that Britain would grant Rhodesia its independence in the near future. Arnold Smith, then a senior Canadian diplomat, recognized the problems developing within the Commonwealth and advised Prime Minister Lester B Pearson to manage this problem at the London CHOGM, 1964. It was rumoured that Britain would try to avoid the Rhodesian question at the 1964 Conference, much to the chagrin of the Commonwealth's Afro-Asian members. Pearson, however, in a speech drafted by Arnold Smith, raised the matter through a statement on the value of a multiracial Commonwealth and re-iterated principles of democratic and racial equality that had been raised in 1961 with South Africa. This statement was important as it lent support to the Afro-Asian caucus that was developing in the Commonwealth.[442] Canada then lent support to the proposal for the creation of a Commonwealth Secretariat.

The Commonwealth Secretariat was created in 1965 after a proposal put forward by President Kwame Nkrumah at the 1964 CHOGM. The reason for creating this new Commonwealth agency was because many of its new members questioned Britain's dominance over Commonwealth Heads of Government Meetings (CHOGM) and its handling of the Rhodesian matter. Canada supported this proposed change to the Commonwealth's structure in an effort to placate the demands of the Afro-Asian majority, which was a deviation from its earlier position on a Commonwealth Secretariat. During the Mackenzie-King era of Canadian foreign policy, Canada had stood firmly against the proposal of a Commonwealth Secretariat for fears that this body would bring Canada once again under the control of Britain. This new proposal, however, was put forth in an attempt to remove British control of the organization, which allowed Canada to support such a project.[443] In the following year, Canada would further support suggestions for granting the Secretariat maximum powers, though this was not to occur.[444] The first Secretary-General of the Commonwealth, however, was to be a Canadian diplomat, Arnold Smith, as a Canadian was the only acceptable person to bridge the rift between the "old" and the "new" Commonwealth.

These events that occurred in 1964 and 1965 were important in that they demonstrated Canada's patronage for the "new" Commonwealth, and this support continued to grow throughout the years that ensued. What is more important, however, was Canada's continued stand for a multiracial Commonwealth, based on democratic and racial equality, which directed its position on Southern Rhodesia in 1966.

Three weeks after the formation of the Commonwealth Secretariat, Arnold Smith faced his first crisis. On 11 November, 1965, Ian Smith, the leader of the ruling party in Rhodesia, the Rhodesian Front, unilaterally declared independence (UDI) from Britain.[445] Once again fears were generated amongst the Commonwealth's Afro-Asian members that Britain would grant Rhodesia its independence. At the end of December 1965, the President of Nigeria called for a conference to look at the Rhodesian problem. This conference was held in Lagos, a few weeks later, January 11-13. The importance of this conference was twofold: it was the first Commonwealth conference to be held outside of Britain since the

Ottawa conference, 1932, and it was the first issue-specific conference in Commonwealth history.

Canada placed itself in a position of "middleman" at the Lagos CHOGM, between the Africans, and other "new" members of the Commonwealth, and the "old" white guard. As early as 1964, Ian Smith had solicited Canada's position on UDI. The response was that the Government of Canada would not recognize, nor condone, such an act. In a statement in the House of Commons, Paul Martin assured Parliament of Canada's position:

> I may say that well over two years ago I, myself had received as Secretary of State for External Affairs two ministers of the Government of Southern Rhodesia in my office in the Department of External Affairs. I had explained to them our attitude toward events in that country, events which were discussed not only at Commonwealth meetings, but in the United Nations itself. May I say that as a result the Government of Mr. Smith was not taken unawares by the action of the Government of Canada . . . I might add that the record will show that the Prime Minister of Canada had urged in private communications, as did I, that the Government of Rhodesia should take full consideration of the implications of the step which it took some time last November.[446]

After UDI, Canada severed its diplomatic links with Rhodesia and placed its own economic sanctions on all but a few products with Rhodesia. Furthermore, in December 1965, in protest against Britain, Tanzania and Ghana severed diplomatic links with Britain, and under diplomatic precedence nominated Canada as their neutral representative to the United Kingdom. Such trust was due to Canada's previous support of African concerns for a multiracial Commonwealth. On the other hand, Canada was still an "old" member of the Commonwealth, sympathetic to Britain's needs and concerns, and the questions of political and economic costs, which were similar to its own. The Africans were calling for military force to be sent into Rhodesia to re-establish British rule until "majority rule" could be established. Canada supported the principle of NIBMAR (No Independence Before Majority Rule), but it did not agree to the use of force. In November 1965, Prime Minister Harold Wilson had told Ian Smith that Britain would not use military force against Rhodesia, and

Pearson was similarly disposed. After UDI both Wilson and Kaunda, the President of Zambia, had asked Canada to send a military force to Zambia to assist in border protection, but Canada refused to do so. Economic sanctions were the tools to be used against Rhodesia.[447]

Canada's first act of bridge-building was to encourage Wilson to attend the Lagos CHOGM in January 1966. As mentioned above, the Lagos meeting had been called by the Nigerian President at the end of December, under influence from Arnold Smith. The sole purpose of the meeting was to discuss the Rhodesian crisis and the use of military force. Wilson had already called for the use of economic sanctions against Rhodesia after UDI in an effort to placate Commonwealth demands and to avoid United Nations interference. "Neither Pearson nor Wilson was pleased with the idea of a special conference because the disagreements that could result might outweigh any benefits of discussing the issue."[448] As JP Schlegel wrote "Canada's views were that if the Lagos meeting was to serve any constructive purpose, it must find some means of re-establishing mutual confidence without forcing the discussion to a clear win or lose for either side."[449] Not to attend, therefore, would have been just as detrimental. In a meeting in Ottawa, Wilson finally agreed to attend. Furthermore, on 3 January, Pearson sent a letter to Arnold Smith reminding him of the neutrality that the office of Secretary-General should hold.

Smith had been very active regarding the Rhodesian crisis in the Commonwealth. It was already known that it was he who prompted the Lagos CHOGM in an effort to avoid the disintegration of the Commonwealth.[450] Smith was also interviewed in *The Times* making statements to this effect and encouraging African members to use the Commonwealth:

> I am convinced that a withdrawal could not help the present crisis and that it would diminish pressures on Britain and elsewhere outside Africa toward adoption of such further measures as may be needed to achieve a just solution: moreover . . . all Commonwealth countries including, Britain are committed to majority rule in Rhodesia. Continued Commonwealth consultation can help hold Governments to this commitment.[451]

Canada's actions were necessary to re-establish the neutrality of this office and to further encourage Britain's attendance.

At the meeting, Canada found itself trying to balance the positions of the African states, which were adamant to use force in Rhodesia, and Britain, which wished to continue the use of sanctions. African states were cynical about the effective use of sanctions in bringing a change to Rhodesia. Wilson, with a new belief in sanctions, believed that they could bring about a quick end to the crisis. Milton Obote, President of Uganda, had suggested taking this matter before the United Nations Security Council, in the hope that if sanctions failed force would then be the next foreseeable step. Britain, however, did not want this matter to be dealt with in the United Nations, as it was still an internal affair over which it hoped to maintain control. Canada played a successful role in maintaining the status quo by encouraging members to allow more time for sanctions to prove effective. This position was premised upon a belief that sanctions would soon bring an end to the Smith regime in Rhodesia. As Paul Martin had stated in a speech about this issue:

> When Mr. Smith's followers realize that the growing economic dislocation resulting from UDI is not a temporary phenomenon but rather that their trade will continue indefinitely and progressively to be damaged by sanctions and that their economic prospects are distinctly bleak, they should realize their mistake in backing this illegal action.[452]

However, as Hayes reported, "neither External Affairs nor any other governmental department had conducted a governmental study to establish whether sanctions would have an impact such that one could properly conclude that they would lead to a change in the regime."[453]

In addition to encouraging the use of economic sanctions against Rhodesia, Pearson proposed to establish a Commonwealth Sanctions Committee to assess continually the usefulness of sanctions and to improve progressively their effectiveness.[454] The first Chairman of this Sanction Committee was Lionel Chevrier, Canada's High Commissioner to London, and the position was given to Canada once again because of its neutral stance. Arthur Bottomley, Britain's Foreign Secretary, preferred Britain to chair this committee, but under protests from the Afro-Asian members, he accepted Canada for its neutrality. This Committee met thirteen times between January and September, 1966. It should be noted that Canada initially was unwilling to become involved further in this aspect of the Rhodesian affair.

Pearson had contributed further to the Lagos CHOGM by suggesting the creation of a second committee to assist in coordinating aid to Zambia, which had been affected greatly by sanctions, as well as to administer a special fund for financial assistance given to Black Rhodesians. Zambia was heavily dependent upon its resources, especially oil, which entered the country through Southern Rhodesia. After the initiation of sanctions against Rhodesia, an airlift was set up by Britain, the United States, and Canada, to supply Zambia with its much needed oil. Paul Martin stated to the House of Commons:

> This airlift has enabled Zambia to maintain and build up its oil stocks to the point where, with increased use of road transportation, the airlift itself may be reduced or become unnecessary in a few weeks time. This has been a useful undertaking and one most effectively carried out by the Royal Canadian Air Force. Our participation was originally intended for a period of one month, starting late in December. We subsequently agreed at the request of the British and Zambian Governments to continue the airlift until the end of April. The position now is being reviewed. I might say that the airlift has cost Canada up to March 31, $1,125 '000.[455]

Canada, along with Britain, had completed an evaluation for the creation of an alternative infrastructural route, either by rail or by road, for Zambia. Eventually a rail line was built between Zambia and Tanzania to give Zambia access to ports. Though surveyed by Canada, this line was built by the Chinese government. In 1969, however, Canada would supply Zambia with the needed trains through a loan.[456]

Canada also gave monies for the education of Black Rhodesians. Pearson realized that if Rhodesia was to gain its independence later on, it would need educated persons to run the country.[457] He, therefore, suggested the creation of the second committee, to be chaired by the Secretary-General, for this expressed purpose. It should be noted that this suggestion came as a result of African concerns for assisting refugees fleeing Rhodesia and it serves to demonstrate the Commonwealth's commitment to majority rule. The committee assessed candidates for postsecondary education and provided finance to institutions to host these students. This project is of particular importance because the majority of Black Rhodesians educated through this scheme other African universities: an example of the South aiding the South.

The importance of Pearson's actions at the Lagos conference were that consensus, through the establishment of the two committees, helped ease the tensions developing within the Commonwealth. It was Pearson's intentions to preserve the integrity and unity of the Commonwealth and the unanimous support that was given to the use of sanctions did just that. Sanctions created the needed compromise that saved the Commonwealth for the time being.

In September 1966, the second CHOGM was held in London. This was the conference initially scheduled for that year, prior to the Lagos CHOGM. Though other issues were discussed at this meeting, the Rhodesian crisis took the spotlight and again created debilitating controversy for the Commonwealth. After the Lagos CHOGM, the African states believed that more action would ensue if sanctions did not achieve their desired results "within a matter of weeks . . ."[458] When the Smith regime continued to survive, the African states within the Commonwealth renewed their calls for the use of force. The embargoes and voluntary sanctions against Rhodesia were having little effect and oil was openly getting to Rhodesia via Lourenco Marques, a Portuguese controlled port.[459] Britain's position at the opening of the September conference, however, had remained the same when Wilson declared that Britain would only use force if there was a break down in law and order in Rhodesia. Wilson was also adamant that he would not support mandatory sanctions, but suggested the increase in voluntary sanctions to plug loopholes, along with the use of diplomatic pressures to be applied to Portugal and South Africa.[460] There is some irony in this, as it was revealed through the Bingham Report in 1978 that Britain was exporting oil to Rhodesia, through South Africa, during this time period.

A further crisis arose over the issue of NIBMAR. Wilson had declared that Britain would continue to negotiate with the Smith regime to seek a means of granting Rhodesia constitutional independence, as set out in principles established in 1964.[461] The Afro-Asian position wanted more from Britain, calling for mandatory sanctions or the use of military force, and that independence only be granted to Rhodesia upon the principles of majority rule and "one man, one vote." By 8 September, Zambia implicitly threatened to leave the Commonwealth and a division had formed within the Commonwealth along racial lines. The non-white Commonwealth, with the exceptions of Malawi and Malaysia, had caucused in opposition to Britain. It was Pearson who once again drew the Commonwealth together by seeking compromise in the meeting by convincing Kaunda of the Commonwealth's value to Zambia.[462]

Pearson pointed out that, on the following day, there was actually unanimity on the point of majority rule for Rhodesia, but opinions differed as to the best means to achieve this goal.[463] Pearson went on to describe the situation as a "duality of purpose" with the first objective being the dismantling of "the illegal Smith regime [and] according to most speakers, our next objective . . . is to bring majority rule as the basis for independence."[464] Pearson went on to explain the best means that, in his view, could be utilized to bring about the downfall of the Smith regime. He explained how the use of force could be legitimized if this matter was to be taken before the Security Council, but then went on to explain the moral principle of not using such force for selfish principles:

> I do not consider that the use of force as part of police action, or force used under international authority with a UN mandate, or to repel an aggressor, is wrong in any way in itself. It is wrong when used exclusively for selfish national purposes, or whenever the objective can be achieved without force, or when good results are not likely to be achieved, or achieved only at a prohibitive cost. Results must always be related to the means of achieving them. So each situation must be considered on its merits.[465]

Believing that force would be too costly and possibly hurt those they were trying to help, Pearson suggested that economic sanctions be given more time. To encourage African support, he added if sanctions failed then he would be willing to consider the use of force.[466]

In describing the use of sanctions, Pearson referred to limited mandatory sanctions imposed by the United Nations. This stance allowed for a number of compromising points which helped gain acceptance of his ideas. The first was that by taking this matter before the UN it appeased African desires for more to be done. As Obote had pointed out earlier at the conference, once the matter was before the Security Council it would become easier to initiate the use of force. Mandatory sanctions also forced those states which had ignored voluntary measures to comply and stop importing goods from Rhodesia. The fact that these measures were also limited assisted in bringing on line states like Britain, which did not want to go before the Security Council on this matter, and the United States, which itself had continued to trade with Rhodesia. Finally, limited mandatory sanctions were easier to control and would not have adverse effects upon other minority regimes in Southern Africa which then might break these sanctions.[467]

With the second point of contention, that of NIBMAR, Pearson assumed the meaning of this to be the principle of political and racial equality, which all members agreed upon. This was accepted by all parties, including Britain's prime minister, who had been given a free hand on this matter by Cabinet.[468] Over the week-end of the conference, the Canadian delegation continued to draft a proposal that would be acceptable to all parties. The final proposal suggested that majority rule could be installed without necessarily implying "one man, one vote." This statement made Pearson's suggestion more acceptable and practical in the end. It was this proposal that was used as a template for formulating the Commonwealth's final statement on the matter. A committee struck at the conference to compile this statement was headed by Pearson who had the confidence of all the other delegates.

It is important to note that though there had not been total consensus on all matters at the London CHOGM, on the two most contentious issues involving Rhodesia, collapsing the Smith regime and majority rule, Canada was able to use its influence. It has been noted that these matters threatened to dissolve the Commonwealth, but through the utilization of sanctions, Canada once again preserved its existence.[469] Limited mandatory sanctions were a compromise by all parties. Britain went further than it intended, and it was implicit that measures would be increased if sanctions continued to prove ineffective. At the time of the conference Pearson set a deadline to test the effectiveness of sanctions until the end of the year. On 1 January, 1967, Canada took a two-year seat on the Security Council. After sanctions continued to fail, the question of the use of military force was taken before the Security Council by a resolution of the General Assembly. In the ensuing vote, though Pearson previously had stated that he would use force if so deemed necessary by the United Nations, Canada abstained upon this matter. It was never Canada's intention to use force, but rather to utilize limited mandatory sanctions as a means of preventing the breakup of the Commonwealth.[470]

Pearson recognized that sanctions were a suitable tool for dealing with the Rhodesian crisis, and that this problem would not disappear overnight. Canada's next step, however, was to avoid committing itself to another meeting of Commonwealth Heads of Government. These meetings had proven to be acerbic, creating further tensions along racial lines within the organization. This would have led to the Commonwealth's dissolution, and not aided it in resolving the Rhodesian issue. As an internal memo from the Department of External Affairs stated, "In fact if one were to be held soon [CHOGM], it would be difficult to prevent Rhodesia being a principal subject of discussion. It is hard to see what this could usefully achieve."[471] The Department of External Affairs memo then went on to promote the United Nations Security Council and the Commonwealth Sanctions Committee as the more appropriate mechanisms for dealing with Rhodesia.[472]

1969 to 1973

The Heads of Government of the Commonwealth did not meet again until 1969. By this date the political picture within Canada had changed. Pearson had retired from politics in 1968, and Pierre Elliot Trudeau was Canada's new Prime Minister and leader of the Liberal Party. Though he was a well educated and travelled man, he knew very little, in comparison to Pearson, about international politics. As a French-Canadian it was also feared that he would not be as supportive of the Anglo-centric Commonwealth, as were his predecessors. It was initially Trudeau's intention not to attend the 1969 London CHOGM. Trudeau rightly believed that this meeting would be dominated by African concerns over Rhodesia and Nigeria, which were of no concern to Canada in his opinion. Initially Trudeau was going to send Mitchell Sharp, his Minister of External Affairs, but after a suggestion by Gordon Robertson, Secretary to the Cabinet, Trudeau attended the London conference.[473]

Trudeau's attitude to the Commonwealth meeting was one of indifference, and the meeting itself was tame in comparison to the previous CHOGMs in 1966. Once again the meeting was centred on African concerns, but this time the Afro-Asian caucus would not win any concessions from Britain. Sanctions had continued to prove ineffective against Rhodesia, with many states continuing to break them. On the list of known offenders were Britain, the United States, China, the USSR, Japan, South Africa, Portugal, Zambia and members of the European Economic Community. Oil was still being exported to Rhodesia through Mozambique and South Africa, though under a mandate from the Security Council Britain had established a naval blockade around the port of Beira.[474]

Between 1966 and 1968, Britain continued to negotiate with the Smith regime to bring an end to this crisis. In 1966, negotiations on *HMS Tiger* had failed to reach an agreement,[475] and there were also pressures placed upon Britain by the Afro-Asian caucus of the Commonwealth to grant Rhodesia independence only after fulfilling six principles. It was the sixth principle that had caused contention at the London CHOGM in 1966—NIBMAR. At this CHOGM, the Commonwealth had secured Britain's support for this principle, however reluctantly, through Pearson's careful use of semantics. The talks upon *HMS Fearless,*[476] however, were to undermine the Commonwealth's confidence in Britain once again when it abandoned the sixth principle in an offer made by Wilson to Smith.[477] Such a move generated much concern amongst the Afro-Caribbean members of the Commonwealth, but they were poorly organized, and at a Commonwealth Sanctions Committee meeting convened to discuss their concerns, George Thomson, Minister without Portfolio, was able to undermine their efforts.[478] In the end Ian Smith declined Wilson's proposals, though they were left on the negotiation table for a few more months.

The London CHOGM, 1969, held in January dealt almost exclusively with the Rhodesian crisis and the Nigerian civil war. Wilson's objectives had changed and so had British opinion. The cost of sanctions to Britain was high compared to other states and Wilson was facing another election. In 1966, economic problems at home distracted Wilson at the Commonwealth's meetings, and the fear of its disbandment ran high. By 1969, however, the British public had grown tired of the Rhodesian issue and of its former colonies dictating terms to it.[479] With a forthcoming election that same year Wilson made a stand against the Afro-Asian faction to much support.[480]

Trudeau's actions at this meeting were also of media concern. *The Economist* asked the question, "would Mr Trudeau spend his energy exhorting Mr Wilson to abandon the *Fearless* proposals and come back to NIBMAR, or, like Mr Lester Pearson in 1966, in persuading the Africans to be patient a little longer?"[481] His apathy presented prior to the CHOGM was known, but questions were raised as how he would act within the Heads of Government meeting. His predecessor had worked hard to mediate between the two factions of "old" and "new" members at the previous two CHOGMs, but Trudeau would not follow suit. William Dobell, commenting on this CHOGM, wrote:

> Knowing that Canadians share some part of the revulsion Prime Minister Trudeau of Canada must have pondered before his flight to London how far beyond the cautious, optimistic and trusting policy of his predecessor it was prudent to go.[482]

It became apparent that Canada's new directions in foreign policy did not place much value in Canada's role as a "helpful fixer" in international affairs.[483] At the London CHOGM Trudeau took a firm stand alongside Wilson criticizing Nyerere, Kaunda and other Commonwealth leaders for their lack of realism and foresight. The result of such measures was to draw other states, such as Australia, New Zealand and Singapore "on side" in his critique of the Afro-Asian position. Further demonstrations of Trudeau's attitude towards the Commonwealth meeting were demonstrated in his "playboy" performances outside of the Commonwealth, which were to attract media attention. Though his actions indicated disdain for this organization, on his return to Canada, Trudeau applauded the Commonwealth, admitting his conversion to the support of this organization, as it appealed to his intellectualism and flamboyant character. Further to this, he noted in his book with Ivan Head that the Commonwealth acted as a "crystal ball", allowing one to judge the mind-set of the Third World in international affairs.[484] Trudeau's true commitments to the Commonwealth, however, would ensue in the following year.

Trudeau's attitude towards the 1969 CHOGM was an echo of Canadian sentiments, both within the halls of Government and in the public. Canadians were tired of the role Canada played in international affairs, believing that Canada was at the "beck-and-call" of the United Nations, and Trudeau wanted to make Canadian foreign policy more innovative.[485] It was also well known that sanctions were failing. The Sanctions Committee had noted this but no guilty parties were named.[486] Canada had avoided earlier calls for another CHOGM as early as February

1967. Arnold Smith was looking to hold another meeting but Pearson and External Affairs felt that another CHOGM would only be concerned with African issues, namely Rhodesia and Nigeria, both considered disruptive to the Commonwealth's well-being. Canada, through its aid to black Rhodesians and to Zambia believed that it was doing everything in its power that suited Canadian concerns.[487] Canada had been minimizing its costs, maintaining the Commonwealth as a low budget enterprise, and it was all of this briefs in mind that Trudeau that, prior to the London CHOGM, made him cynical of the import of the Commonwealth and this conference.

In June 1970, the Conservative government in Britain was returned to power under the leadership of Edward Heath. As early as 1967/68 they were predicting their own victory and had resolved to re-initiate arms sales to South Africa under the Simonstown Agreement, 1955. In this treaty, Britain handed over the Simonstown naval base to South Africa and agreed to supply South Africa with a number of ships to patrol the Cape. In December 1963, Wilson had stopped arms deals with South Africa under a voluntary ban by the United Nations and only supplied spare parts so that South Africa could maintain its own defences. After increased Soviet activities in the Indian Ocean, and after lost revenues from its previous arms trade with South Africa,[488] Heath vowed that he would honour the Simonstown Agreement. This created controversy amongst Commonwealth members with renewed threats that some members would leave the organization.

In contrast to his earlier attitude to the Commonwealth, and to Canada's new foreign policy position as a "helpful fixer", Trudeau sent his personal foreign policy advisor Ivan Head to discuss this new Commonwealth crisis with the African members. Ivan Head, a former Dean of the Faculty of Law at the University of Alberta, was chosen by Trudeau to work within the Prime Minister's Office to offset the bureaucracies of Canadian government. Head played a crucial role in trying to keep the Commonwealth together. This started with the Finance Ministers meeting in Nicosia in September, when African leaders became quite concerned by the Heath government's proposed plans. On his way back to Guyana, Shridath Ramphal felt that this was an important issue and sought assistance from the Canadian government. Ramphal, stopping in Toronto to visit family on his return from this conference, contacted Head on the Friday asking for a meeting. Head met him that Sunday where he was informed of the events that had occurred in Nicosia. This had generated his own concern for the matter, and Head took this news to Trudeau on the Monday morning. Though Trudeau's recent foreign policy stance had been to change Canada's image of a "helpful fixer," he looked at this matter pragmatically, sending Head to Africa to meet with Nyerere and Kaunda. It was feared that if Tanzania and Zambia were to leave the Commonwealth, this would cause other Caribbean and Asian states to follow, dissolving the organization.[489] Head was sent to Africa to convince these two African leaders of the importance of the Commonwealth.[490]

Canada's concerns over South Africa predated the September meeting. It had strongly supported the voluntary arms embargo against South Africa in 1963, but Canada still shipped spare parts to this country. In 1970, however, this action was to be challenged by Ghana in the Security Council. This matter preceded a decision by the Security Council to intensify the arms embargo.[491] On 15 October, Canada abstained on a General Assembly resolution that backed this decision by the Security Council, though it implemented a spare parts embargo on arms to South Africa on 2 November, 1970. Canada's position on this matter was not based upon moral principles, but rather it was an effort to preserve the Commonwealth.[492]

Canada's efforts to mediate the impending crisis started as early as 29 June, 1970, two weeks after the Conservative victory in Britain. Mitchell Sharp, Canada's Minister of External Affairs had met with Sir Colin Crowe, Britain's High Commissioner to Canada, to discuss this matter. Further discussions ensued with other Commonwealth countries to solicit their positions, and on 17 July Trudeau sent a personal letter to Heath relaying the fact that arms sales to South Africa would damage Commonwealth affairs. However, on 20 July, 1970, Sir Alex Douglas-Home was to announce Britain's renewed arms trade with South Africa in spite of Canadian protestations.[493] As Redekop stated, "The Canadian government began to press actively for some compromise that would enable the Commonwealth to survive."[494]

Canada was once again launched into a mediating role between the two hardened positions of Britain and the African Commonwealth. Trudeau had already warned Heath in his letter that, quote in *The Times*, stated ". . . I have serious misgivings about your decision to resume sales of certain types of arms to South Africa . . . I . . . fear attention is more likely to be focused on the fact of the resumption of arms sales . . . than on the nature of the supplies involved."[495] True to his prediction this had become the case. On 27 November, Sharp released a conciliatory press statement regarding the arms issue to open the way for face saving measures for both sides,[496] and in December Ivan Head would be sent as Trudeau's personal envoy to have meetings with Nyerere and Kaunda. Canada's position was clearly that of Bridge-builder between the two parties, and Trudeau was publicly committed to condemning the arms deal. He also displayed support for Britain by announcing that the Commonwealth was a forum of consultation and cooperation that should not be used to "bind other countries so that they can't carry out what they believe to be in their own interests."[497] This became a key point at the Singapore CHOGM, as it cleared the way for compromise between the two factions. Before this occurred, however, much ground work needed to be done.

As mentioned above, Trudeau sent Ivan Head to visit Nyerere in Tanzania, and Kaunda in Zambia to discuss these matters. These states, along with Ghana, had threatened to quit the Commonwealth should Britain persist in its arms sales to South Africa. Head was also due to travel to Ghana but because of a military coup that occurred, this portion of his mission was cancelled. These meetings proved crucial in encouraging the attendance of these major African actors at the Singapore CHOGM, which was necessary to inspire confidence at the conference. Nyerere and Kaunda were definite leaders within the Commonwealth framework and set the position for the Afro-Asian caucus.[498]

As Trudeau's personal envoy, Head carried a letter stating that he was authorized to speak on behalf of Trudeau. This would be tested by Nyerere during his visit when Head was asked to give his support of a statement of principles, which later formed the basis of the Singapore Declaration. Forced into a position by the Tanzanian president, Head acquiesced to this demand reluctantly, but this was to secure both Kaunda's and Nyerere's attendance at Singapore in January.[499] The statement to which Canada now lent its support, set out six principles outlining the Commonwealth's support for such matters as racial, political, and economic equality as ensconced in the democratic principles, which many Commonwealth states were founded upon, as well as a commitment to international values such as peace and security. The motive behind this statement was to secure a Commonwealth position firmly behind these values, and to force Britain into a compromising position where it chose either the Commonwealth or

South Africa. This support for its Afro-Asian counterparts was in keeping with the lines of the liberal tradition in Canadian foreign policy.[500]

This liberal tradition also voiced itself domestically with a strong position from an organization called *Just Canadian Policy Toward African*, made up of academics, churchmen, and trade unionists, which took a hard line stance, as did the African states, dictating that Canada should leave the Commonwealth if the arms sales continued.[501] As stated before, however, it was not Trudeau's position to make a moral stand against *apartheid*, but rather to preserve the Commonwealth. The position suggested by the African proposal was inflexible to Britain's needs. Canada's role as mediator needed to consider the position of both parties.

The January CHOGM in Singapore was already set to be an argumentative occasion. Heath attended the meeting from a position similar to Wilson's in 1969: he was not willing to concede to the hostile demands of the African states and was indignant to their interference in Britain's foreign relations. He, therefore, approached the conference with an indifference to the meeting. It was proposed in some news articles at the time that Heath's position was an act,[502] and that Trudeau and the Commonwealth Secretariat were over-sensitive to the African states' threats to leave the Commonwealth, as it was known that "Commonwealth states would do what was in their own interests."[503] Whatever the case, a compromise was needed to save face for all the parties concerned.

Unlike the Rhodesia matter, sanctions were not a viable option as Britain already had shown that it could not afford to lose its trade links with South Africa. Another tool for agreement needed to be found. The Declaration of Commonwealth Principles was partially acceptable, but interfered with Britain's sovereignty to make its own foreign policies. An amendment, however, suggested by Trudeau, helped secure the loophole needed "which would permit the British to implement their policy of arms sales to South Africa."[504] The amendment was the addition of the words "in its own judgment directly" added to the clause dealing with aid to a racist state. This allowed Britain the freedom to assess its own foreign policy goals without contradicting principles that it had bound itself to. The acceptance of the amended Declaration of Commonwealth Principles helped bridge the rift that had developed between the Afro-Asian and the British caucuses within the Commonwealth.

The second instrument used to preserve the Commonwealth was the establishment of a study group to assess the Soviet activity in the Indian

Ocean. The justification used by Heath for why Britain needed to re-initiate its arms agreement with South Africa in the first place was due to the increase in Communist, and more exactly, Soviet activities that threatened its economic links in the region. After Britain ceded the Simonstown naval base in 1955, it was no longer capable of defending its economic interests in the region. This was clearly demonstrated by Britain's loss at Suez in 1956. This study group was struck up to assess this situation, and it was made up of eight Commonwealth member states and chaired by Canada. However, this group never met, and as early as February 24, 1971, Nigeria, and then India, pulled out from this study group after Britain agreed to sell South Africa a number of Wasp Helicopters needed for its naval fleet.[505] Regardless of the outcome of this study group, it was used as a compromise needed to hold the Commonwealth together at the Singapore CHOGM.[506]

The next Commonwealth CHOGM was held in Ottawa in 1973 and the stage was once again set for another turbulent meeting. However, Trudeau defused this matter by changing the Commonwealth agenda. The previous conferences of the Commonwealth had drawn around divisive factions regarding the Rhodesia and South African matters. As the membership of the Commonwealth grew, its friendly informality had been replaced with a caucus styled forum found in the United Nations. A meeting once centred on consultation and cooperation, where states with a common history could share views and ideas to improve the standards of living within their own countries, was now meeting along hardened battle lines. In 1973, it was Britain that threatened not to attend the conference for fears of the ensuing battle on Rhodesia.

In the previous year, 1972, the Pearce Commission was established to assess local opinions within Rhodesia as to a proposed settlement plan. Controversy was once again generated within the Afro-Asian caucus that the opinions of the average black African would be suppressed by the Government appointed Chiefs and not be truly representative of African opinion. Pressures were once again placed upon Britain to ensure that the voices of detained black Africans, like Joshua Nkomo and Reverend Sithole would be heard. Prior to the Pearce Commission findings, Canada was asked to help in this process, and Ivan Head visited many African states to ensure its openness by all sides.[507] The Pearce Commission would report to London that the black Africans of Rhodesia would only be happy with a representative government based upon majority rule, and that the white Rhodesians believed that black Africans were incapable of managing the Rhodesian economy.[508] Britain feared harassment at the forthcoming CHOGM. Britain's interests within the Commonwealth had also waned with fading memories of empire, and its new interests rested with the EEC which it had joined on 1 January, 1973.[509] To secure British participation, Trudeau invited Queen Elizabeth II to open the proceedings.

The structural changes that Trudeau introduced at the Ottawa CHOGM helped remove the barriers of formality and pre-set speeches which caused the Singapore CHOGM to drag on, and returned the Commonwealth to a conference premised upon informality and functional cooperation. Much resentment had been expressed at the Singapore CHOGM to this structuralism that had encroached upon CHOGMs and Trudeau had managed to secure the topic of "procedures" on the Commonwealth agenda for Ottawa.[510] The issue of "inflexibility" at Commonwealth conferences had long become a concern of the Canadian government that constantly asserted the fact that the Commonwealth was a "functional association" that needed to be flexible to achieve its goals of consultation and cooperation. The history of this concern dated back to 1966 when Pearson had expressed displeasure at CHOGMs being held for specific issues, which threatened the existence of the Commonwealth. In mind were the Rhodesian and Nigerian conflicts that polarized the Commonwealth. It would not be until 1971 that Trudeau would secure the advantage of addressing this matter within a Commonwealth forum that would allow him to confront this matter at Ottawa.

At the Ottawa CHOGM, Trudeau went forward with his plan of reducing the number of plenary sessions to two—at the beginning and end of the conference—and introduced a number of seminar styled forums where the Heads of State could share ideas. Finally, Trudeau initiated the use of the "weekend retreat" at Commonwealth conferences, which removed the Commonwealth leaders from the still formalized forum of the CHOGM to an informal and relaxed environment where they could discuss matters at their leisure. According to Michael O'Neill, this progress on the CHOGM's structure assisted in mediating difficult issues including the Rhodesian crisis.[511] Finally, Trudeau introduced a new item for discussion at the conference, which served to benefit all the leaders present. This was the subject of "comparative techniques of government" which allowed members to share and air their grievances of leadership. This was adopted at subsequent CHOGMs. These seminar fora were restricted to the Heads of State only, allowing for more open discussion around matters of concern to Commonwealth leaders, and represented Trudeau's own desire for more informal and intellectual talks.

A Commonwealth Communique was produced to re-affirm the position of all member states towards the situation of Rhodesia at Ottawa. As mentioned above, it was accepted by all members of the Commonwealth that Rhodesia was no longer a short-term crisis but rather a long-term problem. The Communique served the purpose of ascertaining agreement upon the chosen course of action while not evoking any disruptive discussions on the matter. In reality, the Communique was nothing more than a hollow gesture, but it served an important purpose of obtaining consensus. The African states already had resigned themselves to the fact that this crisis could not be resolved through peaceful means.[512] It was inevitable that force was going to be applied through increasing guerrilla activities in Rhodesia. The Africans tried to elicit support for these "freedom fighters" but Britain was not supportive of any action that transgressed the rules of law. Britain supported the Communique on the basis that it re-affirmed its own position. The most important support for the Communique came, however, from Australia and New Zealand which were trying to develop their links with the Third World members of the organization. Their positions were changing, as their economic interests moved further away from Britain.[513]

The importance of this period, 1969 to 1973, demonstrated Canada's change in perspective on the matters of Rhodesia and South Africa. Under the Pearson administration, Canada sought to preserve the Commonwealth through the use of sanctions and mediation skills. Trudeau, on the other hand, was initially ambivalent to the concerns of the Afro-Asian caucus of the Commonwealth. By 1970, however, when the "arms sales" issue threatened to dissolve the Commonwealth, Trudeau took an active position to improve the integrity of the organization. The introduction of the structural changes at the Ottawa CHOGM, 1973, assisted in displacing the animosity found at Commonwealth conferences and returned the Commonwealth to its previous stature as an organization based on functional consultation and cooperation. Through the use of entrepreneurial and technical skills, consensus was returned to the Commonwealth conference.[514] As a letter from Shridath Ramphal, then Foreign Minister for Guyana, to Mitchell Sharp, summarizing the Ottawa CHOGM, stated:

I am convinced that Ottawa has reaffirmed the validity of the Commonwealth in the contemporary international system and given it a new vitality to play its role effectively. For these important results Canada must take the major credit and I wish you to know how conscious we are of our indebtedness to you and your colleagues.[515]

1973 to 1985

In the previous section this paper demonstrated the efforts made by the Trudeau administration to preserve the Commonwealth. In the following, section it will be shown that Canada's efforts towards Rhodesian and South African issues waned. This is mainly because they posed no threat to the stability of the organization, nor did they make any impact upon Canadian society. Rhodesia and South Africa would remain on the "back burner" of Commonwealth interests, surfacing, from time to time at the CHOGMs, but they evoked little response from Canada.

At the Kingston CHOGM, 1975, Trudeau was more interested in the new issue of Third World development and the New International Economic Order. Trudeau was always looking for new themes to champion that were pushing, the edge of political concerns. With the recent oil crisis in 1973, and the introduction of the NIEO in 1974, Trudeau's concerns were centred mainly upon these issues. This was heightened by the fact that Ivan Head, his foreign policy advisor, and Canada's commitment to the CFTC, re-directed Canada's interests toward such matters. The most notable support for the Rhodesian and South African crises came with Canada's economic support given to Mozambique upon it obtaining its independence during the conference.[516] This event did not threaten the existence of the Commonwealth, and it only obtained superficial support from Canada in relation to the problems in southern Africa.

At the following CHOGM in London, 1977, Canada once again was forced to make a stand at the Commonwealth conference, but its position was directly motivated by its own self-interest. In 1976, the New Zealand "All Blacks" Rugby team went to South Africa on an official sporting tour.[517] This prompted a negative response from the African members of the Commonwealth who considered such sporting relations as implicit support for the government of South Africa, and, after the Soweto Massacre that same year, such support was intolerable. In protest for these actions, they boycotted the Olympic Games held in Montreal. This publicized event went on to damage the prestige that Canada would have gained from this international event and added to the negative publicity that Canada was already receiving over not allowing the Taipei government to participate under its own flag.[518] At the London CHOGM, 1977, the African states threatened to boycott the Commonwealth Games in Edmonton, Alberta, 1978, if nothing was done upon the matter.[519] A compromise was offered by Britain, at this conference, with the assistance of the Commonwealth Secretary-General,[520] which introduced the Gleneagles Agreement at the weekend retreat to Scotland. In this accord member states agreed not to engage in sporting events with a segregated South African team.

Canada acquiesced to this agreement to protect its interests at the Commonwealth Games in Edmonton. At Montreal, 1976, the African boycott was noticeable by the empty lanes at running events, but the impact was minimal due to the number of states competing. At the Commonwealth games, however, the number of participating states was much less, and a foreseen recurrence of empty lanes would have a greater impact, maligning any prestige that might be obtained by this international sporting event. Canada could also agree to the sports sanctions against South Africa because of the two sports highlighted in the Gleneagles Agreement—rugby and cricket—neither of which were important to the average Canadian, but were significant sports to white South Africans. This made it easier for the Canadian government to prohibit these sports with South Africa.

The next CHOGM took place in Lusaka, 1979, and once again the Rhodesian issue rose to the surface. In 1977, the Commonwealth Secretariat published a report detailing how the British detailing government was responsible for breaking its own oil sanctions against Rhodesia.[521] A British follow-up report, the Bingham Report, 1978, found that the Labour government in 1967 was aware that Shell and British Petroleum, two oil companies in which the British government had substantial shares, were trading oil to Rhodesia during the time of the embargo.[522] Initial attempts to stop this illicit trade were circumvented through trade alliances made with French and South African oil companies. The end result was that during this whole period Britain was trading with Rhodesia.

Sanctions busting, with regard to Rhodesia, was well known and attempts to deal with it were superficial. As early as 1967, during the first year of sanctions against Rhodesia, it was evident that certain countries were breaking sanctions. At that time, the only sanctions which proved truly effective were those levied against tobacco, but this was due to an already flooded market. Goods, such as chromium ore needed for the production of stainless steel, were constantly being bought thus undermining the sanctions. In the earlier years of the Rhodesia sanctions very little was reported about these violations. Some reasons expressed were that a number of states were unsure whether their own nationals were breaking sanctions as well as the tight control certain governments held on their media. The net result of these matters was that companies or individuals were tried regarding sanctions-breaking. The most vigilant state was Britain.

These reports on sanctions-breaking, however, arose at a time when Britain had formulated a settlement with the Rhodesian government. The agreement was based on a pact between Muzerowa and Ian Smith, which allowed for a slow integration of black Rhodesians into government under the drafting of a new constitution.[523] This settlement was disregarded by the African caucus of the Commonwealth, which stated that this agreement was not representative of the wishes of Rhodesians as a whole. A report produced by the Commonwealth Secretariat supported this claim with further evidence obtained from an analysis of the proposed constitution itself. The reality of the constitution was that though blacks would be admitted into government, their powers would be superficial and non-representative and the true control of government would continue to rest with the white minority.[524] At the Lusaka CHOGM pressures were placed upon the new Thatcher government to re-appraise the situation and to hold a referendum within Rhodesia to ascertain the support from the majority. Prime Minister Margaret Thatcher, initially advised not to attend the meeting by the Foreign and Commonwealth Office,[525] agreed to re-open talks and to seek an acceptable settlement for Rhodesia. These became known as the Lancaster House Talks, 1979/80, and eventually led to a settlement of the Rhodesian crisis and the birth of Zimbabwe in April 1980.

Canada had recently had an election that put the Conservative party in government under the leadership of Joe Clark. As the government had only been in office for six weeks prior to the Lusaka conference it did not really have time to prepare for this meeting or to establish its own foreign policy. Thus, it followed the precedents set by the Trudeau administration and continued its position on Rhodesia. Clark played only a minor role at the Lusaka conference, which was over-shadowed by that of Nyerere, Fraser, and others of the Commonwealth. It was, however, consistent with Canada's position on southern Africa: though it did not agree with the politics of these countries, it kept a low profile upon the matters, assuming responsibility only when necessary.

After the release of the Bingham Report, 1978, and the statements from the British government regarding the granting of independence to Rhodesia under the Smith/Muzerowa alliance, problems were expected to arise within the Commonwealth.[526] Paul Martin, in his memoirs, tells of his fears that the new Clark Conservatives might back Thatcher, and this would add fuel to this Commonwealth issue. The new Administration, however, wisely reserved its position until Lusaka.[527] At Lusaka, Clark would later be called on at the conference, but only in a minor capacity.

During the conference, a compromise needed to be found to deal with the Rhodesian crisis in its newest form. Thatcher could not guarantee that the Conservatives in Britain would renew sanctions against Rhodesia. It had been one of their mandates to resolve the Rhodesian matter and resume trade relations with that state. At the weekend retreat, the Secretary-General, Sonny Ramphal, asked a few of the Heads of Government to stay behind from the scheduled visit to Victoria Falls. Canada was not one of those states, as Ramphal felt that its presence would only increase pressure upon Thatcher who already found the meeting a stressful enterprise. Ramphal also believed that Clark's presence was not needed as Canada was already supportive of the Commonwealth's general position. At this meeting a compromise was found that led to the Lancaster House Conference later that year. After the Saturday weekend retreat, however, Clark played a crucial role in selling the compromised agreement to the rest of the Commonwealth. At the meeting at Lusaka, Clark had an informal meeting with the Heads of Government from the Caribbean. It was recognized that Canada had much influence with these states, as Australia had within Southeast Asia, due to its geographical proximity and aid relations with this region. Many Caribbean states were closely aligned with their African counterparts on the Rhodesian issue and needed to be convinced of the feasibility of the Lancaster talks. It fell upon Canada's shoulders to sell this arrangement to other Commonwealth Heads of Government, and once again Canada played a mediatory role.[528]

The following CHOGMs were of similar importance to Canada's position on southern Africa and Commonwealth affairs. There was no other occasion between 1980 to 1985 where Canada played a substantive role within Commonwealth affairs and South Africa. At the 1981 CHOGM in Melbourne, Trudeau was concerned to use the Commonwealth as a "sounding board" for the forthcoming UNCTAD conference in Cancun, Mexico, 1982. Trudeau was asked to be joint chairman with the Mexican president after Britain and the United States showed disinterest in the concerns of the Third World. It was hoped that Canada's presence would encourage the attendance of these two states. The Cold War, however, was entering its final phase, that of the SDI (Space Defense Initiative), which detracted monies from the Official Development Assistance given to the Third World. The result was that Cancun failed in its objectives to re-vitalize concerns for the Third World.

In this final section it was shown that Canada played a minor role in southern African affairs. Apart from aid given to assist blacks in southern Africa, a programme initially targeting Rhodesians, but then later expanded to included Mozambique (1975), South Africa, and Namibia (1977), it did very little. The explanation was that there was no immediate threat to the Commonwealth that warranted its full attention. Though the Canadian government did not agree with *apartheid,* it did not want to hurt its own interests. However, this changed in 1985.

1985-1987

In 1984, the Conservative government again took office in Canada, but under the leadership of Brian Mulroney. A new generation of Canadian politics was about to take shape and one area where it expressed itself was in the Commonwealth. At the Nassau CHOGM, 1985, Canada joined the Afro-Asian caucus of the Commonwealth in taking an aggressive stand against *apartheid.* After the much publicized riots and killings within South Africa, Canada, under the personal direction from Mulroney took a stand against *apartheid,* deviating from Canada's traditional policies on South Africa.

Canada's traditional policy on South Africa was different from that taken against Rhodesia. Throughout the Rhodesia crisis Canada took a position of sanctions in the hope that economic pressures would change the minds of the political leadership of the country. With South Africa, however, the opposite position was taken. After the London CHOGM in 1977, where Canada signed the Gleneagles Agreement, Canada reviewed its policies toward South Africa. In this review, it believed that more good would come from trade relations with South Africa, and that through an approach of "quiet diplomacy" Canada would be able to change the political position of the South African government. Canadian trade with South Africa, therefore, increased rather than decreased after 1977.[529] The crucial barrier that occurred, however, was for Canada to use its trade to influence South Africa's domestic affairs, which rested simply upon the fact that its total value of trade with South Africa was not that high, especially when compared to that of the United States or Britain. Canada, therefore, had very little economic leverage over South Africa.

Another factor relating to this point was that the United States and Britain did have an economic advantage over Canada. The volume of trade between these countries and South Africa was much greater, affording them more influence over South Africa. However, in the 1970's and early 1980's they chose not to apply it to deal with the issue of *apartheid*. Indications of these two states strong support for South Africa were present as early as 1976 when Henry Kissenger tried to negotiate the Rhodesian problem in the Geneva Agreements. These talks tried to enforce the sanctions levied against Rhodesia, and in an effort to increase the economic pressures upon that state, Kissenger told the Vorster government of South Africa that it should stop its support of the Smith regime. The threats implied were that similar sanctions could be raised against South Africa if it did not comply. After the British and the American's position was made clear South Africa joined the world in trying to encourage Ian Smith to seek a settlement to the Rhodesian crisis.[530]

It should be noted that it was not really in Britain's or the United States' interest to place sanctions against South Africa. After the recent independence of Mozambique and Angola, there were renewed fears of Communism within the region. South Africa, with its extremely anti-Communist government, was, therefore, a preferred ally. They, therefore, wanted to do very little that would hurt this state. Furthermore, their own economic interests were at stake, especially for Britain, and they did not wish to hurt these either.

The interests of the United States and Britain in this region would influence Canadian decisions throughout the 1960's, 1970's, and early 1980's. These two states were Canada's predominant trading partners and it would not do anything to negate its own trade interests with these states. Furthermore, with regard to Rhodesia, Canada did not want to use force for fears that this would draw South Africa into a prolonged "hot" war. It was not within the interests of Canada, Britain, or the United States that the situation should develop in this fashion. Canada's policies on southern Africa were, therefore, much in alignment with those of Britain and the United States.

After the election victory of Canada's Conservatives in 1984, fears were growing in other Commonwealth countries that Canada would also adopt a similar "conservative" approach as Reagan and Thatcher had done in the United States and Britain. This would mean closer ties between Canada and South Africa. Mulroney, however, in an effort to allay these fears, sent Bernard Wood, the director of the North-South Institute, as a personal emissary to southern Africa. The purpose of this mission, stylized in the African tradition of sending, emissaries to neighbouring tribes, was to relay messages to the Front Line states and South Africa of Canada's new position on southern Africa. A study had been performed to assess the strategic advantages of employing sanctions against South Africa, and how best to make them effective. It was realized that the greatest cost would be incurred by the Front Line states such as Zambia, Zimbabwe, Mozambique, and Malawi, and in order to make sanctions work this factor needed to be taken into account. It was Bernard Wood's duty to assure the Africa states on South Africa's border that they did not have to do anything and that Canada would help these states overcome any affects incurred through sanctions against South Africa. Wood also informed the Government of South Africa that Canada did not accept its practice of *apartheid*.[531] By October 1985, Canada's position was well established.

At the Nassau CHOGM in October 1985, Mulroney took Canada in a new foreign policy direction with regard to South Africa. Mulroney, who had been adamantly *anti-apartheid* used this forum to express his views. The Commonwealth had always been a forum within Canadian politics where the Prime Minister could have a latitude of freedom from the influences of government bureaucracies, and he used the Commonwealth for this purpose, taking a stand against *apartheid* and firmly placing his support with the Afro-Asian caucus of the Commonwealth.[532] Malcolm Frazer of Australia did the same.[533] Britain was isolated on its policies on South Africa. At the conference, however, little was done to achieve Britain's support for this movement, which was still trying to protect its own economic interests in South Africa. The calls made within the Commonwealth were for sanctions to be placed upon South Africa using economic pressures to change the domestic situation within this state. In compromise to Britain, however, it was decided that an Eminent Persons Group (EPG)[534] would be sent to South Africa with a set of six demands for changes to be made. These included the release of political prisoners, such as Nelson Mandela; the independence of Namibia, which South Africa controlled illegally; and, of course, the call for the recognition of Majority Rule within South Africa.[535]

After the EPG[536] reported that no action had been taken by South Africa in 1986, Canada unilaterally took further measures by applying its own sanctions on South Africa.[537] These were announced at a mini-summit of Commonwealth Foreign Ministers, which was chaired by Joe Clark. Clark initially had been more cautious in Canada's approach to South Africa, advising Mulroney not to make too many hasty statements or decisions.[538] After the findings of the EPG, however, Canada itself initiated a number of measures for economically isolating South Africa and a further list of changes that it demanded. The objective of these measures was to isolate financial institutions within South Africa, placing the economic burden upon those who were in power—namely the white South Africans.[539] Though Canada did instruct its private sector to sever ties with South Africa, it tried to encourage a voluntary boycott, though it did produced a published list of companies trading with South Africa. Another domestic measure introduced by the Federal Government of Canada was the introduction of a list on which persons could register their protests to the actions of the South African government. The ground was being cleared for the Vancouver CHOGM, 1987.

The Vancouver CHOGM of the Commonwealth produced the memorable Okanagan Statement. This was a statement by the Heads of Governments at the conference of their condemnation of the practices of the South African government and a list of demands for changes within this state. It further called for sanctions to be levied against South Africa. What is most memorable of this action taken within the Commonwealth was the dissent of Britain upon this matter that would bring Mulroney and Thatcher into direct conflict with one another. Thatcher accused Canada and Australia of using sanctions against South Africa to increase their trade in raw materials, primarily those needed for the production of defensive weapons (Uranium). These were publicly refuted but nonetheless generated animosity. The end result was a Commonwealth position accepted "without the consent of Britain." The importance of this, however, would not be that Britain disagreed with the measures against South Africa but rather that the Commonwealth would take measures to implement these changes called for in the statement without the consensus of its members. This had never before occurred in Commonwealth history.

Canada's position on *apartheid* changed drastically in 1985 compared to its position prior to Mulroney becoming Prime Minister of Canada. Nossal attributed this fact to the personality of Canada's leaders of the time, all of whom were of the same generation.[540] Though Canada's position on South Africa slackened in 1988 after realizing that it could not sustain this position or role in international society, it is a demonstration of middle power leadership. It is also a clear demonstration of how Canada used the Commonwealth for its own political agenda.

In a review of Canadian foreign policy by the Standing Committee on Canada's International Relations in 1985, it was suggested that Canada use the Commonwealth to further its objectives on human rights, especially with regard to *apartheid* and South Africa.[541] Where previously Canada had played the mediatory role in an effort to preserve the institution with all its integrity, Mulroney led the Commonwealth on a path that itself could have been contentious. Whether this contention would have caused a rift within the institution is doubtful, as Britain was isolated and could no longer rely on the support of Australia and New Zealand.

The Commonwealth also served as a coalition legitimizing Canada's actions in other avenues as it sought to bring changes regarding *apartheid*. South Africa, for a long time, had been protected by the United States and Britain from international sanctions. The Canadian government used its position to lobby the United States Congress to further isolate Britain and to gain support for its actions in the Security Council of the United Nations.

Summary

When assessing the political influence that Canada exerted within the Commonwealth from 1963 to 1987, its objective must be remembered. The Commonwealth had served Canada as an international forum since 1931, preserving its trade relations with Britain at that time. As time changed the Commonwealth, its value to Canada changed. No longer a forum reflecting trade relations, it was a link to a newly emerging world that had become a part of Canada's traditional foreign policy strategies. It was also a forum that set Canada apart from the United States, supporting Canada's national identity. It was, therefore, Canada's objective to preserve this organization from dissolving due to the crises that arose within it. The means that Canada chose to deal with these matters, the Rhodesian and South African crises, varied. Sanctions played a very important role, as did the use of envoys and other mediation practices. What remained consistent however, were Canada's efforts to bridge the rift developing between the "old" and "new" members along racial lines.

The use of sanctions against Rhodesia and South Africa reflect a normative position demonstrating Canada's abhorrence to racism. This was ancillary, however, to Canada's primary concern—the preservation of the Commonwealth. Canada initially used sanctions as a means of compromise between the two sides. The demands made by the Afro-Asian caucus for the use of force against the Smith regime was unacceptable to Britain and Canada as it was believed that these measures would be too costly and ineffective. On the other hand, to do nothing, would cause the demise of the Commonwealth. Sanctions served, therefore, to demonstrate the support for black Rhodesians and the condemnation of constitutional racism. More importantly, however, sanctions served the Commonwealth by demonstrating its unity. Throughout the Rhodesian crisis, even when sanctions were known to fail, the continued support over sanctions helped to draw the Commonwealth together. Examples of this occurring were in September 1966 at the London CHOGM, when Canada encouraged the prolongation of time in order to allow sanctions to work, and after 1972, when it was known that sanctions were failing, they were still used to demonstrate the Commonwealth's unchanging position on Rhodesia.

With South Africa, however, sanctions did not become an option for Canada until after 1985. When the South African crisis came to the forefront of Commonwealth affairs in the 1970's, Canada avoided the use of sanctions but chose instead to coerce the South African government to mend its ways through economic relations. The reasons for not applying sanctions were based on a number of factors. Primarily Canada wished to maintain good relations with Britain and the United States, which supported South Africa because it was an anti-communist state. South Africa also became an important supplier of precious ores needed for both states' economies. Finally, there were fears that if sanctions were levied against South Africa they would force South Africa closer together with Rhodesia making the resolution of that matter even harder for the Commonwealth. Sanctions were, therefore, impractical for Canada and the Commonwealth at that time. In 1985, however, in an effort to allay the fears of its Commonwealth partners, sanctions were called for by Canada in an effort to consolidate the Commonwealth's position on *apartheid*.

Sanctions therefore served a number of functions. They demonstrated the abhorrence of the Commonwealth to racism, and were used to punish the Smith regime for its illegal declaration of independence. Canada's support of sanctions also demonstrated its commitment to the Commonwealth by acquiescing to the demands of this coalition. The primary purpose of sanctions within the Commonwealth was their symbolic position demonstrating the unity of the organization on the issue of *apartheid*. Though they proved to be ineffectual in Rhodesia, they served to unify the Commonwealth.

Just as important as Canada's support for sanctions, however, were the other measures employed by Canada to preserve this organization. Canada used its political influence to change the structure of the Commonwealth and that of Commonwealth meetings as a means of preserving the organization. Its first structural initiative was that of its support for the Commonwealth Secretariat. Britain's dominance over agenda items in the early 1960's had created mistrust amongst its Commonwealth partners. The creation of the Commonwealth Secretariat helped restore confidence within the Commonwealth through the removal of Britain from the central control of the organization. This action by Canada also elevated its standing amongst the African members of the Commonwealth.

The second important structural contribution that Canada made to the Commonwealth was its initiative to introduce the weekend retreat to CHOGMs. The introduction of the weekend retreat at the Ottawa CHOGM, 1973, negated some of the United Nations styled formalities which had become prevalent within Commonwealth conferences. These formal actions by states added to the tensions found in CHOGMs and decreased the likelihood that compromise could be found in Commonwealth meetings. This initiative by Trudeau returned the Commonwealth to its informal beginnings and this retreat later served as a useful tool for achieving compromise at later Commonwealth meetings.

Through the use of emissaries, such as Ivan Head and Bernard Wood, Canada also exploited its good standing amongst its Commonwealth partners to discover their political needs to mediate and encourage support for the Commonwealth. The most notable case of this was in December 1970, when it was feared that Tanzania, Ghana, and Zambia would leave the Commonwealth over Britain's proposal to renew arms sales to South Africa. Trudeau sent Ivan Head to Tanzania and Zambia in order to negotiate with these states and to ascertain their objectives. This action led to Canada's support for the Declaration of Commonwealth Principles, later to be accepted at the Singapore CHOGM with one amendment, which helped reconfirm the political principles on which the Commonwealth was founded. This in turn helped to preserve the Commonwealth at the acrimonious Singapore CHOGM in January 1971.

Bernard Wood's visits to southern Africa in 1985 and 1986 were of a similar nature. In this case, however, he was sent to this region in order to demonstrate Canada's support for black Africa and its demands upon the Commonwealth. This action helped to instill confidence amongst the Commonwealth and allowed Canada to air its position on South Africa.

Finally, the actions of various Canadian Prime Ministers, from Pearson to Trudeau, all helped to mediate and preserve the Commonwealth at various CHOGMs. These actions helped to create the necessary bridge needed by the Commonwealth to deal with the crises which it faced. Through its acts, Canada demonstrated its commitment to the Commonwealth by its support for the concerns of the "new" members of the Commonwealth. This was necessary to remove the image of the "old boys club" which the Commonwealth was perceived to be. Through bridging the gap between the "old" and the "new" members of this organization, Canada was able to keep both sides within the Commonwealth. When taking all of Canada's various political actions within the Commonwealth together, it becomes apparent that Canada's political influence within the organization was to serve as the much needed bridge between the "old" and the "new" members of this association. By doing so Canada served its own political interests by preserving and shaping the Commonwealth.

Conclusion

Middle Power Structural Leadership?

IN THE YEARS surveyed, 1963 to 1987, three specific issues were focused upon: the patronage that Canada lent the Commonwealth; Canadian aid to its Commonwealth partners; and the mediating role that Canada played within the southern African crises. In all three areas, Canada served in a pivotal capacity to preserve the Commonwealth. Drawing upon the empirical evidence presented, it can be concluded that Canada played a structural role within the Commonwealth that can be described as "leadership."

Leadership has never been defined properly in International Relations,[542] hindering the possibility for a clear operational definition.[543] For our purposes, however, the two categories of coercive and passive leadership will be used to help confine the issue, as put forth by others,[544] as these two classifications of leadership are both causative. Measured by the evidence of followership, leadership becomes defined as the ability of a leader to get others to do what it wants them to do through persuasive actions.[545]

The theory on middle power leadership to be applied here has been derived from the works of Cooper, Higgott, and Nossal.[546] Their hypothesis, an adaptation of Oran Young's theory of leadership,[547] has been premised upon the fact that middle powers act as leaders on issue-specific themes within secondary and tertiary agenda issues in the international system. Of the three forms of leadership described by Young—structural, entrepreneurial, and intellectual—Cooper, Higgott, and Nossal believe that middle powers act only as entrepreneurial and technical leaders.[548] Through the use of bargaining skills and innovative ideas, middle powers act as catalysts, facilitators, and managers in the international system to shape bureaucracies. They are also capable of building coalitions as a means to deal with common concerns, relying on the self-interest of states. However, Cooper, Higgott, and Nossal state that due to the limited resources of middle powers, they are unable to make structural changes to the international system. It is for this reason that middle powers maximize their resources and apply them to issue-specific themes.

Cooper, Higgott, and Nossal hypothesize that middle powers furnish a leadership role in these realms through acting as catalyst, facilitator, and manager within the international system. These behavioural characteristics of middle power states reflect the entrepreneurial and intellectual leadership skills that Oran Young described. They are active in the description of the catalyst role of middle power behavior as, "Entrepreneurial middle powers may act as a catalyst with respect to a diplomatic effort, providing the intellectual and political energy to trigger an initiative and, in that sense, take the lead in gathering followers around it."[549] The facilitator role is described as that of "agenda-setting" and the promotion of "associational, collaborative, and coalitional activity."[550] Middle powers adopt this leadership strategy as they do not have the resources of great powers needed for structural leadership. The development of these coalition groups serves to subsidize middle power states lack of power through the creation of collective leveraging power.[551] The final behavioural role of middle powers is that of manager in the international system. Middle powers may use their skills to stabilize the system through confidence-building measures and mediating disputes as they arise. To a lesser extent, though Cooper, Higgott, and Nossal emphasized this aspect of management, middle powers may use their skills to build certain regimes, though most of these energies are directed to the creation of norms and conventions rather than establishing institutions. They may, however, shape the bureaucracies of these institutions through innovative measures.[552]

The roles of catalyst, facilitator, and manager reflect the entrepreneurial and intellectual leadership styles that Oran Young provided. Added to this, Cooper, Higgott, and Nossal introduced the idea of technical leadership that provides for much of the mediatory and managerial skills which middle powers are best known. These include the specialized skills needed to participate within international bureaucracies. These abilities are "not the sole preserve of middle powers . . ."[553] as many great power states also have well developed bureaucracies. These states also have much broader commitments that stretch their resources. Middle powers, however, apply their resources to more specific tasks, effectively optimizing their resources.

Another characteristic of middle power leadership mentioned by Cooper, Higgott, and Nossal, is that of the application of their technical skills. Middle power states predominantly concentrate their international efforts in a number of specific issue areas that reflect their own social concerns. As mentioned above, these are concentrated upon the second and third agenda issues of economics, environmentalism, and human rights, which reflect the concerns of their societies and can directly affect their own standards of living. "The influence of middle powers in agenda setting and policy coordination will be constrained by structural pressures; their influence will vary issue by issue, by institutional arena, and by the openness and receptivity to initiatives from other sources."[554] Cooper, Higgott, and Nossal examined throughout their book this specific approach of middle power states in the international system. They utilize particular regimes to protect their interests within the international environment.

In assessing whether Canada has acted as a middle power leader, and more to the point a structural leader, with regard to the Commonwealth, will now be examined. The assertion being made in this book is that Canada, as a middle power, has played a leadership role in the Commonwealth. The second question that follows on from this is whether or not Canada's actions constitute structural leadership. The facts to support these arguments will be from the information presented in previous chapters.

Building the Modern Commonwealth

Canada's actions within the Commonwealth lead one to ask whether it has acted as a leader within this organization. According to Cooper, Higgottt, and Nossal's hypothesis on middle power leadership, Canada acted as a catalyst in the establishing of the Commonwealth Secretariat in 1965. The idea for the transformation of this association, controlled by Britain, to an organization with no one state at its core, was suggested by the Afro-Asian caucus. The disagreement between this group and the old members of the Commonwealth over Rhodesia, however, inhibited the chance of the Afro-Asian caucus gaining support for their proposal. Canada's position on the matter gave the Afro-Asian caucus the support they needed to foster legitimacy for their suggestion. As part of the old guard with the Commonwealth, Canada's support for the creation of a Secretariat lent credibility to this idea by easing the tensions felt by the "old" members of the Commonwealth. It was for this very reason that the first Secretary-General was a Canadian.

According to Cooper, Higgott, and Nossal, a middle power acts as a catalyst when it is able to provide the needed "political energy to trigger an initiative, and in a sense, take the lead in gathering followers around it."[555] What enabled Canada to take this lead, however, was its position, or proximity, to both groups within the Commonwealth, which gave legitimacy to its actions. This matter of position is of structural significance for it enabled Canada to create the needed confidence in both camps. It was this relational factor which allowed Canada to influence the "old" members of the Commonwealth to accept the concept of a Secretariat.[556]

Further credibility was given to Canada's actions as it helped provide some of the economic support needed to realize this objective of a Commonwealth Secretariat. Britain had been at the centre of the Commonwealth from its inception in 1931, and the Afro-Asian caucus distrusted its former imperial master. They, however, were economically powerless to support the concept of a Commonwealth Secretariat without the financial assistance of Britain. Canadian economic contributions instilled confidence to the Afro-Asian caucus adding legitimacy to the Secretariat, as Britain was no longer the sole contributor. In a moralistic endeavour to boost the confidence of the Secretariat, Smith tried to choose a balance of persons from all Commonwealth members to fulfil the bureaucratic functions of this organization. At first these persons came from the "old" members of the Commonwealth, but later the Secretariat would incorporate persons from other Commonwealth countries. These actions helped to boost the legitimacy of the Secretariat in the eyes of its "new" members.

Canada's leadership role in the Secretariat facilitated the building of needed cooperation to ensure the survival of the Commonwealth. Its provision of technical skills, the managerial talents of Arnold Smith, gave the leadership needed to encourage the "new" members of the Commonwealth to follow. These are both characteristics of middle power leadership as set out by Cooper, Higgott, and Nossal. They state, though, that middle powers act as facilitators in coalition-building because of their lack of economic resources. In this scenario, it was the ability of Canada to provide economic resources that enabled it to develop the cooperation needed to build the Secretariat. Canada's leadership role within the Commonwealth was structural in that it took it upon itself the responsibility to provide the needed funds that, in conjunction with Australia and Britain, allowed the Secretariat to function. Britain could not take on this role alone because its historical role of authority created its own impotency. It therefore needed the support of a middle power, Canada and Australia, to legitimize its efforts.

The second matter of Canadian leadership within the Commonwealth came with its initiatives to create the Commonwealth Fund for Technical Cooperation (CFTC) and the Commonwealth Youth Programme (CYP) in 1971, and the Division for Women's Issues in Development in 1981. In these cases, Canada clearly acted as an entrepreneurial leader generating the initiative for the CFTC and the CYP. Unlike the Secretariat whose budget is based upon assessed contributions from its membership, the CFTC and the CYP are funded by voluntary contributions. When Trudeau suggested the creation of these two organs of the Commonwealth in 1971, it was to maintain the confidence of the Afro-Asian caucus in the Commonwealth as an institution that looked after their concerns. At this time the Commonwealth was facing a crisis over Britain's plans to resume arms sales to South Africa. In an effort to mediate the growing division between Britain and the Afro-Asian caucus, Canada pointed out that Britain, as a sovereign state, had the right to decide its own trade and foreign policies. This looked as if Canada was now siding with Britain, especially after Trudeau's position at the 1969 London CHOGM, over African concerns in southern Africa. These two Commonwealth organs were established to re-affirm Canada's concern for Third World issue. By making the contributions to this forum voluntary, Canada hoped to encourage the southern hemisphere to assist itself. To lend impetus to this proposal, Canada pledged to double the contributions made by Third World states to the CFTC.

In these initiatives, Canada displayed leadership that was relational and had structural consequences. To maintain a sense of balance and fairness within the Commonwealth, Canada needed to support Britain for there were strong fears that Britain would leave the Commonwealth. Impartiality was needed if Canada was to continue to mediate these problems within the Commonwealth. Canada used its economic resources to encourage the Afro-Asian caucus to remain within the Commonwealth. In doing so, it changed the face of this organization and altered its functional direction. These changes were derived from Canada's ability to utilize its structural resources to change the face of the Commonwealth.

In 1981, Canada introduced the idea of a new Commonwealth Division to look at Women's Issues in Development. This was one of the first international organizations to structurally link aid and women's rights. This was Canada's first step in developing a human rights policy within the Commonwealth, and would eventually lead to the adoption of a Human Rights Initiative at the Harare CHOGM, 1991. Women's issues had been a domestic issue within Canada since the 1960's and the projection of these Canadian values was a natural progression in its own identity. It's the realization of this initiative in the form of a new Commonwealth Division was an act of leadership, as the face of the Commonwealth exhibited a preference for a male-centred world. Canada's ability to encourage these states to follow its lead, and accept its values, initiated an eventual change in Commonwealth policy.

Developing the Commonwealth.

Traditionally, middle powers have been viewed as the champions of Third World causes, and this chapter examined Canada's role in the Commonwealth and its position on Third World matters. Since 1948, Canada has participated in development programmes offering bilateral assistance to its Commonwealth partners. In the mid-1960's, the Canadian government recognized that aid was the primary role that the Commonwealth played in its foreign policy, which culminated with Trudeau's call for Social Development in the foreign policy white paper in 1970. In 1975, at his Mansion House address in London, Trudeau followed up this approach with his call to re-assess how the First World gave aid to the Third World. The nature of his speech was to petition on behalf of the Third World for the First World to offer better trade agreements rather than just development. This speech was inspired from the Group of 77's (G-77) demands at UNCTAD, the previous year, for a New International Economic Order, and preceded the change in the Commonwealth's policies on aid at the Kingston CHOGM, with the appointment of Sonny

Ramphal as Secretary-General. This position by Canada's Prime Minister gave weight to the demands of the G-77 as this middle power stood up for the Third World cause. Its behavior demonstrated a moral position that encouraged discussion of this matter internationally.

Canada's efforts helped to motivate these discussions, which eventually facilitated finding a resolution to this matter in 1979 with the introduction of the Common Fund. The objective behind the Common Fund was that First World countries would offer preferential import tariffs to Third World countries, allowing them to generate revenues to develop their industries on their own. Within UNCTAD, however, Canada's actions would undermine its position before the academic community as it opposed many of the changes suggested. Adopting a liberal internationalist approach, which was in close alignment with Britain and the United States, Canada demonstrated its vulnerability to changes in the international economic system and how it was still a "follower". Many of the changes proposed at UNCTAD meetings, giving preferable trade agreements to Third World industries, created direct competition for Canadian industries. This meant that if Canada supported these proposals, its own national industries would be placed in jeopardy. Canada could not, therefore, support the changes.

Trudeau's actions at Mansion House, however, led to this matter becoming an agenda issue in international fora, including the Commonwealth. By this fact, Canada's actions encouraged discussion of this matter within the Commonwealth, and eventually led to an amicable solution to be found for this problem. Its actions, by Cooper, Higgott, and Nossal's definition of middle power leadership, gave impetus to this matter.[557]

Preserving the Commonwealth

In this chapter Canada clearly demonstrated entrepreneurial and technical leadership in line with that envisaged by Cooper, Higgott, and Nossal. Between 1961 and 1987 the Commonwealth faced two major crises that continually threatened to dissolve this institution. These were the Rhodesian and the South African conflicts. Both were centred upon the issue of constitutional racism, *apartheid*, but two differing approaches were used to resolve these problems. For Canada's part, its role was to try and preserve the Commonwealth and this is how it performed its task of middle power leadership.

Canada's first step in trying to solve the crisis that had arisen in the Commonwealth over Rhodesia was to support the concept of a Commonwealth Secretariat. Its intentions were to defuse the animosity that had developed between the old and the new members of the Commonwealth. The initial problem was seen to be the control that Britain exerted over the Commonwealth as its core and dominant actor. The problems generated by the Rhodesian conflict continued, however, and in 1965, with Rhodesia's unilateral declaration of independence, the matter erupted within the Commonwealth. In 1966, the Commonwealth held two conferences to deal with this matter: the first in Lagos, Nigeria in January, and the second the planned London CHOGM in September. Both conferences were acrimonious affairs with the Afro-Asian caucus challenging Britain to resolve this matter. There was, however, no quick solution.

Canada's Prime Minister, Lester Pearson, played an important role in bridging the rift that had developed between these two sides. He did not seek to resolve the Rhodesian issue, but rather to preserve the Commonwealth. At the January CHOGM Pearson found compromise in the solutions proposed by both parties. The Afro-Asian caucus wanted Britain to use force to resolve this matter, and Britain wanted to negotiate a solution. This aroused fears within the Afro-Asian caucus that Britain would ignore their concerns and grant Rhodesia its legal independence. Britain, on the other hand, saw this matter as an international security issue that was beyond the concern of the Commonwealth. Neither side was prepared to back down and it was Pearson who offered the solution to this problem. Pearson pointed out that both sides ultimately sought the same goal and that only their means to achieve this goal varied. Pearson's solution was to use sanctions to bring pressure upon the Smith government in Rhodesia so that an equitable solution could be found for all parties, and he reworded a Commonwealth statement that would reflect these concerns. Pearson also suggested the creation of a fund to help Black Rhodesians and the creation of a Committee to review sanctions. Again these suggestions were amenable to all parties, and enabled the Commonwealth to survive another CHOGM. Though sanctions would fail to bring an end to the Rhodesian situation by September, they served a purpose in defusing the situation at Lagos.

At the London CHOGM in September, Pearson once again used his diplomatic talents to bring resolve to the meeting. Sanctions and negotiations had failed and once again the Afro-Asian caucus was calling for force to be used to end the crisis in Rhodesia. Again Britain sought alternative means to end the matter. Force was an impractical solution, for it was neither in Britain's or Canada's interest to send troops to Rhodesia, but the African members of the Commonwealth were talking of bringing their own forceful measures. The implication was closer ties to Communist countries. Pearson's solution was to suggest the extension of sanctions until the end of the year where the matter could then be taken before the Security Council of the United Nations if sanctions continued to fail. Implied in this solution was Canada's decision to use force for it would become a representative on the Security Council in January 1967. After the September meeting, Pearson refused to commit Canada to another ad hoc CHOGM as he saw them as destructive to the Commonwealth, as they were too.

Pearson's actions within the Commonwealth demonstrated technical leadership which was needed to preserve the Commonwealth over these issues. His mediation talents helped to find temporary solutions to a continuing problem, maintaining the Commonwealth. These leadership efforts were representative of the management skills which Cooper, Higgott, and Nossal attribute to middle power leadership. Canada used its influence to build confidence in sanctions as a means to diffuse pressures within the Commonwealth. It also helped to generate confidence in the Commonwealth asa forum to deal with the Rhodesian crisis, ultimately facilitating the resolution of this crisis in 1980.

The second crisis that threatened the Commonwealth was South Africa which would come to the forefront of Commonwealth affairs at the Singapore CHOGM, 1971. In 1969, the Commonwealth would meet for the first time since the London CHOGM in 1966, and this break helped to diffuse the problems facing the Commonwealth. Trudeau reluctantly attended this meeting, believing that the agenda issues of Rhodesia and the Nigerian Civil War were of little interest to Canada. At this meeting Trudeau found himself siding with Britain, condemning the suggestions of his African counter-parts as irrational. His position helped to put into perspective the long-term matter which Rhodesia would become. In 1970, after the Nicosia Finance Ministers' meeting, a new problem would arise, Britain's renewed arms sales to South Africa. Once again the Afro-Asian caucus saw this as indicative of Britain's support for *apartheid*, but this time there were threats that these states would leave the Commonwealth.

Trudeau's response was to send Ivan Head, his foreign policy advisor, to talk with the two key African leaders, Nyerere and Kaunda. It was Head's purpose to encourage the attendance of Commonwealth Africa at the Singapore conference and in order to do so he needed to convince these states of the importance that the Commonwealth served. In order to obtain their agreement to attend the conference, Head agreed on Trudeau's behalf to support a declaration of Commonwealth principles that highlighted the Commonwealth's stand for equal rights. This acceptance of the proposal encouraged African leaders to attend the conference, building confidence in the Commonwealth.

The Singapore conference was still an acrimonious affair, with Britain's trade policies being singled out for attention. Trudeau was able to draw a compromise within the conference asserting Britain's right to design its own trade policies, and Britain supported the Singapore Declaration, supporting the wishes of the African delegates at the conference. Touted as a success, the Commonwealth limped on temporarily resolving itself of this new crisis, but Rhodesia and South Africa would remain as agenda-issues for the next two decades.

The Ottawa conference, 1973, gave Trudeau an opportunity to divert Commonwealth attention from these crises, allowing it to focus upon other matters of concern. Since 1961, the Commonwealth had focused upon the single concern of African states, *apartheid*. Trudeau noted as well that the Commonwealth had adopted a United Nations styled caucus system. This debilitated the Commonwealth from dealing with matter and looking for solutions: the Commonwealth offered its members a forum designed to facilitate cooperation and consultation, but the United Nations stylized caucus system prevented such discussions. Trudeau set out to change this at this CHOGM.

With the opportunity to structure the agenda of this conference, Trudeau changed the face and the tempo of the CHOGMs for years to come. His first step was to limit the speeches made by the Heads of Delegations by creating an informal retreat in which only the Head of each delegation could attend. By limiting the persons attending, it enabled the Commonwealth to discuss issues in a smaller forum where there would be no "grandstanding" to the media or their nationals. This allowed the

Commonwealth to focus on issues of general concern to all members. Trudeau also introduced the idea of Heads of State sharing their problems of leadership. Unable to avoid the issues of southern Africa, Trudeau helped to shape the Commonwealth Communique that condemned constitutional racism. Though many of the African states believed that the Commonwealth could no longer solve the Rhodesian issue, this statement did help in fostering Commonwealth unity on these issues.

Canada once again played an important part in maintaining the Commonwealth in this time period. Its effort in bridging the gap between Britain and the African bloc helped to sustain the Commonwealth in this difficult time. Using its resources, the managerial skills of Head and Trudeau, and its economic initiatives in the CFTC and CYP, Canada was able to broker confidence in this organization, again displaying leadership qualities as set out by Cooper, Higgott, and Nossal.

Canada's final act of leadership touched upon in this thesis ws its stand against Britain in the Vancouver CHOGM, 1987, which instigated the Commonwealth's stand against South Africa. In 1985, Mulroney set Canada in a new direction in its Commonwealth foreign policy when he decided to take issue with *apartheid*. At the Nassau CHOGM, 1985, Canada suggested the sending of an Eminent Persons Group to South Africa, making demands for change. These included the granting of independence to Namibia; the release of Nelson Mandela; and the end of *apartheid*. The following year, Mulroney sent his own personal envoy, Bernard Wood, to meet with Front Line States, and the South African President. The purpose of these visits was to establish the grounds for sanctions to be used against South Africa. At the Vancouver CHOGM, 1987, after appeals to South Africa failed, the Commonwealth called for sanctions, with the exception of Britain.

Canada played a key role in directing this Commonwealth effort. For years within the Commonwealth, Canada had "side-stepped" the issue of South Africa in an attempt to reconcile the differences between the two sides within this organization. In 1985, however, it took steps to build the needed coalition to deal with this matter. Cooper, Higgott, and Nossal recognize this effort as forming an act of middle power leadership, as it was Canada's change in policy which facilitated the building of the coalition against South Africa.[558] This ability to place pressure upon Britain and to reason and negotiate with the United States also implies a relational or an approximate position to these states. To have influence in these matters, Canada needed to be able to use its resources as a middle power to bring about change, and these changes eventually altered the face of the international community.

Middle power Structural Leadership

In assessing Canada's role within the Commonwealth, it has acted as a catalyst, facilitator, and manager within issue-specific themes. Two questions that can be raised, however, are whether the acts of mediation truly constitute leadership, and whether Canada has acted as a structural leader? In answering these questions, it is believed that mediation can constitute an act of leadership, though this will obviously vary from case to case. As for the second question, middle powers can perform a limited form of structural leadership, but this term in itself is inadequate in describing the actions Canada and the Commonwealth.

The question of whether the act of mediation constitutes leadership is very interesting. Oran Young drew the distinction between entrepreneurial leadership and mediation by noting that mediators were disassociated third parties.[559] Alternatively, the entrepreneur was a party to the matter being negotiated. However, mediators, in an attempt to resolve conflicts must occasionally provide incentives to the disputants, as well as introduce innovative ideas, offering alternative solutions to the problems being mediated. In both instances, the causative effect of the mediators' actions will induce the disputants to follow their lead. This would, therefore, constitute leadership in both a structural and entrepreneurial form. Mediation can, therefore, be a form of leadership.

On various occasions in the Commonwealth, Canada played both a leading and mediating role. In offering a compromise solution at the two CHOGMs in 1966, Pearson helped to mediate the impasse that had arisen over Rhodesia, allowing the Commonwealth to survive. The solutions that Pearson offered, however, were also resourceful and set the Commonwealth on a certain track for dealing with this matter. Trudeau's actions leading up to, and during, the 1971 Singapore CHOGM, were also mediatory as he tried to prevent the collapse of the Commonwealth over Britain's decision to renew its arms sales to South Africa. Once he had succeeded in encouraging the attendance of certain African states at the CHOGM, he then used his influence to build a compromise between the two disputants. Through his inventiveness, he was able to achieve the settlement which allowed the CHOGM to end on a successful note. This would not have been the result, however, if the two juxtaposed parties had not decided to follow his suggestions.

The second question to be raised is whether the theory of middle power leadership adequately explains the structural influence that Canada had within the Commonwealth. Cooper, Higgott, and Nossal described middle power leadership as technical and entrepreneurial but stated that middle powers only played a limited structural leadership role. They dismissed the structural elements in international leadership, and in doing so they seem to confuse Oran Young's definition of structural leadership with that of hegemonic leadership:

> The essence of our argument is that under conditions of waning hegemony (or, to use Ruggie's term, hegemonic defection) there is a need to pay much more attention to other sources of leadership. In particular, we examine what Oran Young has termed technical and entrepreneurial definitions of leadership, a leadership style that contrasts with more traditional—and structurally determined—definitions of leadership that tended to prevail in the post-1945 period.[560]

The result is that they rule out the possibility that middle power states play a structural role within the international system:

> We start with the assumption that the sources of leadership in global politics are both systemic and domestic . . . As a consequence, our first concern is to extend the analysis to increase the number of actors which might have the potential to exercise non-structural forms of leadership. Second, we are attempting to widen the range of issue areas in which this non-structural leadership may be forthcoming.[561]

What their theory seems to ignore is that the very essence of the middle power state's capabilities rests in structure itself. As Iver Neumann points out in his work on regional leadership, many middle powers are regional hegemons playing significant roles in various regions which invariably effect the international system as a whole.[562] It is the fact that middle powers have certain resources that allows them to act within the international system. At times these resources can be used to exact leverage to secure compliance,[563] though this is on a much lesser scale than seen with great power sates, but more importantly these resources allow middle power states to interact within the international system, performing entrepreneurial and technical leadership.

Canada, however, is not in a position to become a regional leader because of its proximity to the United States. Nor does Canada possess adequate resources to create international fora to project its ambitions internationally. It utilizes, therefore, pre-existing international fora as a means to express its concerns. Through agenda setting, and the introduction of new programmes in these fora, Canada is able to shape these organizations so that they reflect its concerns. The Commonwealth is an example where Canada has initiated structural changes in an international forum, reshaping the organization to reflect its concerns. The introduction of the CFTC and the CYP were instigated for a number of reasons, but more importantly they re-defined the value of the Commonwealth for both Canada and its other Commonwealth partners. Further structural innovations, the introduction of the summit retreat at CHOGMs, was part of Trudeau's ambition to return CHOGMs to their informal nature that they had prior to decolonization, and to make these meetings more personable. The idea introduced at the Ottawa CHOGM in 1973 could have been a one-off event, but because of its success, subsequent CHOGMs followed this practice. What is most notable of these summit retreats is their use to discuss contentious issues that continually threatened to create a rift in the Commonwealth. Trudeau used the first retreat to create a positive outlook on the Commonwealth, but subsequent meetings, such as the London CHOGM, 1977, and the Lusaka CHOGM, 1979, used these retreats to deal strategically with the contentious matter of apartheid.

A caveat that should be mentioned is that the structural changes introduced by Canada in the Commonwealth, or which could be introduced into any other international fora, are of a limited nature similar to that expressed by Cooper, Higgott, and Nossal. They stated that:

> The evolution of cooperation—and the processes of regional institutionalization— . . . demonstrates the importance of alternative forms of leadership to those . . . envisaged under hegemony . . . [T}he essence of these forms of leadership lies less in their reliance on structural—or power-driven—bases of

international leadership associated with hegemony and more with forms of persuasion that come from the development of significant technical, intellectual, and entrepreneurial skills (often by secondary actors in the system) . . . in the absence of positive leadership from great powers, middle power diplomacy applied in a regional context fostered limited economic cooperation.[564]

Extrapolating from their view on regional leadership and applying this to international organizations, the changes that Canada introduced within the Commonwealth do not, in themselves, affect the international system. To say unequivocally that these actions by Canada constitute structural leadership would be wrong. However, by the very nature that these structural changes helped to preserve the Commonwealth from collapse in some cases, and introduced moralistic themes such as Women's issues in others, it could be said that there was a knock-on effect, however ancillary, upon the international system as a whole.

Through the application of its resources, it could be said that Canada gave entrepreneurial and technical leadership to this organization. Yet, the culmination of its efforts to preserve this forum also lead one to speculate that it played a structural leadership role as well. To test this hypothesis further, one could look to other international fora and examine the roles played by middle powers. Though their roles may be limited, they are still significant actors whose actions cannot be disregarded. Whether they act to stabilize or destabilize the international system, their actions will affect the very structure of that system. Should this be called structural leadership as defined by Oran Young would be misleading, but the theory offered by Cooper, Higgott, and Nossal also proves inadequate.

As a note to end this book, the introduction set out the period of study between the years 1963 to 1987. As noted above, these years were significant in that the Commonwealth went through its evolution with decolonization and the creation of the Secretariat. Canada's role, during these years, was one of leadership, as it tried to preserve and shape this organization. Over these three decades, there were three administrations—under Pearson, Trudeau, and Mulroney—that played a part in this process. After 1988, however, Canadian foreign began a process of re-focusing. With its new policies on trade that saw it building a closer relationship with the United States and with the end of the Cold War in

1991, the Commonwealth's importance to Canada began to wane. This diminishing role was furthered by the lack of interest in foreign policy by Canada's subsequent Prime Ministers—Jean Chretien, Paul Martin, and Stephen Harper. The leadership on its foreign policy was to come from Canada's Ministers of Foreign Affairs, most notably Lloyd Axworthy, who focused upon Human Security issues. Though the Commonwealth had a potential role in this arena, and in fact it would develop its own human rights agenda, as an organization, it was of more importance to Prime Ministers than Ministers of State. It is no wonder then that its significance was overlooked. Canadian leadership in the Commonwealth cannot be denied, but, sadly, it seems this legacy has been forgotten.

Endnotes

1   Margaret Doxey, "Canada and the Modern Commonwealth", *Behind the Headlines* Vol. XL, No 2 (1982); "Strategies in Multilateral Diplomacy: Canada, the Commonwealth and the NIEO", *International Journal* (1980) pp. 329-56; "Canada and the Commonwealth", in John English and Norman Hillmer (eds), *Making a Difference? Canada's Foreign Policy in a Changing World Order* (Toronto: Lester, 1992) pp. 34-53.

2   Evan Potter, "Canada in the Commonwealth" *The Round Table* (2007) 96:4, pp. 447-463; W.D. McIntyre "Canada and the Commonwealth", in M. Appel Molot and N Hillmer (eds), *Canada Among Nations 2002: A Fading Power* (Don Mills, Ontario: Oxford UP, pp. 281-298; David Black "Canada and the Commonwealth: The Multilateral Politics of a "Wasting Asset"" Canadian Foreign Policy, (Spring 2010) 16:2, pp. 61-77.

3   Ivan Head and Pierre Trudeau, *The Canadian Way: Shaping Canada's Foreign Policy, 1968-1984*, (Toronto: McClelland & Stewart, 1995); John W Holmes, *The Shaping of Peace: Canada and the Search for World Order, 1943-1957*, Vol. 2, (Toronto: University of Toronto Press, 1982) see Chapter 8; Louis Delvoie "The Commonwealth in Canadian Foreign Policy", 310, *The Round Table* (1989) pp. 137-143.

4   Ian O Cameron, "Canada, the Commonwealth and South Africa: National Foreign Policy-Making in a Multilateral Environment", Vol. 18, No 2, *Millennium* (1989) pp. 205-225; Frank Hayes, "Canada and Southern Rhodesia" in KR Nossal (ed) *An Acceptance of Paradox: Essays on Canadian Diplomacy in Honour of John W Holmes* (Toronto: Canadian Institute of International Affairs, 1982) pp. 141-173; Clarence Redekop "Trudeau at Singapore: The Commonwealth and Arms Sales to South Africa" in KR Nossal (ed) (1982), *ibid*, pp. 174-195.

5   JL Granatstein and Robert Bothwell, *Pirouette: Pierre Trudeau and the Canadian Foreign Policy* (Toronto: University of Toronto, 1989); Tom Keating, *Canada and World Order: The Multilateralist Tradition in Canadian Foreign Policy* (Toronto: McClelland & Stewart, 1993).

6   D Dewitt and J Kirton, *Canada as a Principal Power*, (Toronto: Wiley and Sons, 1983); MK Hawes, *Principal Power, Middle Power, or Satellite?* (Toronto: York University Press, 1984); N Hillmer and S Stevenson (ed), *Foremost Nation: Canadian Foreign Policy and a Changing World*, (Toronto: McClelland and Stewart, 1977)

7   Bernard Wood, *The Middle Powers and the General Interest*, (Ottawa: The North-South Institute, 1988) p. 18

8   JL Granatstein, *Canadian Foreign Policy Since 1945: Middle Power or Satellite?*, (Toronto: Copp Clark, 1973); Arther Andrews, *The Rise and Fall of a Middle Power: Canadian Diplomacy from King to Mulroney*, (Toronto: Lorimer Co., 1993); Michael Hawes, *op.cit.*.

9   John Holmes (1966), *op.cit.*; John Holmes, *Canada: A Middle-Aged Power*, (Toronto: McClelland and Stewart, 1976); John Holmes (1983), *op.cit.*; John Holmes (1984), *op.cit*; Cooper, Higgott, and Nossal, *op.cit.*.

10 Clair cutler and Mark Zacher, *Canadian Foreign Policy and International Economics Regimes*, (Vancouver: UBC, 1992) pp. 3-4.

11 Jock Finlayson, *op.cit.*.

12 Ivan Head and Pierre Trudeau, *op.cit.*.

13 Bernard Wood, "Canada and Southern Africa: A Return to Middle Power Activism" *The Round Table* (1989), 315, pp. 280-90.

14 Department of Foreign Affairs and International Trade (DFAIT), File # 23-1, Vol. 10, September 10, 1974: Draft report for the Commonwealth Finance Ministers Meeting.

15 AE Thorndike, "Regionalism and the Commonwealth", in AJR Groom and P Taylor (eds), *The Commonwealth in the 1980's*, (London: Macmillan, 1984) pp. 40-54.

16 MM Ball, *The "Open" Commonwealth*, (Durham, NC: Duke University Press, 1970); M Doxey, *The Commonwealth Secretariat and the Contemporary Commonwealth*, (Basingstoke: Macmillan, 1989); A Smith (with Clyde Sanger), Stitches in Time, (London: Andre Deutsch, 1981).

17 Commonwealth Secretariat, *Annual Report of the Commonwealth Secretary-General*, (London: Commonwealth Secretariat, 1966), p. 16.

18 KC Wheare, Constitutional Structure of the Commonwealth, (Oxford: Clarendon Press, 1960).

19 Whether or not there are grounds for distinction in this area could be discussed at a later date, but it is tangential in this context.

20 MM Ball, *op.cit.*, p. 3; N Mansergh, *The Commonwealth Experience*, (London: Weidenfeld & Nicolson, 1969) p. 349, quoting Winston Churchill.

21 MM Ball, *op.cit.*, p. 3.

22 JN Kinnas, *The Politics of Association in Europe*, (Frankfurt: Campus Verlag, 1979) p. 11, p. 162; JN Kinnas, "Associations", in AJR Groom and P Taylor (eds), *International Organizations*, (London: Pinter, 1978) p. 159; See also AJR Groom and Paul Taylor, *Frameworks for International Co-operation*, (London: Pinter, 1990).

23 This is the position put forward by Sir William Dale, *The Modern Commonwealth*, (London: Butterworths, 1983); MM Ball, *op.cit.*; and Stephen Chan, "The Commonwealth as an International Organization: Constitutionalism, Britain and South Africa", *The Round Table* (1989) Vol. 312, pp. 393-412.

24 AJR Groom, "The Commonwealth as an International Organization", in AJR Groom and Paul Taylor (eds), The Commonwealth in the 1980's, (London: Macmillan, 1984) pp. 293, 296.

25 Clive Archer, *International Organizations*, (London: Allen and Unwin, 1983) p. 33. Also see M Wallace and D Singer, "Intergovernmental Organization in the Global Syste, 1815-1964", *International Organization* (1970) pp. 245-7.

26 C Archer, *ibid*, pp. 34-5.

27 C Archer, *ibid*, p. 35.

28 AJR Groom, "The Setting of World Society", in AJR Groom and P Taylor, Frameworks for International Cooperation, (London: Pinter, 1990) pp. 3-11, p. 4.

29 Stephen Chan, "The Commonwealth as an International Organization: Constitutionalism, Britain and South Africa" Round Table, Vol. 312, (1989) pp. 393-412, pp. 398-400; MM Ball, *op.cit.*, pp. 79, 111-112.

30 N Mansergh, op.cit., pp. 30-58. Canada was the first colony of Britain to be granted its independence. The manner in which constitutional power was transferred became a model for other colonies.

31 MM Ball, *op.cit.*, pp. 33-34.

32 MM Ball, *ibid*, p. 33; AJR Groom, *op.cit.*, pp. 293, 296: KC Wheare also put forth an argument that the Commonwealth was not constitutionally based due to his definition of a constitution. However, Sire William Dale argued that the definition used by Wheare referred to a domestic constitution which

would be in applicable to an international organization; Sir William Dale, *The Modern Commonwealth*, (London: Butterworths, 1983) p. 52; KC Wheare, *op.cit.*

33 See M Doxey, "Constructive Internationalism: A Continuing Theme in Canadian Foreign Policy", *The Round Table*, Vol. 311 (1989) pp. 295-298; MM Ball, *op.cit.*, p. 12; AJR Groom (1984), *op.cit.*, pp. 293, 297.

34 MM Ball, ibid, p. 33; HJ Harvey, *Consultation and Co-operation in the Commonwealth*, (Oxford: Clarendon Press, 1952) pp. 3-4.

35 MM Ball, *ibid*, p. 33.

36 MM Ball, *ibid*, p. 33.

37 MM Ball, *ibid*, p. 33.

38 MM Ball, *ibid*, pp. 33-34.

39 O Akinrinade, "The 1971 Declaration of Commonwealth Principles After 20 Years", *The Round Table*, Vol. 321 (1992), pp. 23-35; S Chan, *op.cit.*, p. 401.

40 S Chan (1989), *ibid*, pp. 400-401; These principles are: international peace and support for the United Nations; liberty and equal rights for all; the denouncement of racial discrimination; support the principles of self-determination; the creation of a more equitable international society; and international cooperation as a means to achieve these goals: see S Chan, *The Commonwealth in World Politics, 1965-1985*, (London: Lester Crook, 1988) pp. 85-86.

41 S Chan (1989), *ibid*, p. 401.

42 S Chan (1989), *ibid*, p. 401.

43 M Doxey (1989), *op.cit.*, p. 3.

44 See A Smith, *op.cit.*,

45 Due to some of the resentment that was generated at the outset of the creation of this post, the Commonwealth Secretariat is limited to an administrative role fulfilling the ambitions dictated by its membership. Though there is a modicum of room for innovation from this office, its primary role is one of organizing and overseeing the various functions ascribed to the Commonwealth.

46 M Doxey (1989), *op.cit.*, p. 49.

47 This is a traditional position which has been maintained throughout the Commonwealth's existence, though there is some precedence set where the Secretariat may involve itself in internal matters of a member state through a non-public forum, or if it is in the general interest of the Commonwealth as a whole. M Doxey (1989), *ibid*, pp. 48-53.

48 M Doxey (1989), *ibid*, p. 37.

49 Included in this office are the international, legal, and the information gathering and distributing functions.

50 This office is responsible for economic affairs, export market development, and food production and rural development. M Doxey (1989), *ibid*, p. 26.

51 AJR Groom "The Setting of World Society" in AJR Groom and P Taylor (London: Pinter, 1990), *op.cit.*, p. 4.

52 MM Ball, *op.cit.*, p. 58; GEH Palmer, *Consultation and Co-operation in the British Commonwealth*, (London: Oxford UP, 1934) pp. 190-191.

53 AJR Groom, "The Commonwealth as an Organization", in AJR Groom and P Taylor (eds), *The Commonwealth in the 1980's*, (London: Macmillan, 1984) pp. 293-304.

54 GEH Palmer, *op.cit.*, pp. 191-192.

55 GEH Palmer, *ibid*, pp. 164-166.

56 A Smith (with Clyde Sanger), *op.cit.*, pp. 106-129.

57 D Mitrany, *A Working Peace System*, (London: National Peace Council, 1946).

58 M Doxey, "Strategies in Multilateral Diplomacy: The Commonwealth, Southern Africa, and the NIEO", *International Journal* (1982) p. 333; Inis Claude, *The Changing United Nations*, (New York, 1966) pp. 73-102.

59 M Doxey (1982), *ibid*, p. 333.

60 RO Keohane and J Nye, *Power and Interdependence: World Politics in Transition*, (Boston: Little and Brown, 1977) p. 11; SD Krasner (ed), *International Regimes* (Ithaca: Cornell UP, 1983) pp. 5-9.

61 Krasner, *op.cit.*, p. 2.

62 AC Cutler and MW Zacher, *Canadian Foreign Policy and International Economic Regimes*, (Vancouver: UBC Press, 1992) p. 3; F Kratochwil and JG Ruggie, "International Organization: A State of the Art on an Art of a State.", *International Organization*, Vol. 40, No. 4, (Autumn 1986) p. 759.

63 AJR Groom and P Taylor (1984), *op.cit.*, p. 10.

64 Through the manipulation of agenda issues and norms, then, states may control the regime and/or an international organization: see RO Keohane, International Instiitutions and State Power, (London: Westview, 1989) p. 161; MP Karns and KA Mingst, "International Organizations and Foreign Policy: Influence and Instrumentality" in J Roseneau et all (eds) New directions in the Study of Foreign Policy (London: Harper-Collins, 1987) p. 468.

65 See N Mansergh, *op.cit.*.

[66] In 1897 there was some encouragement to all greater trade amongst the colonies and the former colonies. N Mansergh, *ibid*, p. 131.

[67] I Drummond and N Hillmer, *Negotiating Freer Trade*, (Waterloo, Ontario: Wilfred Laurier Press, 1989).

[68] N Mansergh, op.cit., pp. 131, 138-144, 242-245, 324.

[69] JJ Schott, *The Uruguay Round: An Assessment*, (Washington, DC: Intstitute for International Economics, 1994) p. 6.

[70] C Kindleberger, *The World in Depression: 1929-1939*, (Berkeley: UP California, 1973).

[71] S Gill and D Law, *The Global Political Economy: Perspectives, Problems and Policies*, (London: Harvester-Wheatsheaf, 1988) pp. 132-135.

[72] N Mansergh, *op.cit.*, p. 243.

[73] R Gilpin, *The Political Economy of International Relations*, (Princeton: Princeton UP, 1987) pp. 131, 372; Gill and Law, *op.cit.*, p. 134.

[74] See the Duncan Report, 1969.

[75] *The Economist*, 16 January, 1971, pp. 27-30

[76] RJ Harrison, "By Way of Comparison: French Relations with Former Colonies", in AJR Groom and P Taylor (1984), *op.cit.*, pp. 179-180.

[77] There were four conventions with the first in 1975 and the last in 1989.

[78] M Doxey, "The Commonwealth Secretariat", in AJR Groom and P Taylor (1984), op.cit., p. 28

[79] These were Canada, New Zealand, Australia, India, Pakistan, Malaysia, and Singapore.

[80] Prior to this project, member states were responsible fiscally for their own development and research projects.

[81] The Colombo Plan was mainly a political action by Britain to show its commitment to the Commonwealth. N Mansergh, *op.cit.*, p. 410.

[82] For example India and Pakistan. N Mansergh, *ibid*, p. 410.

[83] For example Malaysia and Singapore.

[84] A Kilgore and J Mayall, "The Residual Legatee: Economic Co-operation in the Contemporary Commonwealth", in AJR Groom and P Taylor (1984), *op.cit.*, p. 150.

[85] A Smith, *op.cit.*, pp. 106-129.

[86] The Commonwealth Trade and Economic Conference, 1958, offered some preliminary work towards global development. This led to the 1963 Commonwealth meeting on trdae, the GATT discussion, and a further meeting at UNCTAD in 1964. See RA Higgott and AF Cooper, "Middle Power Leadership and Coalition Building: Australia, the Cairns Group, and

the Uruguay Round of Trade Negotiations", International Organization, Vol. 44, No. 4, (Autumn 1990) p. 610.

[87] O Akinrinade (1992), *op.cit.*, pp. 30-31.

[88] Canada, which gave the initial funding to the CFTC asked for the right to have one of its own people placed in charge of the Commonwealth agency and this was granted. This demonstrates the political nature of economic support within the Commonwealth. A Smith, *op.cit.*, p. 119. For a breakdown of financial contributions by member states see M Doxey (1989), *op.cit.*: and Appendix A, *infra.*

[89] CP Kindleberger, "Dominance and Leadership in the International Economy", *International Studies Quarterly*, Vol. 25, No. 2, (1981) pp. 242-254.

[90] N Mansergh, *op.cit.*, pp. xv, 120-155.

[91] N Mansergh, *ibid.*, pp. 30-59.

[92] N Mansergh, *ibid.*, pp. 155-156, 159-186.

[93] N Mansergh, *ibid.*, pp. 220-221.

[94] Gerard Bergeron, *op.cit.*, p. 786.

[95] Though Canada wasa full member of the League of Nations, decisions were made on its behalf by Great Britain.

[96] A collective foreign policy, as OD Skelton told MacKenzie-King, involves a "maximum responsibility and a minimum of control." N Mansergh, *op.cit.*, p. 223.

[97] N Mansergh, *ibid.*, pp. 269-294.

[98] This was the concept of the Smuts Plan, 1943, for rising against the growing tide of Communism.

[99] N Manserrgh, *op.cit.*, pp. 342-343.

[100] Hugh Tinker "Migration in the Commonwealth" in AJR Groom and P Taylor (1984), *op.cit.*, p. 248.

[101] It should be noted, however, that there was a racial element to this freedom of movement with most of the immigration taking place amongst *white* citizens of the Commonwealth. H Tinker, *ibid.*, pp. 244-259.

[102] H Tinker, ibid, p. 248.

[103] This compromise was maintained through the London Declaration, 1949, and set the precedent for Commonwealth states to become Republics, but membership was conditional upon the consensus of Commonwealth states. The Monarch remained the figurehead of the organization. N Mansergh, *op.cit.*, pp. 28-29.

[104] Canada, (and South Africa and the Irish Free State), from 1931 to 1947, disapproved of a Secretariat as it saw this organ detracting from Canada's independence and creating a new era of imperial control. JBD Miller, The Commonwealth in the World, 3rd.ed., (London: Duckworth, 1965) pp. 43, 79.

[105] A Smith, *op.cit.*, p. 16.

[106] This was alleged by the Duncan Report, 1969. MM Ball, *op.cit.*, pp. 26-27.

[107] The Government at this time in Britain was Labour and believed in hanging on to the old Disraelian ideals, set out by the Tory leader Benjamin Disraeli. The Conservative Government that followed, however, would be thankful for removal of responsibility that the Secretariat would offer. M O'Neill, "Continuity Without Consensus: The Commonwealth Heads of Government Meetings, 1971-1981" in AJR Groom and P Taylor (1984), *op.cit.*, p. 198.

[108] Simultaneous to this growing fear of the break up of the Commonwealth, was Britain's ambition to join the EEC. As stated above, this evidently occurred in 1973, and the Lome Convention was an effort to maintain British interests within its old Empire. See *The Economist*, January 16, 1971, pp. 13, 27-30; *The Economist*, July 3, 1971, pp. 40, 62.

[109] The specific issue that challenged Britain was its arms sales to South Africa that offended the other Commonwealth states, causing them to place pressure upon Britain to change its foreign trade policy.

[110] MM Ball, *op.cit.*, pp. 33-34.

[111] M O'Neill, *op.cit.*, pp. 185-224; O Akinrinade, *op.cit.*, pp. 24-27.

[112] South Africa voiced fears that the Commonwealth was no longer a "white-man's club". JDB Miller, *op.cit.*, pp. 54-55.

[113] All except Britain: S Chan, *Twelve Years of Commonwealth Diplomatic History: Commonwealth Summit Meetings, 1979-1991* (Lewiston: Edwin Mellon, 1992) pp. 55-62.

[114] M Doxey (1992), *op.cit.*, pp. 329-356.

[115] Interview with Carolyn McAskie, Vice-President CIDA (Multilateral Aid Division), Hull, Quebec, 12 September, 1996.

[116] Gerard Bergeron, "Foreign Affairs", in JMS Careless and RC Brown (eds), *The Canadians: 1867-1967* (Toronto: Macmillan, 1967) pp. 785-805.

[117] KR Nossal, *The Politics of Canadian Foreign Policy*, 2nd.ed. (Scarborough, Ontario: Prentice-Hall, 1989)

[118] Denis Stairs notes that this influence upon the "substance" of foreign policy is quite limited, but the public pressure that it can generate will affect the

policy-makers. "The Press and Foreign Policy in Canada", *International Journal*, Vol. 33 (Spring 1976), p. 238; D Stairs, "Public Opinion and External Affairs: Reflections on the Domestification of Canadian Foreign Policy", *International Journal*, Vol. 34 (Winter 1977-78) pp. 130-138.

119 The Canadian government called in Arnold Smith, the Commonwealth Secretary-General, to help explain the events of the Nigerian Civil War. Smith confirmed that the atrocities projected by the media were never evidenced during his investigations. A Smith, *Stitches in Time*, (London: Andre Deutsch, 1981) pp. 100-101.

120 Interview with Bernard Wood, Prime Minister Mulroney's Special Envoy to Southern Africa, Paris, France 10 June, 1996.

121 KR Nossal (1989), *op.cit.*, p. 115, fn97; Don Munton and TM Shaw, "Apartheid and Canadian Public Opinion", *International Perspectives* (September/October 1987) p. 11.

122 KR Nossal (1989), *op.cit.*, pp. 91-94.

123 J Granatstein and R Bothwell, *Pirouette: Pierre Trudeau and Canadian Foreign Policy*, (Toronto: University of Toronto, 1990) p. 290.

124 Department of Foreign Affairs and International Trade (DFAIT), File # 23-1, Vol.1, 20 December, 1967.

125 KR Nossal (1989), *op.cit.*, pp. 162-163; James Eayrs, *The Art of the Possible: Government and Foreign Policy in Canada*, (Toronto: McClelland and Stewart, 1995) p. 98.

126 KR Nossal (1989), *op.cit.*, pp. 163-64.

127 Ivan Head and Pierre Trudeau, The Canadian Way: Shaping Canada's foreign policy, 1968-1984, (Toronto: McClelland and Stewart, 1995) p. 98.

128 Kim Nossal referred to this influence as the pre-eminence of the prime minister stemming from the personal ambitions of the individual. *Op.cit.*, (1989) pp. 164-184; Walter D Young, "Leadership and Canadian Politics", in John H Redekop (ed), *Approaches to Canadian Foreign Policy* (Scarborough, Ontario: Prentice-Hall, 1978) p. 283: David Dewitt and John Kirton, *Canada as a Principle Power*, (Toronto: Wiley and Sons, 1983).

129 Ivan Head and Pierre Trudeau, op.cit., p. 134.

130 KR Nossal (1989), *op.cit.*, p. 176.

131 Quoted in KR Nossal (1989), *op.cit.*, pp. 217-18; Mitchell Sharp, "Civil Service recollections", *Ottawa Journal*, 12-13 December, 1985; Interview with Mitchell Sharp, former Minister of Foreign Affairs and Foreign Policy Advisor to Prime Minister Jean Chretien, Ottawa, Ontario, 23 July, 1996.

132 KR Nossal (1989), *op.cit.*, pp. 217-218.

[133] Flora Mac Donald, "Cutting Through the Chains", *The Globe and Mail,* 7 November, 1980, p7; KR Nossal (1989), *op.cit.,* p. 218.

[134] *Hansard: Canadian Parliamentary Debates,* Vol. VIII (Ottawa: Queen's Printer, 1966) 30 August, 1966, pp. 7791-2.

[135] Hansard: Canadian Parliamentary Debates, Vol. VIII (Ottawa: Queen's Printer, 1966) 2 September, 1966, pp. 8008-16.

[136] KR Nossal (1989), *op.cit.,* pp. 231-253.

[137] Quoted in KR Nossal (1989), *op.cit.,* p. 27.

[138] Richard Lipsey, "Canada and the United States: The Economic Dimensions", in Charles F Doran and John H Sigler, *Canada and the United States: Enduring Friendship, Persistent Stress,* (Englewood, NJ: Prentice-Hall, 1985) p. 81.

[139] Canada has always benefitted economically from its geographic proximity to the United States and Britain in what was commonly referred to as the "North Atlantic Triangle". John Bartlet Brebner, *North Atlantic Triangle: The Interplay of Canada, the United States and Great Britain,* (Toronto: McClelland and Stewart, 1966).

[140] Tom Keating, *Canada and World Order: The Multilateralist Tradition in Canadian Foreign Policy,* (Toronto: McClelland and Stewart, 1993) p. 60.

[141] M Haas, *International Conflict,* (Indianapolis: Bobbs-Merrill, 1974) pp. 324-331.

[142] M Doxey, "Strategies in Multilateral Diplomacy: The Commonwealth, Southern Africa, and the NIEO", *International Journal* (Spring 1980) pp. 329-56: R Keohane, "Multilateralism: An Agenda for Research", *International Journal,* Vol. 45, No. 4 (Autumn 1990), p. 731: T Keating, *op.cit.*

[143] Ian O Cameron, "Canada, the Commonwealth and South Africa: National Foreign Policy-Making in a Multilateral Environment", *Millennium,* Vol. 18, No. 2 (1989), pp. 205-225, at p. 205.

[144] Quoted in T Keating, *op.cit.,* p. 12. R Keohane (1990), *op.cit.,* p 731.

[145] T Keating, *ibid,* p. 12; JG Ruggie, "Multilateralism: The Anatomy of an Institution", *International Organization,* Vol. 46, No. 3 (Summer, 1992) p. 567.

[146] Interview with Mitchell Sharp, Ottawa, Ontario, 23 July, 1996; Editorial "Canada: Trends in External Policy", *The Round Table,* (1954/1955) pp. 179-186.

[147] Evan Luard, *A History of the United Nations: The Age of Decolonization, 1955-1965,* 9Vol. 2 (London: Macmillan, 1989) p. 176.

[148] *Ibid,* p. 120.

[149] *Ibid,* p. 121.

[150] These resided mainly in the Pacific region. *Ibid,* p. 131.

[151] *Ibid*, p. 179. Also find reference in RJ Vincent, Foreign Policy and Human Rights (Cambridge: Cambridge University Press, 1986).

[152] For an interesting overview of these problems of statehood, see Robert Jackson, *Quasi-states: Sovereignty, International Relations, and the Third World* (Cambridge: Cambridge University Press, 1990). He proposed that because of their general inabilities to govern themselves, these newly independent countries are only quasi-states.

[153] FH Soward, "Canada, the Elevent General Assembly, and Trusteeship", *International Journal* (Summer 1957) pp. 167-181; ET Rowe, "The Emerging Anti-Colonial Concensus in the United Nations", Journal of Conflict Resolution, Vol. 8 (September 1964) pp. 209-230.

[154] It was not until the Trudeau era that Canada would re-assert its independence from American influence: Lawrence Martin, *The Presidents and the Prime Ministers*, (Toronto: Doubleday, 1982).

[155] WJ Hudson, *Austalia and the Colonial Question at the United Nations* (Sydney: Sydney UP, 1970) pp. 7, 33, 60.

[156] WJ Hudson, *ibid*, p. 99; ET Rowe, *op.cit.*, p. 214 (ff8)

[157] J-P Therien, "La Francophonie" in John English and Norman Hillmer (eds), *Making A Difference: Canada's Foreign Policy in a Changing World Order* (Toronto: Lester Publishing, 1992) pp. 59-61.

[158] As Arnold Smith indicated in his book *Stiches in Time* (London: Andre Deutsch, 1981), Canada, as a fiscal leader within this organization, was forced to accede to this pressure brought forward by the African delegations as it was a matter of saving face. It should be mentioned, however, that Canada's initial response was to denounce this idea as she was in fear that this would once again subject her to imperial domination: p. 16.

[159] John W Holmes, "A Canadian's Commonwealth: Realism out of Rhetoric", *The Round Table*, Vol. 56 (1965/66) pp. 335-347, at pp. 336-338.

[160] GL Reuber, "Why Canadian Foreign Aid?", *International Journal* (Winter 1958/1959) pp. 11-20.

[161] *Foreign Policy for Canadians: International Development* (Department of External Affairs White Paper, 1970)

[162] Michael Pearson, Gregor Mackinnon, and Christopher Sapardanis "'The World is Entitled to Ask Questions': The Trudeau Peace Initiative Reconsidered", *International Journal* (Winter 1985/6) pp. 129-158; A Bromke and KR Nossal, "Trudeau Rides the "Third Rail"", *International Perspectives* (May/June 1984) pp. 3-6.

[163] David Taras, "Brian Mulroney's Foreign Polcy: Something for Everyone", *The Round Table* (1985) pp. 35-46, at pp. 37-38.

[164] Ulrich Fanger, "Canada's Foreign Policy in the Eighties: Continentalism and Internationalism", *Aussenpolitik* (1988) pp. 86-101, 96-97, 100-101.

[165] Interview with Derek Ingram, Commonwealth Journalist, London, 6 May, 1996.

[166] Human rights was an issue presented to the Commonwealth by Chief Emeka Anyaoku, who succeeded Ramphal as Secretary-General of the Commonwealth. According to Ivan Head, he was Canada's choice for Secretary-General over the Australian candidate Malcolm Fraser. It is not unlikely, therefore, that this initiative was pushed by Canada: Interview with Ivan Head, former Advisor to Prime Minister Trudeau, Vancouver, B.C., 17 October, 1996; Margaret Doxey, "Canada and the Commonwealth", in John English and Norman Hillmer (eds), *op.cit.*, pp. 34-53, 38; Kathleen E Mahoney, "Human Rights and Canada's Foreign Policy", *International Journal* (*Summer* 1992) pp. 555-594.

[167] Department of Foreign Affairs and International Trade (DFAIT), File # 23-1, Vol. 6, 15 August, 1973. Internal memo.

[168] Stephen Chan, *The Commonwealth in World Politics: A Study of International Action, 1965-1985*, (London: Lester Crook, 1988. 24-25.

[169] Arnold Smith also possessed the political skills and knowledge needed to stand against Whitehall. Stephen Chan (1988), *ibid*, p. 25; Derek Ingram, *The Imperfect Commonwealth* (London: Rex Collings, 1977) p. 24.

[170] Commonwealth Secretariat, Annual Report of the Commonwealth Secretary-General, 26 August, 1966.

[171] In 1965, the Commonwealth Secretariat budget for the 1965/66 year was £176,000; by 1987, the budget was £6, 299, 705. *Ibid.*

[172] It should be mentioned that Pakistan left the Commonwealth in 1972.

[173] DFAIT, File # 23-5-1, Vol. 5, 30 May, 1966. Internal memo.

[174] In a telex from Canada's High Commission in London, as part of the suggestions at the Commonwealth Law Ministers meeting for a legal division included the creation of a Commonwealth Appeal Court and Commonwealth legislation. Both of these matters were not acceptable to Canada. DFAIT, File # 23-5-1, Vol. 5, 4 May, 1966.

[175] DFAIT, File # 23-5-1, Vol. 5, 30 May, 1966. Internal memo. The projected cost of this new division was to be £22, 000 of which Canada's costs would be £4, 312.

[176] DFAIT, File # 23-5-1, Vol. 5, 8 August, 1966. Letter from AG Campbell to AR Menzies, High Commissioner (Canberra).

[177] DFAIT, File # 23-5-1, Vol. 5, 30 May, 1966. Internal Memo.

[178] Initially, Britain's Foreign Secretary, Douglas-Home, suggested that the Committee meetings of the Commonwealth should only have regional representatives attending. This was unacceptable to a number of Commonwealth states. In a letter from Pearson to Douglas-Home, Pearson advised that all Commonwealth members should be represented at Committee meetings dealing with the Commonwealth Secretariat. DFAIT, File # 23-5-1, Vol. 1, 1 September, 1964. Letter from Pearson to Douglas-Home.

[179] DFAIT, File # 23-5-1, Vol.5, 5 August, 1966. Internal memo.

[180] Commonwealth Secretariat, *Annual Report of the Commonwealth Secretary-General*, 26 August, 1966, p. 17.

[181] DFAIT, File # 23-5-1, Vol. 1, 11 July, 1964. This was taken from a briefing on the Head of Government Meeting in London, 1964.

[182] A Smith, *op.cit.*, p. 55.

[183] At this time, the Commonwealth Division in the Department of External Affairs was headed by Mr. AG Cambell.

[184] DFAIT, File # 23-5-1, Vol. 5, 20 May, 1966. Letter from AR Menzies to AG Campbell.

[185] On 25 April, 1966, A Bottomley, the British Foreign Secretary directed this question in a message passed on from the High Commission. DFAIT, File # 23-5-1, Vol. 5, 5 May, 1966.

[186] *Ibid.*

[187] DFAIT, File # 23-5-1, Vol. 5, 30 august, 1966.

[188] *Ibid.*

[189] This meeting was to be held in Nigeria, but Smith arranged for it to be transferred to Canada for reasons unknown.

[190] DFAIT, File # 23-5-1, Vol. 5, 28 April, 1966. Letter from Chevrier to Pearson.

[191] DFAIT, File # 23-5-1, Vol. 5, June 1966, Letter from Pearson to Chevrier.

[192] Interview with John English, Professor of History at the University of Waterloo and Member of Parliament, Canterbury, Kent, 10, April, 1996.

[193] A Smith, *op.cit.*, p. 300.

[194] Interview with Clyde Sanger, a former Communications Officer for the Commonwealth Secretariat, Ottawa, Canada, 17 September, 1996.

195 The article was to be published in the December 1967 issue of *Commonwealth Trade and Commerce Journal.* DFAIT, File # 23-1, Vol. 1, 27 November, 1967.

196 DFAIT, File # 23-1, Vol. 1, 27 November, 1967. Letter from D Ingram to LB Pearson.

197 The Sterling began its rapid decline after the Suez Crisis, and Britain was again petitioning to join the European Economic Community. In a circular from the London High Commission, an excerpt from *The Times* commented on the demise of Britain as a world power. DFAIT, File # 23-1, Vol. 2, 24 January, 1968.

198 According to Mitchell Sharp, Britain also wanted Canada to take over much of the lead within the Commonwealth. Interview with Mitchell Sharp, former Minister of External Affairs and the Foreign Policy Advisor to Prime Minister Chretien, Ottawa, Ontario, 23 July, 1996.

199 DFAIT, File # 23-1, Vol. 2, 20 June, 1967.

200 DFAIT, File # 23-1, Vol. 2, 25 August, 1967.

201 DFAIT, File # 23-1, Vol. 2, 16 August, 1967.

202 This was found in a review paper on the Commonwealth Secretariat noting the problems that Canada saw with this organization. One interesting point noted in this paper were two occurrences where Arnold Smith's role as Secretary-General was mentioned in a negative light, but these were both crossed out with a pen. DFAIT, File # 23-5-1, Vol. 6, 11 January, 1968; Stephen Chan (1988), *op.cit.*, p 25, also alludes to Smith exceeding his duties outlined in the *Agreed Memorandum.*

203 This review committee was established in June 1965 to oversee more than 250 Commonwealth Organizations. By 1967, these had been reduced to ten organizations dealing mainly with economic and education issues. A Smith, *op.cit.*, p. 47.

204 A confidential report drafted by Paul Martin sets out many of the reasons for not having the Secretary-General chair Committee meetings. DFAIT, File # 23-5-1, Vol. 6, 25 March, 1967.

205 DFAIT, File # 23-5-1, Vol. 6, 22 March, 1967. Telex from London High Commission.

206 In Smith's memoirs *Stitches in Time*, the year given to these reviews was 1966. All of the evidence shows that they occurred in 1967. *Op.cit.*, p. 47.

207 *Ibid*, p. 47.

208 DFAIT, File # 23-5-1, Vol. 6, 27 December, 1967.

209 Commonwealth Secretariat, *Second Report of the Commonwealth Secretary-General*, November 1968, p. 74.

210 DFAIT, File # 23-5-1, Vol. 6, 29 March, 1968.

211 DFAIT, File # 23-5-1, Vol. 6, 1 May, 1968.

212 DFAIT, File # 23-5-1, Vol. 8, 21 October, 1968. This was a report of a meeting that occurred on 11 October, 1968, between Arnold Smith and representatives from the Department of External Affairs.

213 DFAIT, File # 23-5-1, Vol. 8, 21 October, 1968.

214 *Ibid.*

215 *Ibid.*

216 *Ibid.*

217 DFAIT, File # 23-5-1, Vol. 8, 4 November, 1968.

218 *Ibid.*

219 Interview with CJ Small, former Assistant Secretary-General and Canadian Diplomat, Ottawa, Ontario, 14, September, 1996.

220 Interviews with Carolyn McAskie, Hull, Quebec, 12 September, 1996 and CJ Small, Ottawa, Ontario, 14 September, 1996.

221 Interview with Carolyn McAskie, Hull, Quebec, 12 September, 1996.

222 The Economist, 16 January, 1971, pp. 27-30. Edward Heath was quoted as stating "that he felt he had caught them [the African members of the Commonwealth] making demands on him that he would never be allowed to make on them."

223 Interview with Ivan Head, former Advisor to Prime Minister Trudeau, Vancouver, BC, 17 October, 1996.

224 Arnold Smith in *Stitches in Time* said that he gave the Managing Directorship to George Kidd, a Canadian, primarily because of Canada's commitment. *Op.cit.*, p. 119.

225 Interviews with John English, Canterbury, Kent, 10 April, 1996; Carolyn McAskie, Hull, Quebec, 12 September, 1996; CJ Small, Ottawa, Ontario, 14 September, 1996; and Robert McLaren (telephone interview0, former Assistant Secretary-General, Victoria, BC, 7 October, 1996.

226 Interviews with John Harker, Ottawa, Ontario, 10 September, 1996; Clyde Sanger, Ottawa, Ontario, 17 September, 1996; and Carolyn McAskie, Hull, Quebec, 12 September, 1996.

227 DFAIT, File # 23-1, Vol. 18, 1 June, 1978.

228 LS Trachtenberg, "The Commonwealth Youth Programme and Youth-oriented Activites" in AJR Groom and P Taylor (eds), *The Commonwealth in the 1980's* (London: Macmillan, 1984) pp. 55-63.

[229] DFAIT, File # 23-5-1, Vol. 21, (no date: between 1 May, 1979 and 31 December, 1982). Memorandum for Mr. Morgan; Interview with Ivan Head, Vancouver, BC, 17 October, 1996.

[230] Commonwealth Secretariat, *Report of the Commonwealth Heads of Government Meeting in Nassau, 1985.*

[231] DFAIT, File # 23-1, Vol. 8, 11 January, 1974. An internal memo prepared for a meeting between the SSEA and Arnold Smith.

[232] Interview with CJ Small, Ottawa, Ontario, 14 September, 1996.

[233] In a report on the Commonwealth by External Affairs, the Secretariat was seen to be a strong forum in which to convey women's issues to developing countries. DFAIT, File # 23-1, Vol. 22, 1 July, 1987.

[234] M Doxey (1989), *op.cit.*, p. 96.

[235] DFAIT, File # 23-3-1985, Vol. 2, 12 July, 1985.

[236] Interview with Flora MacDonald, former Minister of External Affairs, Ottawa, Ontario, 9 September, 1996.

[237] The Commonwealth of Learning, *The Memorandum Of Understanding on The Commonwealth of Learning as agreed by Commonwealth Governments—September 1988.* Available on the Internet Uniform Resource Locator (URL): http://www.col.org/mou.htm. Empasis added.

[238] Telephone Interview with Robert McLaren, Victoria, BC, 7 October, 1996.

[239] Interview with John Harker, Ottwawa, Ontario, 10 September, 1996. According to Harker, this person was a friend of Ramphal and his posting caused some resentment from Canada and Britain; this was further supported by S Chan, *Twelve Years of Commonwealth Diplomatic History* (Lewiston: Edwin Mellen, 1992) pp. 87-88.

[240] DFAIT, File # 23-1, Vol. 8, 15 March, 1974. In an internal note from Mr. Moffat of the Commonwealth Division in External Affairs.

[241] In a confidential memo from the USSEA to the London High Commission, on the matter that some Commonwealth Organizations and Conferences were still serviced by the British Government. DFAIT, File # 23-5-1, Vol. 16, 16 December, 1975.

[242] One of the reasons why Britain liked to maintain the largest contributions to the Secretariat, at 30% of its annual budget, was that it offered it control. Interview with Derek Ingram, former Commonwealth journalist, London, 4 May, 1996. According to Robert McLaren, however, Britain was very conscious of its contributions in the Secretariat and its former imperialist image, and for this reason tried to distance itself from Commonwealth

activities. Telephone Interview with Robert McLaren, Victoria, BC, 7 October, 1996.

[243] Canada had sponsored Ramphal for Secretary-General in 1975 on the condition that he would not remain for more than one term, refusing to support Arnold Smith for another term because they believed that the organization would become too static and bureaucratized. Interview with Ivan Head, Vancouver, BC, 17 October, 1996.

[244] DFAIT, File # 23-1, Vol. 14, 26 March, 1976. Telex 535.

[245] DFAIT, File # 23-1, Vol. 14, 29 March, 1976.

[246] DFAIT, File # 23-1, Vol. 14, 7 April, 1976.

[247] *Ibid.*

[248] Sptephen Chan, *The Commonwealth in World Politics: A Study of International Action, 1965 to 1985* (London: Lester Crook, 1988. Pp. 23-26.

[249] Telephone Interview with Robert McLaren, Victoria, BC, 7 October, 1996.

[250] DFAIT, File # 23-1, Vol. 15, 18 June, 1976.

[251] *Ibid.*

[252] *Ibid.*

[253] S Chan (1988), *op.cit.*, pp. 23-26.

[254] DFAIT, File # 23-1, Vol. 19, 8 April, 1980.

[255] Ibid.

[256] Ibid.

[257] Interview with John Harker, Ottawa, Ontario, 10 September, 1996. Interview with Ivan Head, Vancouver, BC, 17 October, 1996.

[258] According to Flora MacDonald, as soon as the Conservatives were elected into office, Ramphal was in contact to solicit Canadian Ministers' support. Interview with Flora MacDonald, Ottawa, Ontario, 9 September, 1996. Interview with Ivan Head, Vancouver, BC, 17 October, 1996.

[259] DFAIT, File # 23-1, Vol. 19, 19 September, 1979.

[260] DFAIT, File # 23-1, Vol. 19, 29 November, 1979.

[261] DFAIT, File # 23-1, Vol. 19, 27 March, 1980.

[262] DFAIT, File # 23-1, Vol. 18, 1 June, 1978.

[263] Interview with CJ Small, Ottawa, Ontario, 12 September, 1996.

[264] Interview with John Harker, Ottawa, Ontario, 10 September, 1996.

[265] Interview with CJ Small, Ottawa, Ontario, 12 September, 1996.

[266] Interview with Clyde Sanger, Ottawa, Ontario, 17 September, 1996.

[267] Interview with Shridath Ramphal, London, 26 June, 1996.

[268] Telephone Interview with Robert McLaren, Victoria, BC, 7 October, 1996.

[269] DFAIT, File # 23-1, Vol. 19, 5 September, 1979.

270 S Chan (1988), *op.cit.*, p. 19; Telephone Interview with Robert McLaren, Victoria, BC, 7 October, 1996.

271 Telephone Interview with Robert McLaren, Victoria, BC, 7 October, 1996.

272 Interviews with Carolyn McAskie, Hull, Quebec, 10 September, 1996, and Robert McLaren, Victoria, BC, 7 October, 1996.

273 Interview with CJ Small, Ottawa, Ontario, 14 September, 1996.

274 DFAIT, File # 23-1, Vol. 20, 31 August, 1982. In a CIDA evaluation of the CFTC, it was stated that "there is a weakness in the organizational interrelationship between CFTC and the Secretariat wherein CFTC totally funds several Secretariat programs but has limited day to day management control over these Divisions."

275 Telephone Interview with Robert McLaren, Victoria, BC, 7 October, 1996.

276 DFAIT, File # 23-5-1, Vol. 21, (no date on document) Confidential Memorandum for Mr Morgan of External Affairs on his visit to the Commonwealth Secretariat.

277 Ibid.

278 Commonwealth Secretary-General Reports, 1966 to 1987.

279 O Akinrinade, "The Commonwealth and its Secretariat: An Essay on Leadership and Influence in an International Organization." *Quarterly Journal of Administration*, Vol. 26 (April-July 1992) p. 85.

280 Interview with CJ Small, Ottawa, Ontario, 14 September, 1996

281 Interview with Carolyn McAskie, Hull, Quebec, 12 September, 1996.

282 Report on a meeting between JC Best, Director of Programme for Applied Studies in Government, Commonwealth Secretariat and External Affairs. DFAIT, File # 23-5-1, 3 February, 1976.

283 Inis L Claude, Jr., *Swords Into Plowshares: The Problems and Progress of International Organizations*, 4th.ed., (New York: Randon House, 1984) p. 191.

284 DFAIT, File # 23-5-1, Vol. 6, 4 January, 1967.

285 Ibid.

286 DFAIT, File # 23-5-1, Vol. 6, 5 January, 1967

287 DFAIT, File # 23-5-1, Vol. 16, 3 February, 1976.

288 Ibid.

289 DFAIT, File # 23-1, Vol. 18, 1 June, 1978.

290 DFAIT, File # 23-5-1, Vol. 16, 17 December, 1975.

291 DFAIT, File # 23-5-1, Vol. 21 (No date on document—Between 1 May, 1979 and 31 December, 1982).

292 Telephone Interview with Robert McLaren, Victoria, BC, 7 October, 1996.

[293] Interview with John Harker, Ottawa, Ontario, 10 September, 1996.

[294] Ramphal never sated this reason outright, but he did say that he did not like Secretariat employees with "two paymasters.' Interview with Shridath Ramphal, London, 26 June, 1996.

[295] This is an adaptation on Hedley Bull's statement on influence being applied to Canada and the Commonwealth: *The Anarchical Society: A study of Order in World Politics* (London: Macmillan, 1977) p. xiii.

[296] DFAIT, File # 23-5-1, Vol. 16, 3 February, 1976.

[297] Ivan Head and Pierre Trudeau, *The Canadian Way: Shaping Canada's Foreign Policy, 1968-1984* (Toronto: McClelland and Stewart, 1995) pp. 147-148.

[298] LA Delvoie, "The Commonwealth in Canadian Foreign Policy", *The Round Table*, Vol. 310 (1989) pp. 137-143; RO Matthews, "Canada's Relations With Africa", *International Journal* (Summer, 1975) p. 539.

[299] MM Ball, *The "Open" Commonwealth* (Durham, NC: Duke UP, 1972) p. 159

[300] *Ibid*, pp. 71-73

[301] For example, the Caribbean and Latin American states are grouped together, as are the South-East Asian and Oceanic states.

[302] K Spicer, *A Samaritan State* (Toronto: University of Toronto, 1960) p. 54; T Keating, *Canada and World Order: The Multilateralist Tradition in Canadian Foreign Policy* (Toronto: McClelland, 1993) p. 132; Department of Foreign Affairs and International Trade (DFAIT), *Department of External Affairs Annual Report* (1963, p. 26) and (1964, p. 71.

[303] MM Ball, *op.cit.*, p. 202.

[304] Quoted in T Keating, op.cit., p. 131; Keith Spicer, "Clubmanship Upstaged: Canada's Twenty Years in the Colombo Plan", International Journal (Winter, 1969-70) p. 22.

[305] MM Ball, o*p.cit.*, p. 33

[306] *Ibid*, pp. 201-216.

[307] DFAIT, *Department of External Affairs Annual Reports* (Ottawa: Queen's Printers, 1963) p. 38.

[308] *Ibid*, p. 38.

[309] *Ibid*, p. 38.

[310] *Ibid*, p. 38.

[311] *Ibid*, p. 38.

[312] DFAIT, *Department of External Affairs Annual Report* (Ottawa: Queen's Printers, 1964) p. 16

[313] *Ibid*, p. 18.

[314] DFAIT, *Department of External Affairs Annual Report* (Ottawa: Queen's Printers, 1966) pp. 30-31.

[315] DFAIT, *Department of External Affairs Annual Report* (Ottawa: Queen's Printers, 1967) p. 27.

[316] DFAIT, *Department of External Affairs Annual Report* (Ottawa: Queen's Printers, 1964) p. 16.

[317] *Ibid*, p. 21.

[318] DFAIT, *Department of External Affairs Annual Report* (Ottawa: Queen's Printers, 1968) pp. 14-15.

[319] DFAIT (1968), *op.cit.*, p. 12.

[320] MM Ball, *op.cit.*, p. 176.

[321] DFAIT (1963), *op.cit.*, p. 39.

[322] *Ibid*, pp. 26, 39.

[323] DFAIT, (1964), *op.cit.*, p. 19.

[324] *Ibid*, pp. 14, 16, 19.

[325] *Ibid*, p. 18.

[326] DFAIT, Department of External Affairs Annual Report (Ottawa: Queen's Printer, 1966) p. 31; DFAIT, Department of External Affairs Annual Report (Ottawa: Queen's Printer, 1967) p. 20; DFAIT, Department of External Affairs Annual Report (Ottawa: Queen's Printer, 1968) pp. 13-14.

[327] DFAIT (1968), *op.cit.*, p. 14.

[328] *Ibid*, p. 15.

[329] *Ibid*, p. 12.

[330] At the time this commitment was made, Canada's aid budget was only 0.3% of its GNP. JC Mills, "Canada at UNCTAD", *International Journal*, Vol. 20 (1964-65) p. 216; T Keating, *op.cit.*, p. 132.

[331] T Keating, ibid, p. 132.

[332] A Andrew, *The Rise and Fall of a Middle Power: Canadian Diplomacy from King to Mulroney* (Toronto: Lorimer Co., 1993) p. 94-96.

[333] DFAIT, *Foreign Policy for Canadians: International Development* (Ottawa: Queen's Printer, 1970) p. 11.

[334] In 1969, the Colombo Plan was extended to 1976. Canadian International Development Agency (CIDA), *CIDA Annual Review: '69* (Ottawa: Queen's Printer, 1969) p. 35.

[335] India exploded a nuclear device in 1974, breaching an agreement that India signed with Canada prior to te transfer of a CANDU Nuclear Reactor. JL Granatstein and R Bothwell, *Pirouette: Pierre Trudeau and Canadian Foreign Policy* (Toronto: OF T Press, 1993) p. 294.

336 In 1972, $500 Million was invested in this region by Canadians. P Dobell, *Canada in World Affairs: 1971-1973*, Vol. xvii (Toronto: Canadian Institute of International Affairs, 1985) p. 197.

337 *Ibid*, p. 197.

338 DFAIT (1970), *op.cit.*, p. 21.

339 P Dobell, *op.cit.*, pp. 179-182.

340 *Ibid*, pp. 179-182.

341 JL Granatstein and R Bothwell, *op.cit.*, p. 294.

342 CIDA, *CIDA Annual Reports, 1972* (Ottawa: Queen's Printer, 1972)

343 CIDA, *CIDA Annual Reports, 1974* (Ottawa: Queen's Printer, 1974)

344 JC Mills "Canada at UNCTAD", *International Journal*, Vol. 20 (1964-65) p. 216.

345 DFAIT (1970), *op.cit.*, pp. 5-6.

346 CIDA, *CIDA Annual Reports*, (1969-1975)(Ottawa: Queen's Printer).

347 JL Granatstein and R Bothwell, *op.cit.*, p 288.

348 *Ibid*, pp. 288-291.

349 CIDA, *CIDA Annual Reports* (1969-1976) (Ottawa: Queen's Printer).

350 *The Economist*, 17 October, 1970, p. 38.

351 Ivan Head confirmed that the CFTC was created to re-affirm African confidence in the Commonwealth; Interview with Ivan Head, form Foreign Policy Advisor to Prime Minister Trudeau, Vancouver, BC, 17 October, 1996.

352 P Dobell, op.cit., p. 201.

353 A Smith, *Stitches in Time* (London: Andre Deutsch, 1981) p. 245.

354 M O'Neill, "Continuity Without Consensus: The Commonwealth Heads of Government Meetings, 1971-81", in AJR Groom and P Taylor, *The Commonwealth in the 1980's* (London: Macmillan, 1984) pp. 200-201.

355 A Smith, *op.cit.*, pp. 246-255.

356 *Ibid*, p. 254.

357 *Ibid*, p. 255.

358 M O'Neill, *op.cit.*, p. 211.

359 A Smith, *op.cit.*, p. 255.

360 Mitchell Sharp, Canada's Minister of External Affairs at this time, actually stated that Canada's interest in the Commonwealth was waning. P Dobell, *op.cit.*, p. 209.

361 In 1975, CIDA published a reviewed strategy for international development entitled *Strategy for International Development Cooperation: 1975-1980.* (Ottawa: Queen's Printer, 1975)

[362] Though Canada continued to give aid to Asia and South-East Asia, Commonwealth States in this region had managed to develop their economies and were actively trading with Canada. DFAIT, *Department of External Affairs Annual Report* (Ottawa: Queen's Printer, 1978) pp. 90-96.

[363] GK Helleiner, "Canada and the New International Economic Order", *Canadian Public Policy*, Vol. II, No. 3, (1976) pp. 258-260.

[364] DFAIT, *Department of External Affairs Annual Report* (Ottawa: Queen's Printer, 1979) p. 25.

[365] DFAIT, *Department of External Affairs Annual Report* (Ottawa: Queen's Printer, 1975) p. 28.

[366] *Ibid*, pp. 27-28.

[367] DFAIT (1978), *op.cit.*, p. 69.

[368] DFAIT, *Department of External Affairs Annual Reports* (1976, p. 24; 1977, p. 36; 1978, p. 67; 1979, p. 51) (Ottawa: Queen's Printer)

[369] CIDA, *CIDA Annual Reports*, 1978/79 (Ottawa: Queen's Printer, 1978/79)

[370] DFAIT, *Department of External Affairs Annual Report* (Ottawa: Queen's Printer, 1979) p. 60.

[371] CIDA, *CIDA Annual Reports* (Ottawa: Queen's Printer, 1975-1980)

[372] *Ibid*.

[373] DFAIT, Department of External Affairs Annual Reports (Ottawa: Queen's Printer, 1975-1979).

[374] DFAIT (1970), *op.cit.*

[375] AF Cooper, RA Higgott, and KR Nossal, *Relocating Middle Powers: Australia and Canada in a Changing World Order* (Vancouver: UBC Press, 1993) pp. 38-42; Chapter 2.

[376] DR Morrison, "Canada and North-South Conflict" in MA Malot and BW Tomlin, *Canada Among Nations: The World of Conflict, 1987* (Toronto: Lorimer, 1988) pp. 136-158.

[377] DFAIT, *Department of External Affairs Annual Report* (Ottawa: Queen's Printer, 1980) p. 47.

[378] *Ibid*, p. 24.

[379] DFAIT, *Department of External Affairs Annual Reports* (Ottawa: Queen's Printer, 1981) p. 11

[380] DFAIT, *Department of External Affairs Annual Reports* (Ottawa: Queen's Printer, 1982/83) pp. 20-21; DFAIT, *Department of External Affairs Annual Reports* (Ottawa: Queen's Printer, 1983/84) p. 31.

[381] DFAIT (1980) *op.cit.*, pp. 35, 53.

[382] DFAIT (1983/84) *op.cit.*, p. 27.

[383] DFAIT (1982/83) *op.cit.*, pp. 17-19.

[384] *Ibid*, pp. 17-19.

[385] DR Morrison, *op.cit.*, pp. 137-144.

[386] AL Allahar, *op.cit.*, p. 313; T Barry, B Wood and D Preusch, *The Other Side of Paradise* (New York: Grove Press, 1984) p. 222.

[387] DFAIT, *Department of External Affairs Annual Reports* (Ottawa: Queen's Printer, 1984/85) p. 36.

[388] DFAIT, Department of External Affairs Annual Reports (Ottawa: Queen's Printer, 1984/85-1987/88)

[389] DFAIT (1987/88) *ibid*, p. 3.

[390] P Dobell, *op.cit.*, pp. 215-216.

[391] MM Ball, *op.cit.*, pp. 177-180.

[392] *Ibid*, p. 96.

[393] A Kilgore and J Mayall, "The Residual Legatee: Economic Cooperation in the Contemporary Commonwealth", in AJR Groom and P Taylor (eds) *The Commonwealth in the 1980's* (London: Macmillan, 1984) pp. 150-153.

[394] A Smith, *op.cit.*, pp. 118-119, 297-298.

[395] *Ibid*, p. 119.

[396] A Kilgore a J Mayall, *op.cit.*, pp. 150-153.

[397] CIDA, *CIDA Annual Reports* (Ottawa: Queen's Printer, 1972/1973) p. 67.

[398] CIDA, *CIDA Annual Reports* (Ottawa: Queen's Printer, 1975/1976) p. 125.

[399] CIDA, *CIDA Annual Reports* (Ottawa: Queen's Printer, 1987/1988) p. 118.

[400] *Ibid*, p. 120.

[401] MM Ball, *op.cit.*, p. 50

[402] T Keating, *op.cit.*, p. 124.

[403] MM Ball, *op.cit.*, p. 50

[404] M O'Neill, *op.cit.*, p 206; A Smith, *op.cit.*, pp. 292-293.

[405] M O'Neill, *ibid*, p. 207.

[406] *Ibid*, p. 207.

[407] A Kilgore and J Mayall, *op.cit.*, p. 155.

[408] *Ibid*, pp. 155-156.

[409] *Ibid*, p. 156.

[410] *Ibid*, pp. 156-157; MM Ball, *op.cit.*, pp. 60-61.

[411] JC Mills, *op.cit.*, p. 215.

[412] T Keating, *op.cit.*, p. 124.

[413] CIDA, *CIDA Annual Reports* (Ottawa: Queen's Printer, 1969).

[414] CIDA, *CIDA Annual Reports* (Ottawa: Queen's Printer, 1969-1988)

[415] JC Mills, *op.cit.*, p. 216.

[416] GK Helleiner, *op.cit.*, pp. 452-455.

[417] *Ibid*, p. 455.

[418] *Ibid*, pp. 456, 458-460.

[419] Andrew Cohen, "Canada in the World: The Return of the National Interest," *Behind The Headlines*, Vol. 52, No. 4 (1995) pp. 1-2; M O'Neill, *op.cit.*, p. 206.

[420] GK Helleiner, *op.cit.*, pp. 455-456.

[421] A Kilgore and J Mayall, *op.cit.*, p. 151.

[422] *Ibid*, pp. 155-156.

[423] GK Helleiner, *op.cit.*, pp. 456, 458-464.

[424] AL Allahar, *op.cit.*, p. 306; M Catley-Carson, "Aid: A Canadian Vocation," *Daedalus*, Vol. 117, No. 4 (1988) p. 320.

[425] AL Allahar, *ibid*, p. 306; T Barry, B Wood and D Preusch, *op.cit.*, p. 224.

[426] DR Morrison, *op.cit.*, pp. 136-158.

[427] AL Allahar, *op.cit.*, p. 306.

[428] *Ibid*, p. 306.

[429] M Catley-Carlson, *op.cit.*, p. 320; AL Allahar, *op.cit.*, p. 306.

[430] KR Nossal, "Mixed Motives Revisited: Canada's Interest in Development Assistance", *Canadian Journal of Political Science*, Vol. XXI, No. 1 (1988) pp. 35-56.

[431] RR Paragg, *op.cit.*, p. 330-331.

[432] *Ibid*, pp. 323-343.

[433] C Lane, "Wheat At What Cost? CIDA and the Tanzania-Canada Wheat Program", in J Swift and B Tomlin (eds) *Conflicts of Interests: Canada and the Third World* (Toronto: Between the Lines, 1991) pp. 133-160.

[434] GR Berry, *op.cit.*, p. 350.

[435] Lorne Kavik, "Canada and the Commonwealth: Sentiment, Symbolism and Sel-interest", *The Round Table*, Vol. 65 (1975), pp. 37-39.

[436] GR Berry, *op.cit.*, pp. 351-357.

[437] Report of the Special Joint Committee on Canada's International Relations: "Independence and Internationalism" (Ottawa: Queen's Printer, 1985) p. 24

[438] *Ibid*, p. 25.

[439] Lord Garner, "The Commonwealth Under Strain: Problems of Expansion and Attrition" *The Round Table*, Vol. 65 (1975) p. 212.

[440] Nicholas Mansergh, *The Commonwealth Experience: From British to Multilateral Commonwealth*, Vol. 2 (London: Macmillan, 1982) pp. 181-183, 187.

441 JP Schlegel, "Ottawa's Achilles Heel: Formulating Policies in Southern Africa" *The Round Table*, Vol. 69 (1979) p. 143.

442 Lord Garner (1975), *op.cit.*, p. 212.

443 T Keating, *Canada and World Order: The Multilateralist Tradition in Canadian Foreign Policy* (Toronto: McClelland, 1993) pp. 103-105

444 S Chan, *The Commonwealth in World Politics: A Study of International Action, 1965 to 1985* (London: Lester Crook, 1988) p. 24.

445 N Mansergh, *op.cit.*, p. 188.

446 Paul Martin, *Hansard: Parliamentary Debates* (Ottawa: Queen's Printer, 1966) 3 February, 1966, pp. 695-696.

447 N Mansergh, *op.cit.*, pp. 188-194.

448 FR Hayes, "Canada, the Commonwealth, and the Rhodesian Issue", in KR Nossal (ed), An Acceptance of Paradox: Essays on Canadian Diplomacy in Honour of John W Holmes (Toronto: CIIA, 1982) p. 155.

449 JP Schlegel, *op.cit.*, p. 144.

450 FR Hayes, *op.cit.*, pp. 167-168.

451 *The Times*, 27 November, 1965; quoted in FR Hayes, *ibid*, p. 153.

452 *Statements and Speeches* (Ottawa: Queen's Printer) 66/16, p. 5.

453 FR Hayes, *op.cit.*, p. 156.

454 *The Economist*, 15 January, 1966, p. 185.

455 *Statement and Speeches* (Ottawa: Queen's Printer, 1966) 66/16, p. 6 (4 April, 1966); Robert C Good, *UDI: The International Politics of the Rhodesian Rebellion* (London: Faber and Faber, 1973) pp. 109-110.

456 RC Good, *ibid*, p 93; *The Economist*, 4 September, 1971, p. 36.

457 *The Economist*, 15 January, 1966, p. 185.

458 *Commonwealth Prime Ministers' Meeting in Lagos, 1966*, Cmnd 2890 (London, 1966); M Doxey, *The Commonwealth Secretariat and the Contemporary Commonwealth* (London: Macmillan, 1989) p. 119.

459 Jorge Jardim, *Sanctions Double-Cross: Oil to Rhodesia* (Intervencao, 1978).

460 FR Hayes, *op.cit.*, p. 159.

461 Harold Wilson, *Labour Government: 1964-70* (London: Pelican Books, 1974) pp. 278-279; FR Hayes, *ibid*, p. 159; N Mansergh, *op.cit.*, pp. 189-194, 200.

462 GC Good, *op.cit.*, p. 167.

463 FR Hayes, *op.cit.*, p. 160.

464 *Ibid*, p. 160

465 *Ibid*, p. 160

[466] Wm Dobell, "MR. Trudeau's Rhodesian Policy", *The Round Table*, Vol. 59 (1969) pp. 181-182.

[467] JA Munr and AI Inglis, *Mike: The Memoirs of the Honourable Lester B Pearson: 1957-1968*, Vol. III (Toronto: U of T, 1975) pp. 285-287.

[468] H Wilson, *op.cit.*, p. 282.

[469] W Dobell, *op.cit.*, p. 180.

[470] W Dobell, *ibid*, pp. 181-182.

[471] DFAIT, File # 23-5-1, Vol. * 14 April, 1967, Memo for a UK-Canada Ministers Meeting: *Hansard: Canadian Parliamentary Debates*, 29 January, 1968 (Ottawa: Queen's Printer, 1968) p. 6071.

[472] DFAIT, *ibid*.

[473] Ivan Head and Pierre Trudeau, The Canadian Way: Shaping Canadian Foreign Policy (Toronto: McClelland, 1995) pp. 98-99.

[474] *The Economist*, 11 January, 1969, p. 32; *The Economist*, 21 June, 1969, pp. 16-17; UN S/C Resolution 221, 1966.

[475] N Mansergh, *op.cit.*, pp. 193-194. Negotiations took place in December, 1966.

[476] N Mansergh, ibid, p. 194. These talks took place in October, 1968.

[477] A Smith, *op.cit.*, pp. 12, 26, 27, 64, 72, 234.

[478] A Smith, *ibid*, pp. 60-70; W Dobell, *op.cit.*, 183-184.

[479] Derek Ingram, "Commonwealth Prime Ministers, 1969: The End of Disenchantment?", *The Round Table*, Vol. 58 (1968) pp. 357-364.

[480] *The Economist*, 18 January, 1969, pp. 13-14.

[481] *The Economist*, 11 January, 1969, p. 32.

[482] Wm Dobell, *op.cit.*, p. 179.

[483] DFAIT, Foreign Policy for Canadians (Ottawa: Queen's Printers, 1970) p. 8; Akira Ichikawa ""The Helpful Fixer": Canada's Persistent Image" *Behind the Headlines* (March 1979); Harold von Riekhoff "The Recent Evolution of Canadian Foreign Policy: Adapt, Adopt and Improve" *The Round Table*, Vol. 62 (1972) p. 69.

[484] I Head and P Trudeau, *op.cit.*, p. 134.

[485] H von Riekhoff, *op.cit.*, pp. 63-76.

[486] Wm Dobell, *op.cit.*, p. 183.

[487] Wm Dobell, *ibid*, p. 183.

[488] Clarence G Redekop, "Trudeau at Singapore: The Commonwealth and Arms Sales to South Africa" in KR Nossal (1982), *op.cit.*, p. 175.

[489] *The Economist*, 17 October, 1970, p. 38; H von Riefhoff, *op.cit.*, p. 69.

490 Interview with Ivan Head, Vancouver, BC, 17 October, 1996; I Head and P Trudeau, *op.cit.*, pp. 107-112.

491 S/C res, 23 July, 1970

492 CG Redekop,. *op.cit.*, pp. 176-177.

493 "Britain ends ban on sale of arms" and "Canada continues protest" *Globe and Mail*, 21 July, 1970.

494 CG Redekop, *op.cit.*, p. 178.

495 "Trudeau's letter", *The Times*, 27 July, 1970. CG Redekop, *op.cit.*, p. 178.

496 *Ottawa Citizen*, 28 November, 1970; "UK arms sales" *Globe and Mail*, 25 September, 1970; DFAIT, File # 23-1, Vol.3, 26 November, 1970.

497 "Britain will decide on arms sales" *Toronto Star*, 17 December, 1970.

498 Interview with Derek Ingram, former Commonwealth Journalist, London, 4 May, 1996.

499 CG Redekop, *op.cit.*, p. 188; I Head and P Trudeau, *op.cit.*, pp. 109-110.

500 M O'Neill, "Continuity Without Consensus: The Commonwealth Heads of Government Meetings, 1971-1981" in AJR Groom and P Taylor (eds), *The Commonwealth in the 1980's* (London: Macmillan, 1984) p. 200.

501 CG Redekop, *op.cit.*, pp. 181-187.

502 *The Economist*, 23 January, 1971, pp. 13, 23-26.

503 *Ibid.*

504 CG Redekop, *op.cit.*, p. 188.

505 CG Redekop, *ibid*, pp. 188-189.

506 Interview with Derek Ingram, London, 9 may, 1996.

507 I Head and P Trudeau, *op.cit.*, pp. 114-115; DFAIT, File # 23-1, Vol. 4, 30 September, 1971; DFAIT, File # 23-1, Vol. 4, 29 November, 1971.

508 Roy Lewis, "Rhodesia A Year After Pearce: Britain Needs to Regain the Initiative", *The Round Table*, Vol. 63 (1973) p. 329-338; *The Economist*, 4 August, 1973, p. 31.

509 Editorial, "Yes to Europe: Between Common Market and Commonwealth", *The Round Table*, Vol. 65 (1975), pp. 227-234.

510 P Boehm, *op.cit.*, p. 28: I Head and P Trudeau, *op.cit.*, pp. 117-118.

511 M O'Neill, *op.cit.*, p. 202.

512 *The Economist*, 4 August, 1973, p. 31.

513 Alexander Macleod, "The New Foreign Policy in Australia and New Zealand: The Record of the Labour Governments", *The Round Table*, Vol. 64 (1974), pp. 287-297. *The Economist*, 28 July, 1973, p. 27.

514 P Boehm, *op.cit.*, p. 30.

[515] Letter from Shridath Ramphal, Minister of Foreign Affairs for Guyana to Mitchell Sharp, SSEA, DFAIT, File # 23-1, Vol. ^, 21 August, 1973.

[516] *The Economist*, 10 May, 1975, p. 51; *The Economist*, 6 March, 1976, p. 43.

[517] S Chan, *op.cit.*, p. 50.

[518] I Head and P Trudeau, *op.cit.*, pp. 193-195.

[519] I Head and P Trudeau, *ibid*, pp. 209-210; Stephen Wright, "Nigeria: The Politics of Sport: A Channel for Conflict and a Vehicle for Self-Expression", *The Round Table*, Vol. 68 (1978) p. 362; *The Economist*, 7 August, 1976, p. 43.

[520] S Chan, "Three Birds of Different Feathers: The Commonwealth, the Commonwealth Secretary-General, and the Commonwealth Secretariat", *The Round Table*, Vol. 74 (1984) p. 305.

[521] Martin Bailey and Bernard Rivers, *Oil Sanctions Against Rhodesia: Proposals for Action* (London: Commonwealth Secretariat, 1977).

[522] *The Economist*, 2 September, 1978, p. 20; *The Economist*, 9 September, 1978, pp. 11-13.

[523] Alexander Macleod, "Between Rhodesia and Zimbabwe: A Last Chance to Secure Independence and a Stable Future", *The Round Table*, Vol. 68 (1978) pp. 139-146; Philip Windsor, "Redefining Britain's Foreign Interests: A Case of Boldness Without Conviction", *The Round Table*, Vol. 68 (1978), pp. 37-38.

[524] Commonwealth Secretariat, *An Analysis of the Illegal Regime's Constitution for Zimbabwe-Rhodesia* (London: Commonwealth Secretariat, March 1979).

[525] *The Economist*, 7 April, 1979, pp. 20-21.

[526] Editorial, "Commonwealth Notebook", *The Round Table*, Vol. 68 (1978) pp. 375-377.

[527] Paul Martin, *The London Diaries, 1975-1979* (Ottawa: University of Ottawa, 1988) p. 545.

[528] S Chan, *op.cit.*, p. 36; Lord Soames, "From Rhodesia to Zimbabwe"", *International Affairs*, Vol. 56 (1980) p. 408.

[529] Ian O Cameron, "Canada, the Commonwealth and South Africa: National Foreign Policy-Making in a Multilateral Environment", *Millennium* (1989) p. 207; KR Nossal, *Rain Dancing: Sanctions in Canadian and Australian Foreign Policy* (Toronto: University of Toronto, 1994) pp. 91-110.

[530] Editorial, "Strangled Détente: Between Diplomacy and Violence in Southern Africa", *The Round Table*, Vol. 67 (1977) pp. 3-8; Editorial, "A Deepening Tragedy: The Problem of Detaching MR. Smith's Fate from MR. Vorster's", *The Round Table*, Vol. 67 (1977) pp. 303-313.

531 Interview with Bernard Wood, former Special Envoy to Southern Africa for Brian Mulroney, Paris, 19 June, 1996.

532 DFAIT, File # 23-3-1985-1, 28 June, 1985. Internal memo.

533 Interview with Derek Ingram, London 9 May, 1996.

534 DFAIT, File # 23-3-1985-1, 25 June, 1985, Internal Memo; IO Cameron, *op.cit.*, pp. 11-12; *The Globe and Mail*, 22 October, 1985.

535 S Chan (1988), *op.cit.*, pp. 69-72; Bernard Wood, "Canada and Southern Africa: A Return to Middle Power Activism", *The Round Table*, Vol. 80 (1990) pp. 280-290.

536 Commonwealth Eminent Persons Group, *Mission to South Africa—The Commonwealth Report* (Harmondsworth: Penguin, 1986).

537 KR Nossal (1994), *op.cit.*, p. 106; D Anglin, *Canada and South Africa: Challenge and Response* (Ottawa: Carleton University, 1986) pp. 61-62; Government of Canada, *Report of the Special Joint Committee on Canada's International Relations: Independence and Internationalism* (Ottawa: Queen's Printers, June 1986) pp. 109, 154.

538 KR Nossal (1994), *op.cit.*, pp. 91-110.

539 Interview with Bernard Wood, Paris, 19 June, 1996.

540 KR NOssal (1994), *op.cit.*, p. 109.

541 DFAIT, *Report of the Special Joint Committee on Canada's International Relations: Independence and Internationalism* (Ottawa: Queen's Printers, June 1986)

542 Ralph Stogdill, *Handbook of Leadership*, (New York: The Free Press, 1974) p. 7; James MacGregor-Burns, *Leadership*, (New York: Harper Row, 1978) p. 12; Lewis Edinger, "The Comparative Analysis of Political Leadership", *Comparative Politics*, Vol 7 (January 1975) pp. 254-255; Jarrod Wiener, *Making Rules in the Uruguay Round of the GATT: A Study of International Leadership*, (Aldershot: Dartmouth Publishing, 1995) p. 19.

543 David Rapkin, "World Leadership", in George Modelski (ed), *Exploring Long Cycles* (London: Francis Pinter, 1987) p. 131.

544 Jarrod Wiener, *op.cit.*, p. 19.

545 Jarrod Wiener, *ibid*, pp. 26-27; James MacGregor-Burns, *op.cit.*, p. 445; Lewis Edinger, *op.cit.*, p. 258.

546 AF Cooper, RA Higgott, and KR Nossal, *Relocating Middle Powers: Australia and Canada in a New World Order*, (Vancouver: UBC, 1993).

547 Oran Young, "Political Leadership and Regime Formation: On the Development of Institutions in International Society", *International Organization*, Vol 45, No 3, (Summer 1991) pp. 281-308.

[548] What Cooper, Higgott, and Nossal called technical leadership is a hybrid of Young's entrepreneurial and intellectual leadership. *Op.cit.*, p. 25.

[549] *Ibid.*, p. 24.

[550] *Ibid.*, p. 24.

[551] *Ibid.*, p. 24.

[552] *Ibid.*, p. 25.

[553] *Ibid.*, p. 25.

[554] *Ibid.*, p. 26.

[555] *Ibid.*, p. 24.

[556] Susan Strange, *States and Markets*, (London: Pinter, 1988) p. 24. Strange defines relational power as the ability of A to get B to do what they would not otherwise do; and structural power as the ability to change the structure of the international political economy.

[557] Oran Young, in his description of intellectual leadership, acknowledged that this form of leadership took place over a longer time frame. Nonetheless, ideas suggested in international fora were considered as a form of leadership. *Op.cit.*, pp. 298-299.

[558] Cooper, Higgott, and Nossal, *op.cit.*, pp. 156-159.

[559] Oran Young, *op.cit.*, p. 295.

[560] Cooper, Higgott, and Nossal, *op.cit.*, p. 12.

[561] *Ibid.*, p. 13.

[562] "A region consisting of a contiguous cluster of states is, on the one hand, an isomorphic subsystem of the international system. On the other hand, the lesser scale of the region combines with its defining geographical and cultural traits to make it a specific analytical concern. The region occupies the middle ground between bilateral relations on the one hand, and system-wide relations on the other." Øyvind Øserud, "Regional Great Powers" in IB Neumann (ed), *Regional Great Powers in International Politics* (St. Martin's Press: New York, 1992) pp. 1-15, pp. 1-2.

[563] This is how Oran Young defined structural leadership: *Op.cit.*, p. 288.

[564] Cooper, Higgott, and Nossal, *op.cit.*, p. 84.

Bibliography

Akinrinade, O "The 1971 Declaration of Commonwealth Principles After 20 Years", *The Round Table*, Vol. 321 (1992) pp. 23-35.
- "The Commonwealth and Its Secretariat: An Essay on Leadership and Influence in an International Organization", *Quarterly Journal of Administration*, Vol. 26 (April-July 1992) pp. 62-86.

Allahar, AL "Manuafacturing Legitimacy: Ideology, Politics, and Third World Foreign Policy", in *Conflicts of Interest: Canada and the Third World* edited by J Swift and B Tomlin (Toronto: Between the Lines, 1991) pp. 295-318.

Andrew, A *The Rise and Fall of a Middle Power: Canadian Diplomacy from King to Mulroney* (Toronto: Lorimer, 1993).

Anglin, D *Canada and South Africa: Challenge and Response* (Ottawa: Norman Patterson School, 1986).

Archer, C *International Organizations* (London: Allen and Unwin, 1983).

Ball, MM *The "Open" Commonwealth* (Durham, NC: Duke UP, 1971).

Barry, T
Wood, B and **Preusch, D** *The Other Side of Paradise* (New York: Grove Press, 1984).

Bergeron, G "Foreign Affairs", in *The Canadians: 1867-1967*, edited by JMS Careless and RC Brown (Toronto: Macmillan, 1967) pp. 785-805.

Berry, GR "The West Indies in Canadian External Relations: Present Trends and Future Prospects", in *Canada and the Commonwealth Caribbean*, edited by BD Tennyson (London: UP America, 1988) pp. 347-366.

Black, D "Canada and the Commonwealth: The Multilateral Politics of a "Wasting Asset"" Canadian Foreign Policy, (Spring 2010) 16:2, pp. 61-77.

Boehm, P "Canada and the Modern Commonwealth: The Approaches of Lester Pearson and Pierre Trudeau", *Bulletin of Canadian Studies* (1979) pp. 23-39.

Borden, R *Canada in the Commonwealth: from Conflict to Cooperation* (Oxford: Clarendon, 1929).

Bull, H *The Anarchical Society: A Study of Order of World Politics* (London: Macmillan, 1977).

Cameron, IO "Canada, the Commonwealth and South Africa: National Foreign Policy-Making in a Multilateral Environment", *Millennium*, Vol. 18, No. 2 (1989) pp. 205-225.

Canadian International Development Agency *Strategy for International Development Cooperation: 1975-1980* (Ottawa: Queen's Printer, 1975).

Careless, JMS and **Brown, R** *The Canadians: 1867-1967* (Toronto: Macmillan, 1967).

Catley-Carlson, M "Aid: A Canadian Vocation", *Daedalus*, Vol. 117, No. 4 (1988).

Chan, S *Twelve Years of Commonwealth Diplomatic History: Commonwealth Summit Meetings, 1979-1991* (Lampeter: Edwin Mellon, 1992).

- "The Commonwealth as an International Organization: Constitutionalism, Britain and South Africa", The Round Table, Vol. 312 (1989) pp. 393-412.
- *The Commonwealth in World Politics, 1965-1985* (London: Lester Crook, 1988)
- *The Commonwealth Observer Group in Zimbabwe: A Personal Memoir* (Gweru: Mambo Press, 1985)
- "Three Birds of Different Feathers: The Commonwealth, the Commonwealth Secretary-General, and the Commonwealth Secretariat", *The Round Table*, Vol. 74 (1984) pp. 299-310.

Claude, I *Swords Into Plowshares* (New York: Randon House, 1964).

Cooper, AF
Higgott, RA and **Nossal, KR** *Relocating Middle Powers: Australia and Canada in a Changing World Order* (Vancouver: UBC, 1993).

Dale, W *The Modern Commonwealth* (London: Butterworths, 1983).

Delvoie, LA "The Commonwealth in Canadian Foreign Policy", *The Round Table*, Vol. 310 (1989) pp. 137-143.

Department of Foreign Affairs and International Trade *Foreign Policy for Canadians* (Ottawa: Queen's Printer, 1970).
- *Report of the Special Joint Committee on Canada's International Relations: Independence and Internationalism* (Ottawa: Queen's Printer, 1986).
- *The Commonwealth: Canadian Development Assistance* (Ottawa: Queen's Printer, 1987).
- *Documents on Canadian External Relations, 1947* (Ottawa: Queen's Printer, 1993).
- *Documents on Canadian External Relations, 1953* (Ottawa: Queen's Printer, 1991.

Dewitt, DB and **Kirton, JJ** *Canada as a Principle Power: A Study in Foreign Policy and International Relations* (Toronto: Wiley and Sons, 1983).

Dobell, P *Canada in World Affairs: 1971-1973*, Vol. xvii (Toronto: Canadian Institute of International Affairs, 1985).

Doxey, M "Canada and the Commonwealth", in *Making a Difference: Canada's Foreign Policy in a Changing World Order*, edited by John English and Norman Hillmer (Toronto: Lester Publishing, 1992) pp. 34-53.
- "Meeting New Challenges: Commonwealth Roles and Structure in the 1990's" *The Round Table*, Vol. 328 (1993) pp. 427-442.
- *The Commonwealth Secretariat and the Contemporary Commonwealth* (London: Macmillan, 1989).
- "Constructive Internationalism: A Continuing Theme in Canadian Foreign Policy", *The Round Table*, Vol. 311 (1989) pp. 288-304.
- "The Commonwealth Secretariat", in the *The Commonwealth in the 1980's*, edited by AJR Groom and P Taylor (London: Macmillan, 1984) pp. 15-39.
- "Canada and the Evolution of the Modern Commonwealth", *Behind the Headlines*, Vol. XL, No. 2 (1982).
- "Strategies in Multilateral Diplomacy: The Commonwealth, Southern Africa, and the NIEO", *International Journal* (Spring 1980) pp. 329-356.

English, J and **Hillmer, GN** *Making a Difference: Canada's Foreign Policy in a Changing World Order* (Toronto: Lester, 1992).

Finlayson, JA *Limits on Middle Power Diplomacy: The Case of Commodities* (Ottawa: North-South Institute, 1988).

Garner, Lord "The Commonwealth Under Strain: Problems of Expansion and Attrition", *The Round Table*, Vol. 65 (1975) pp. 205-214.

Granatstein, JC and **Bothwell, R** *Pirouette: Pierre Trudeau and Canadian Foreign Policy* (Toronto: U of Toronto, 1990).

Granatstein, JL *Canadian Foreign Policy Since 1945: A Middle Power or Satellite?* 3rd ed. (Toronto: Copp Clark, 1973).

Groom, AJR "The Commonwealth as an International Organization", in *The Commonwealth in the 1980's*, edited by AJR Groom and P Taylor (London: Macmillan, 1984) pp. 293-304.

Groom, AJR and **Taylor, P** *The Commonwealth in the 1980's* (London: Macmillan, 1984).
- *International Organizations* (London: Pinter, 1978).

Hayes, F "Canada, the Commonwealth, and the Rhodesian Issue", in *Acceptance of Paradox: Essays on Canadian Diplomacy in Honour of John W Holmes*, edited by KR Nossal (Toronto: CIIA, 1982) pp. 141-173.

Head, I and **Trudeau, PE** *The Canadian Way: Shaping Canada's Foreign Policy, 1968-1984* (Toronto: McClelland and Stewart, 1995).

Higgott, RA and **Cooper, AF** "Middle Power Leadership and Coalition Building: Australia, the Cairns Group, and the Uruguay Round of Trade Negotiations", *International Organization*, Vol. 44, No. 4 (Autumn 1990) pp. 589-632.

Holbraad, C *Middle Powers in International Relations* (London: Macmillan, 1984).
- "The Role of Middle Powers" *Cooperation and Conflict*, Vol. VI (1971) pp. 77-90.

Holmes, JW "A Canadian's Commonwealth: Realism Out of Rhetoric", *The Round Table*, Vol. 56 (1965/1966) pp. 335-347.

Ichikawa, A "The "Helpful Fixer": Canada's Persistent Image", *Behind the Headlines* (March 1979).

Ingram, D *The Imperfect Commonwealth* (London: Rex Collings, 1977).
- "If Rhodesia Crumbles: Toward a Commonwealth Presence?", *The Round Table*, Vol. 64 (1974) pp. 451-455.
- "Commonwealth Prime Ministers, 1969: The End of Disenchantment?", *The Round Table*, Vol. 58 (1968) pp. 357-364.

Jackson, RH *Quasi-States: Sovereignty, International Relations and the Third World* (Cambridge: Cambridge UP, 1990).

Kavik, L "Canada and the Commonwealth: Sentiment, Symbolism and Self-Interest", *The Round Table*, Vol. 65 (1975) pp. 37-49.

Keating, TF *Canada and World Order: The Multilateralist Tradition in Canadian Foreign Policy* (Toronto: McClelland and Stewart, 1993).

Kilgore, A and **Mayall, J** "The Residual Legatee: Economic Cooperation in the Contemporary Commonwealth", in *The Commonwealth in the 1980's*, edited by AJR Groom and P Taylor (London: Macmillan, 1984) pp. 140-165.

Kindleberger, CP *The World In Depression, 1929-1939* (Berkeley: UP California, 1973).

Kinnas, JN *The Politics of Association in Europe* (Frankfurt: Campus Verlog, 1979).

Kinnas, JN and **Groom, AJR** "Associations", in *International Organizations*, edited by AJR Groom and P Taylor (London: Pinter, 1978) pp. 69-77.

Kratochwil, F and **Ruggie, JG** "International Organizations: A State of the Art on an Art of a State", *International Organization*, Vol. 40, No. 4 (Autumn 1986) pp. 753-775.

Lane, C "Wheat at What Cost? CIDA and the Tanzania-Canada Wheat Program", in *Conflicts of Interests: Canada and the Third World*, edited by J Swift and B Tomlin (Toront: Between the Lines, 1991) pp. 133-160.

MacGregor-Burns, J *Leadership* (New York: Harper Row, 1978).

McIntyre, WD "Canada and the Commonwealth", in M. Appel Molot and N Hillmer (eds), *Canada Among Nations 2002: A Fading Power* (Don Mills, Ontario: Oxford UP, pp. 281-298

Mansergh, N *The Name and Nature of the British Commonwealth* (Cambridge: Cambridge UP, 1954).
- *Survey of British Commonwealth Affairs: Problems of Wartime Cooperation and Post-war Change: 1939-1952* (London: Oxford UP, 1958).
- *Survey of British Commonwealth Affairs: Problems of External Policy*, 3rd ed. (London: Oxford UP, 1952).

Martin, P *The London Diaries: 1975-1979* (Ottawa: U of Ottawa, 1988).

Matthews, RO "Canada's Relations With Africa", *International Journal*, Vol. 30, No. 3 (Summer 1975) pp. 536-568.

Milburn, JF *Governments of the Commonwealth: covering Australia, Canada, Great Britain, New Zealand and, for Historical Purposes, South Africa* (New York: Harper Rowe, 1965).

Miller, JDB *Survey of Commonwealth Affairs: Problems of Expansion and Attrition, 1953-1969* (London: Oxford UP, 1974).

Miller, R *Aid as Peacemaker: Canadian Development Assistance and Third World Conflict* (London: Oxford UP, 1992).

Mills, JC "Canada at UNCTAD", *International Journal*, Vol. 20 (Spring 1965) pp. 214-220.

Molot, MA and **Tomlin, BW** *Canada Among Nations: The World of Conflict, 1987* (Toronto: Lorimer, 1988).
- *Canada Among Nations, 1984: A Time of Transition* (Toronto: Lorimer, 1985).

Morrison, DR "Canada and North-South Conflict", in *Canada Among Nations: The World of Conflict, 1987*, edited by MA Molot and BW Tomlin (Toronto: Lorimer, 1988) pp. 136-158.

Munton, D and **Shaw, TM** "*Apartheid* and Canadian Public Opinion", *International Perspectives* (September/October 1987).

Neumann, IB *Regional Great Powers in International Politics* (New York: St. Martin's Press, 1992).

Nossal, KR *An Acceptance of Paradox: Essays on Canadian Diplomacy in Honour of John W Holmes* (Toronto: CIIA, 1982).
- *The Politics of Canadian Foreign Policy,* 2nd *ed.* (Scarborough, Ontario: Prentice-Hall, 1989).
- *"Mixed Motives Revisited*: Canada's Interest in Development Assistance", *Canadian Journal of Political Science*, Vol. XXI, No. 1 (1988) pp. 35-56.
- *Rain Dancing: Sanctions in Canadian and Australian Foreign Policy* (Toronto: U of Toronto, 1994).

O'Neill, M "Continuity Without Consensus: The Commonwealth Heads of Government Meetings, 1971-1981", in *The Commonwealth in the 1980's*, edited by AJR Groom and P Taylor (London: Macmillan, 1984) pp. 111-124.

Østerud, Ø "Regional Great Powers", in *Regional Great Powers in International Politics*, edited by IB Neumann (New York: St. Martin's Press, 1992) pp. 1-15.

Painchaud, P *From MacKenzie King to Pierre Trudeau: Forty Years of Canadian Diplomacy* (Quebec: Laval UP, 1989).
- "Middlepowermanship as an Ideology", in *Canada's Role as a Middle Power*, edited by J King Gordon (Toronto: CIIA, 1966) pp. 29-35.

Palmer, GEH *Consultation and Co-operation in the British Commonwealth* (London: Oxford UP, 1934).

Paragg, RR "Canadian Aid in the Commonwealth Caribbean: Neo-Colonialism or Development?", in *Canada and the Commonwealth Caribbean*, edited by BD Tennyson (London: UP America, 1988) pp. 323-345.

Pearson, M
Mackinnon, G and **Sapardanis, C** "The World is Entitled to Ask Questions': The Trudeau Peace Initiative Reconsidered", *International Journal* (Winter 1985-1986) pp. 129-158.

Potter, E "Canada in the Commonwealth" *The Round Table* (2007) 96:4, pp. 447-463

Pratt, C *Middle Power Internationalism: The North-South Dimension* (Montreal: McGill-Queen's UP, 1990).
- *Internationalism Under Strain: The North-South Politics of Canada, the Netherlands, Norway, and Sweden* (Toronto: U of Toronto, 1989).

Redekop, CG "Trudeau at Singapore: The Commonwealth and Arms Sales to South Africa", in *An Acceptance of Paradox: Essays on Canadian Diplomacy in Honour of John W Holmes*, edited by KR Nossal (Toronto: CIIA, 1982) pp. 174-195.

Rothgeb, J *Defining Power: Influence and Force in the Contemporary International System* (New York: St. Martin's Press, 1993).

Ruggie, JG "Multilateralism: The Anatomy of an Institution", *International Organization*, Vol. 46, No. 3 (Summer 1992) pp. 125-145.

Schlegel, JP "Ottawa's Achilles Heel: Formulating Policies in Southern Africa", *The Round Table*, Vol. 69 (1979) pp. 142-153.

Smith, A *Stitches in Time* (London: Andre Deutsch, 1981).

Spicer, K "Clubmanship Upstaged: Canada's Twenty Years in the Colombo Plan", *International Journal* (Winter 1969-1970).
- *A Samaritan State* (Toronto: U of Toronto, 1966).

Stairs, D "Public Opinion and External Affairs: Reflections on the Domestification of Canadian Foreign Policy", *International Journal*, Vol. 34 (Winter 1977-1978) pp. 130-138.

- "The Press and Foreign Policy in Canada", *International Journal*, Vol. 33 (Spring 1976) pp. 223-243.

Stogdill, R *Handbook of Leadership* (New York: Free Press, 1974).

Swift, J and **Tomlin, B** *Conflicts of Interest: Canada and the Third World* (Toronto: Between the Lines, 1991).

Swift, J and **Clarke, R** *Ties That Bind: Canada and the Third World* (Toronto: Between the Lines, 1982).

Taras, D "Brian Mulroney's Foreign Policy: Something for Everyone", *The Round Table*, Vol. 75 (1985) pp. 35-46.

Tennyson, BD *Canada and the Commonwealth Caribbean* (London: UP of America, 1986).
- *Canadian Relations with South Africa: A Diplomatic History* (Washington: UP of America, 1982).

Thorndike, AE "Regionalism and the Commonwealth", in *The Commonwealth for the 1980's*, edited by AJR Groom and P Taylor (London: Macmillan, 1984) pp. 40-54.

Tinker, H "Migration in the Commonwealth", in *The Commonwealth for the 1980's*, edited by AJR Groom and P Taylor (London: Macmillan, 1984), pp. 244-259.

Wheare, KC *Constitutional Structure of the Commonwealth* (Oxford: Clarendon Press, 1960).

Wiener, J *Making Rules in the Uruguay Round of the GATT: A Study of International Leadership* (Aldershot: Dartmouth Publishing, 1995).
- "'Hegemonic' Leadership: Naked Emperor or the Worship of False Gods?", *European Journal of International Relations*, Vol. 1, No. 2 (June 1995) pp. 219-243.

Wood, B "Towards North-South Power Coalitions", in *Middle Power Internationalism: The North-South Dimension*, edited by C Pratt (Montreal: McGill-Queen's UP, 1990) pp. 69-107.

- "Canada and Southern Africa: A Return to Middle Power Activism", *The Round Table*, Vol. 315 (1990) pp. 280-290.
- *The Middle Powers and the General Interest* (Ottawa: North-South Institute, 1988).

Young, OR "Political Leadership and Regime Formation: On the Development of Institutions in International Society", *International Organization*, Vol. 45, No. 3 (Summer 1991) pp. 281-308.

- "The Politics of International Regime Formation: Managing Natural Resources and the Environment", *International Organization*, Vol. 43, No. 3 (Summer 1989) pp. 93-114.